Spiritual Logic

the Hope in

Entrepreneurialism

and the

Game of Money

by

Bill Terry

Spiritual Logic

Copyright © 2017 William A Terry
All rights reserved.
ISBN-13:
978-1542561303

ISBN-10:
1542561302

www.spiritual-logic.net

written for my sanity
... all the while, thinking of yours

Table of Contents

PREFACE	1	
CHAPTER 1	10	Flying Solo
CHAPTER 2	20	A Long Day
CHAPTER 3	38	The Nature of God
CHAPTER 4	50	"But Wait, There's More!"
CHAPTER 5	66	A California Mission
CHAPTER 6	79	So... What About Jesus?
CHAPTER 7	99	A Case for Miracles
CHAPTER 8	113	Our Battle with Perfection
CHAPTER 9	127	The Board of Directors
CHAPTER 10	151	

THE GAME of MONEY PLAYBOOK

10.1	153	The Art of "Not Thinking"
10.2	161	Zero Zero Vision
10.3	162	Rules of Engagement
10.4	163	When to Use the "No-Look" Pass
10.5	165	Trial Game
10.6	176	Determining a Winner
10.7	178	Game Day
CHAPTER 11	185	Spiritual vs Survival Logic
CHAPTER 12	199	A Spiritual Neural-Pathway Rewire
Morning Reprogram	210	
CHAPTER 13	214	Remembering to Remember
Morning Meditation	228	
CHAPTER 14	231	Do Unto Others

CHAPTER 15	251	The Responsibility of Knowledge
CHAPTER 16	270	Be Your Purpose

THE BOOK OF AFFIRMATIONS

Week One – Truth & Wisdom   287

Week Two – Worship   295

Week Three – Counsel   303

Week Four – Knowledge   311

Week Five – Courage   317

Week Six – Understanding   325

Week Seven – Intuition   333

Spiritual Logic

Acknowledgments

I took most of the photos in this book, except the amazing shot of a partial solar eclipse, with a lone seagull casually flying above an unusually calm ocean upon which the sun is spot-lighting through the sea's newly formed clouds, far into forever; a very cool phone-pic; taken by my daughter, Patrick's niece, Samantha Terry Enriquez. Of course, there's the photo shopped self-portrait that Jeff Tucker put together and the selfie taken by my smoke'n hot wife, Sue, with her having climbed on my back and us looking out into the endless Pacific awaiting the great adventure that lay ahead, in which we had just begun in February of 2012. And you must realize the wedding pictures were not taken by me... but by my son, J. Michael Terry, and a close friend of Sue's daughter, Breona, Rachel Hawk.

That pretty much covers it; except to extend a sincere gratitude to an ever-loving Father in Heaven for being interested enough in me, as one of His persons, to put this all together; my life; me and my wife and my family that is. And despite my best efforts to derail the process, even today, He teaches me to recognize His Grace within the daily Miracles designed to save me from me.

Thank you.

Spir·i·tu·al-Log·ic

/spiriCH(oo)əl-läjik/

noun

A Heavenly designed/choreographed reasoning that leads, precisely, to the Heavenly intended effect.

Synonyms

>God's Will
>Love-Logic
>Universal Reality

Antonyms

>Material-Logic
>Fear-Logic
>Wishful Thinking

the Hope in Entrepreneurialism

"Nothing is more subject to Delusion than Piety."

James Madison

"Do not treat prophecies with contempt but test them all; hold on to what is good..."

1 Thessalonians 5:20 - 21

"Don't believe everything you think."

Author Unknown

Spiritual Logic

PREFACE

Be careful of your thoughts, for they become your Words
Be careful of your words, they become your Actions
Be careful of your actions they your Habits
And habits become your Character
Character your Destiny

Chinese Proverb

Tuesday morning, February 3rd, 2003, I awoke to the painful reality of a broken marriage and an emptied home; a dream vacated. The morning of the day prior, on my way out the door leaving for work, I hurried past my two young sons as they sat, innocently, watching Sponge Bob Square

Pants. We caught each other's eyes, smiled and I said good bye – unusual – as we'd normally hug before parting, but this particular morning I had important meetings in North Salt Lake; no time for a goodbye hug.

As I left for the office and had driven out of sight, the boys' mother, Tere, and her parents and brother scurried to pack our belongings into a U-Haul van and, without the courtesy of discussion or chance to say goodbye to my sons, she moved to Washington State; back home. Tere had become a refugee from marriage to a serial-entrepreneur; terrified of being poor.

That next morning, attempting to negotiate the dense fog of confusion, with little sleep, and zero ambition to move I fumbled to justify her reasoning to break up our family and to leave without discussion; secretly. How does a person think this is OK?

A lifelessness rag doll, emotionally, I was weakened to the cellular level and I struggled to pray. And in my anguished and faltering prayers for solace and direction I knew I had to stop. I had to stop thinking. I was making myself crazy; so angry; so confused.

Blindly, I turned to my most reliable survival tools, as if reaching for oxygen to breathe. For fifteen years, nearly every morning, I'd practiced meditation to cool down and calm an overly stimulated A.D.H.D. mind before beginning the day. And on that morning, my thoughts were running wild; out of control, so in a well-rehearsed vigil, I began to think about things I might be grateful for and then pray for the health and welfare of others whom I might serve that day. I prayed for my sons and my mind began to unwind.

With each slow and thoughtful breath, my runaway negativity was being replaced with the peaceful, safe, and loving Thoughts of God. What I was to learn through this timely meditation saved me from lashing out and spiraling into self-destructive behaviors.

Over the years, I'd learned to be suspicious of my original thinking and, through trial and error, to explicitly trust in God's first and creative Thoughts; His being the true source of Wisdom, Inspiration, and my personal and irrefutable Courage to act. His Thoughts have inspired me to serve others and by the knowing intention of selfless-service miracles happen and my unsolvable problems seem to vanish instantly; miraculously.

And as I redirected my thoughts that morning, I could breathe again; physically, emotionally, and spiritually. And, as per usual the miraculous answer came to me; quickly and clearly, but, unexpectedly, in the form of a question.

"What do you want with your life?"

No, it's not like a BOOMING voice from above!

Maybe you've heard Him and didn't know it or think yourself unworthy or unable to hear the voice of God or of one of His trusted Messengers – Angels, perhaps. When a spiritual message is transmitted, the words come not as an audible voice, but as a thought; comfortably recognized as the Truth; a breathless whisper that directs us to the Truth for any given moment or sour-instant we are troubled to endure.

Interesting though...

A hopeful and powerful question! Not the tact I'd expected; me being so fully clothed in "poor me"; alone in an empty house in Utah. I had actually expected God to show me a way to reconnect the broken pieces and reunite me with the boys. Instead, He stepped squarely between me and my misery and posed a terrific question.

And when I heard, "What do you want with your life?" I recognized His brilliance and nearly smiled. I'd instantly been given a choice; to be whipped around by the survival logic that would naturally move me to react quickly in a counter-strike; fueled by fear, loss, and anger or I might choose to think more constructively about how to begin my life today anew, on my terms, with God's cool thinking to guide the Way.

In that time and place in my life, being alone had become a first-class blessing. For in that Holy Instance of solitude, my mind was freed, possibly for the first time in years, from the overseeing negativity of an anxious spouse who feared the great unknowns in starting a business, of which most entrepreneurs find fascinating to solve. And with this Heavenly Authorized uncensored freedom to explore my wants and wishes, I found Hope and my soul could breathe again. I was Instantly released from self-torment; however, much was required of me to inspect my world and make the changes necessary to benefit from the terrible experience of this reality horror-show.

So, I got to work and with pen in hand and open heart and emptied mind, I made columns on a blank page to evaluate the net worth of me. Of what value am I to the world? With hope sprouting, energy increasing, and a clearing mind I began to make an account's journal entries with strengths on one side of the ledger and weaknesses the other. Studying the balance sheet, I searched and could not find my liabilities with the weight to balance the value I placed on my ever-growing relationship with God, which I considered my greatest asset. So, the remainder, my equity, must be the value of my character that had grown from practicing daily meditation and the learned trust, patience, and courage God had instilled in me by this practice.

But, what is it about my character that's of such significance that I should deserve to hope for anything good to come from this particular and seemingly dead moment in my life? What is it about me – specifically – who I am – that may be converted to happiness, now, in this vacated house; emptied of family?

I've come to understand and trust the source of Truth found in these meditatively released Thoughts and throughout this book I'll share with you how I've come to rely and trust in these Thoughts that, through trial and error, I've discovered to be of an Ultimate Truth. Trusting in these brief conversations with God, that they may direct every decision I make – in business and in my personal life – whether in the midst of trial and suffering or at peace in my surroundings. Throughout these chapters, I'll share with you the many miracles that are the direct result of listening and having the Faith to act upon specific spiritual directions. The feelings you get to act on a thing this is more than a feeling, more than a physiologically and emotionally powerful pull to do something; this urge is impossible to dismiss. It's more than an urge – I call these spiritually generated impulses – "Bumps".

And, over the years I've found that by giving up my agendas that mostly distract and mostly create havoc and, as I agree to follow the Spiritual Bumps, I've become more magnanimous in nature. Bumps are selfless Thoughts initiated by the mind of our inner Highest Being. The Spirit of Truth leads us to serve selflessly and to grow exponentially through the many struggles, failures, and long-sufferings necessary to abandon our selfish desires and, instead, seek God and regain and maintain the peace natural to our worlds.

Whether I'm in a battle for peace or contemplating life in meditation, with a simple thoughtful breath, my mind is released from fear and thoughts become more closely knitted with that of God's, a closeness I hope to explain well in the coming chapters; a closeness I pray that may develop for you, well beyond my spiritually-embryonic understandings of how the Universe works.

Long ago I'd lost my faith in the existence of a loving God. However, in October of 1988 I was awakened from a spiritual coma and discovered a loving forgiving God. And since that day, and it hasn't been easy, I've been learning to consciously extract my head from that undesirably smelly place and put my trust in Him; first and last; an Eternal education in trust. And on that seriously confusing morning in February, fifteen years after the moment of realization / head extraction, as I hunkered-down to work on the next phase of my life and to journal this conversation with God, I realized the value in the words I'd written that re-affirmed my belief and trust in His Eternal Love and Forgiveness; for each of us; including me; including Tere.

But, as I'd unexpectedly and quite expectedly found God's Grace in a hopeful conversation with Him, in my dumbed stillness, He wrapped His Love around my mind and soul and helped me think less of my apparent placement into this worst-nightmare-become-real and showered me with Truth and Love. God had given me a means by which to be at my best despite myself and I'd responded to fear with love and hadn't compromised my character and made matters worse in a verbal attack, as I'd loved to have done.

Actually, that evening my first words to Tere weren't so terrible. I asked, "Are you OK?"

Crazy, yet it was perfect to question her wellbeing to ensure that of my sons' and it came from an emotionally-empty perspective and it caught her off guard; as well as it did me. Surprising her with nonresistance was not my intention, but God had put His Team to work to begin the healing in my soul and I'd been relieved of anger. Coming from a place of understanding and love, there was no anger from which to restrain bad action. A miracle had taken place, in that moment in time, to open my heart and mind to forgive; although forgetting wasn't part of the deal, nor need it be.

~

In no way might I prove to you that the improvable God exists, each has his own cherished misunderstandings. And what is controllable in space and time; relative to the Universe and Eternity? But I absolutely believe that He does exist and that He wants for mine, yours, and our success. At the same time, I fear so much of the great unknown that might go so wrong that I become anxious and bewildered as does one who has no belief in God.

So, I have nothing absolutely figured out except that through my experiences survived by prayer and with a "mustard seed of Faith", I've survived insanity to the point that I have something worth writing about and hope that you might appreciate.

And, yes, it's true! I'm one of those openly expressive sorts you might see gazing into the Heavens in prayerful thanksgiving after a great performance or tragedy averted, one who sees himself in the forgotten and I pray, "There but by the Grace of God go I." And I'm one who seems obtusefully unaffected by the train wreck that others shriek in dismay or horror. In prayer, I find peace and comfort in His Promise during the worst of times and I'll show you how.

I also believe that finding God's approval is simpler than religion makes it, having discovered that His Love and Forgiveness is un-earnable. From a multitude of personal experiences and micro-inspection of the reason for these many miracles delivered, of which you'll read later, it's been pounded into my prideful and thickened skull that His Love for you, us, even for me, is free of collateralized debt. In fact, I've written this book to explain, what little I know, how the Universe works in my life to meet every challenge deemed important by Him that I face. I've written several stories of amazing "coincidental meetings" and "serendipitous events" I'm certain are His intentional miracles customized for each new moment in time I struggle to succeed; succeed beyond my fears.

The message worth sharing in this book is the results of years of exploring a relationship with this un-provable and loving God; to offer my experiences that He wants desperately for yours and my happiness complete; to the point of His yearning for it. In Him, I've found the ability to love who it is that I am, have become, and am becoming by my personal and conscious choice to agree with His Plan over my selfish desires; that I am worthy, in my simplicity; and that I might succeed in life in this particular moment in time, playing the role of me. And I, you, and we succeed in this infinitely-dimensional Game of Money with Spiritual Logic being the test and Hope in every Holy Entrepreneurial adventure.

In the quiet and stillness of that early morning in February, in my reflections and openness to accept Truth, after making several objective-based journal entries, I began to write a set of affirmations to more concretely set in my mind the truth I intended to live, as I would have it; starting from scratch. And nearly every day since, over the past fourteen years as I write and re-write this book, I'm reminded of how I met God and of the many accomplishments I've experienced and experience, today, on my spiritual journey to ultimate success in business, from the refuse and loneliness of my many life's failures.

∼

My story may speak directly to the value of forgiveness, patience, and honesty, as well as to not resist your naturally human doubts and fears of which your mind might negatively influence the future, if given the opportunity and energy to over-resist. Rather, with Faith and Hope unleashed by your conscious practice of residing, present, in this Instance, helped by the practice of meditation and prayer, God can pursue His Will through you. And your powerful pre-tangible thoughts are freed to manifest in your brightest destiny revealed.

In this New precise Place and Time, you exist without mistaken emphasis on past mistakes and failures or fears of predicted Armageddon or dreams of life without struggle. Here, in this Holy Place is where you'll find that God exists and – only – right Now, in this moment in time, might you be perfectly who it is that God created you to be; His Beloved; His Genius prepared to be expressed through you; Now-Here.

Listen closely for His breathless unmistakable Thought that leads you to the right places in this world where He needs you to be. He wants for you, me, and us to succeed and gives us renewed courage and strength to confront situations He knows we're prepared well to perform perfectly, selflessly, and fearlessly; in service to others and to the satisfaction of His Will. In this moment – only – may you have no regrets or fear; you're "In the Zone" and you'll see the world as it truly is and may smile and enjoy the fresh air as you glide through a toothache's measure of emotional pain and fail to scream while being shoved towards a cliff by someone you once trusted.

Through the many insane trials, I've faced and survived, I've learned that God's plan is fair, just, and inevitable and that there are no coincidences in life. While mistakes are made and accidents do occur, the effects are surmountable, as "In Him all things are possible" and if I will but ask, I receive.

Yet, the underlying message in this book is one that is forever elusive to master: We succeed in our micro or macro Entrepreneurial Adventures – unconscious of our need to control human endeavor as we consciously agree to accept God's Grace and choose to engage our thought, word, and action in this particular moment in time; only Here and Now. For in this 'Holy Instant' – only – does God reside. And Now and only Here may we achieve greatness within these vessels, these bodies and minds He created so perfectly from which He desires to Shine.

As we enter this new era of hyper-materialism and are required to learn, once again, that our governments, mega corporations, and financial institutions cannot manage God's Will; all the more important it is for each of us to become self-reliant yet securely cooperative in our Holy-Entrepreneurial ventures. Holy-Entrepreneurialism is your Hope for peace and joy, directed by God and un-affirmed by the "keepers of the keys to success" once held solely by "the few". In this era of crowd-funding, 3D printing, and open access to online shopping, marketing, and ordering, free shipping and virtual banking services – every obstacle that might have held us back from entrepreneurial success once controlled by manufactured "barriers to entry" is no longer relevant. "The few" may be made powerless by this rebellion in self-reliance and borderless cooperation.

All good things, promised, happen as you learn to be who you are through your dreams made real in a conscious effort to resist evil, cling to God's blessings, and achieve for Him in business, as well as every part of your life. Play well in the Game of Money with faith that there's plenty of wealth to go around and know that we each receive our share simply by doing our part, each day. And you're rewarded in ways unmistakable, wholly intangible, and Eternally-significant; sourced from a Great, Abundant, uncontrollable, and ever Loving Father in Heaven. He holds "the keys" to inspiration, critical relationships, and valuable material and spiritual resources and it's solely on you, Now, to follow through and succeed for Him that which He has planned for you. As well, it's up to you, me, and to each of us to deny the liars their voice – to save each other from ourselves. Firmly plant your belief in the Eternally Blessed Outcomes you're driven, daily, to achieve – for Him. And you're living your life selflessly successfully completely alive; Purposely Fulfilled.

the Hope in Entrepreneurialism

In humble thanks of His Amazing Grace,

Bill Terry
fellow Adventurer

My entrepreneurial life in a photo-shop metaphor.
Going where most won't nor should they... alone.

CHAPTER 1

Flying Solo

Partial Solar Eclipse at Redondo Beach, California
Photo by Samantha Terry Enriquez

the Hope in Entrepreneurialism

Who is this that speaks to me
So quietly, so certainly

If it is truly You, my Lord
I am Your Servant

If the Spirit of Truth
I am Your Voice

If my Father
I am Your Thought Revealed

And if it is me that speaks to me
Dumb my mind, stub my toe
Wreck me

But if it is You, truly
Place me Here-Now
And speak through me
Be through me

Confident, Now-Here
that I am Your son
I commit myself to You
That I am, in all that I say
All that I do

Empty for You

The life of an entrepreneur is impossible to prepare and for one to fully appreciate without the experience of naming the Company, opening the doors for the first day of business, proudly sweeping the entry in the morning, building a loyal clientele, and inhabiting the lonely task of making payroll and paying taxes from an overly quarried bank account.

Spiritual Logic

Regardless of how great the idea, every business I've started, to do whatever it is I'm been driven to do, has begun cashless. And in a rush to deliver and be paid for the newest solution conjured, I've bootstrapped these businesses with new cash earned by sales. Played well and promises kept, it works.

But, by the winter of 2011, the cash had run out for my newest venture. We'd developed technologies for farming and been selling and supporting them throughout Washington State and, as per usual, the Company was undercapitalized to meet the pressures of a young business, especially during the worst recession since the great depression. I'd struggled to keep the business afloat since January of 2009 when forward motion abruptly stopped and I was forced to let-go of my small but efficient staff. The dream was slowly fading away.

Yes, it was a snowy February morning in 2011 when my entrepreneurial dreams collided with the harsh reality of "cashlessness".

>cash•less•ness
>
>/ˈkaSHləsnəs/
>
>*noun*
>
>the uncherished state in Entrepreneurialism hanging ownership's balls on the line between continuing business or quitting; forcing a commitment towards one or the other.

And as I peered out the window of my two-room apartment, that Sunday morning, my breath frosted the panes of glass. I sat quietly and pondered my fate, as huge flakes of snow fell slowly to the ground; visibly deepening, as is its purpose. It was quiet at 5:30 AM; so quiet, I noticed a slight ring in my ears; maybe too quiet. But it gave me pause to consider this miserably recurring nightmare of financial distress that would cyclically run wild through my entrepreneurial life, as each of my companies had so often struggled to stay afloat. I wrote this, all the while my right eye twitched, again and again. Anxiously, I prayed to God to deliver me the money to pay my bills, run the business, and care for my sons, Matthew and Michael.

It was a beautiful snowfall that morning and, out of habit, I went online to check the snow conditions at Mission Ridge Ski Resort; a great ski mountain just 25 short minutes away from where I sat. Well, it was fifteen degrees at the top and there was 10 new inches of dry "Utah-like-powder" screaming my name to be skied. It was days like these that I wished I had had a "real job" with weekends off and a steady pay-check with benefits. If I had, I'd have been on the lift as it opened. But no, not me, and not that day; for I'd chosen the life of an artist, a go-for-broke entrepreneur and on that day, I was broke, credit shot, I'd accumulated nearly $200,000 in debt, and had zero liquid assets from which to resort. Except for my Canon camera, which I'd pawned twice in the past year for gas money to make appointments across the state.

How'd I get there? Well... like many who live pay-check to pay-check, a cash-poor business experiences the same struggles. If a customer didn't pay on time or there was a single extraordinary expense or project woefully underquoted I might be faced with business closure. This is the reality for many, from the date of company formation to the final sale of its assets; if there's nothing saved for these considerations. And, due to my overly optimistic outlook of future sales justifying the heavy reinvestment of profits into growth, I had saved little in the company coffers for these dips and valleys that ALWAYS occur.

~

Backing up a bit, in August of 2003, I'd moved to Moses Lake, Washington to be near my sons; after six months of living so very far away from them, after their mother's abrupt departure. Alone, I took some time to wrap things up in Utah and say goodbye to the place I'd lived for 48 years. In fact, the morning after my 30-year class reunion and having given a speech to the class of '73, to raise money for scholarships, I was on the road with the balance of my belongings; headed for Washington State. With that speech to 250 of my former classmates behind me, I'd closed the door on regrets from my adolescence and had left nothing undone from a lifetime in Utah; an amazing and long overdue purging of my worst overthought memories.

As I drove north on Interstate 15, I was exhilarated; free to explore a new land; with absolutely no intention of returning to Utah; nor did I have any desire to reconnect with the boys' mother.

However, by the time school had started that fall, Tere and I were back together... let me think... Oh yes, "dumbass" is the word I'm thinking that I was, for making that ill-fated decision. However, looking back I can see why God pushed us together and kept us together for the "bonus years"; to keep a promise to our sons. They were difficult years, but my sons and I grew from the experience in no way might we have, otherwise.

But, our money difficulties, well-honed in Utah, followed us to Washington, as no matter how much I would bring in, it was never enough. We were determined we were due a lifestyle several tax brackets higher than earned. And I allowed the façade to play-out until it could no longer be sustained.

Just after Thanksgiving Day in 2010, we decided to finish what had begun in 2003 and divorced. That troubling Saturday, I moved into a small two room studio apartment and our family was finally split forever.

And as the dust began to settle from the move, I lived within the reality of an extremely difficult financial position, now made more strenuous by the divorce. I'd immediately incurred additional overhead and was financially toppled; broke. By February of '11, I'd run out of money and had over-thought my problems into gnawing headaches and once again I failed to remember to breathe. I'd constantly fight battles in my mind, exploring endless scenarios for a way out of the mess I'd created and many times I'd ask God, "Where's the promised land?" I had no money to run the business, keep the phones on, pay office rent, and to care for my sons.

~

Yes, I'm a poor strategic money manager and would love to blame the boys' mother for my throttled ambition or "the economic downturn" for the failure of my business, but that'd be cheating me of the tough lessons I must fully enjoy; to say nothing of how cowardly it is to blame another for my solely explored misadventures in Businessland. As well, it'd be easy to blame my father for not teaching me how to handle money, responsibly, when it clearly wasn't him who bet the farm on my business plans. It was I; me.

Although, it would've helped to have had a better teacher, if not, role model to help me better understand the cause and effect of the proper use of earnings, passive income, savings, and debt. Even when dad was making relatively good money, with seven kids, and a celebrity's lifestyle, we were poor. He had no concept of how to manage money and because "you can't teach what you don't know," how can I blame him for not imparting simple wisdoms he did not own.

As young children, my three brothers, three sisters, and I watched in shock as strange men jumped from their car and rushed to repossess ours. We were urged to pack quickly as we moved our belongings, with little notice, after being evicted or foreclosed upon. I once overheard my father lie to a prospective landlord about the number of children he had; seven, obviously being too many. And we'd quite often hear, "don't answer that" or "I'm not here" bellowed through the house when the phone would ring – another bill collector avoided.

It didn't take eavesdropping to overhear my parents fight about money. It was a way of life for them. My mother spoke of a time, before I was born, when she answered the door to two strange men demanding the wedding ring from her finger; that too repossessed. She lived in a constant battle to feed and clothe her children and no one can know of her pains but God; to whom she prayed constantly for financial rescue. And she often speaks of God's many answers, with an uneasy mix of pain and gladness in her eyes.

From the late 1950's through the '60s, my father was a well-known disc jockey in Salt Lake City. When the Beatles were making a big splash in America he was caught up in the sensation. He drew a 45 share of the morning radio audience which created a wave of a Rock 'N' Roll celebrity he'd gladly ride. He was a genuine "personality", though. His intellect, love of people, and way with words set him apart and he enjoyed the limelight that had shown brightly upon him. It wouldn't surprise me when someone would ask for his autograph, except once when a classmate in 5th grade asked for a signature on his arm and my father complied. That, I didn't get.

Since his listenership was formidable, the record companies took notice and he was invited to "the party" and it took years and years for him to come back to reality from the wild ride of relative fame and celebrity. He was thrust into "the business" and associated with the stars of the day; Frank Sinatra and Dean Martin to name a few.

As a concert promoter, host, and emcee, he booked groups like the Beach Boys, Herman Hermits, The Doors, Rolling Stones, and many others. He knew the members of the bands, personally. Mick Jagger took time to look him up while in Salt Lake for the Voo Doo Lounge tour in the '90's and they had a "good ole days" conversation. But, dad was not easily impressed by another's fame. He didn't make much of the call. In fact, he hadn't told me of it for several years, until we were talking one day about those "good ole days" and the call came up.

Dad had a way of earning the respect of those extremely famous people, for one, he didn't much care of their opinion of him; he being characteristically non-judgmental, himself. He knew who he was and made the best of his sarcastic, iconoclastic, and sardonic sense of humor.

For example, when he met Frank Sinatra, he was introduced as Bill Terry from Ogden, Utah. Mr. Sinatra looked up at my father and said, "They sure grow you Mormons big." Dad, while still shaking his hand, looked down at him, and with a typical smile in his eyes said, "It's better than being a thin Ginny." Ginny to an Italian is like the N word to a black guy. Mr. Sinatra was taken aback, then laughed and they immediately became friends. For a few years, we actually got Christmas cards from him.

Imagine what it must have been like, invited into the crowd of super celebrities. Surreal, maybe, but dad mistakenly felt obligated to maintain the appearance of greatness and was willing to pay the full price of entry; flying back and forth from Salt Lake to "Vegas" on a whim. Ignoring good sense, he took the family money with him to maintain an image of a well-off celebrity and his children's handed down shoes were, quite literally, stuffed with cardboard to keep the dirt from coming in through the holes in the worn-thin leather soles.

~

While I am not my father, I've developed my very special issues in regards to managing money, as I think one good year in business will continue unabated through to the next. As well, I'd felt obligated to repay the blessings of good business by continually reinvesting the family's profits into the Company, to grow it to a self-sustaining entity, and employ many to share in the wealth; which left no room for an economic hiccup or belch or full-fledged purging, as we'd quickly experienced in 2008 and '09.

Optimism may have its rewards, but living within the reality of the market cycles has been a tough lesson to learn. The marketplace has continually blessed me with just enough good years to keep me coming back for more and I'd become a gambler at the small business craps table; "on a roll" until I eventually crapped out – with everything riding on the come.

By the winter of 2011, that's precisely what happened. My gamble on the business had not yet delivered its pay wagon and I'd lost everything and had become destitute. Yes, I googled it and destitute describes well, the place where I was. My business struggled so badly from the effects of the recession and the lack of cash that I toyed with the idea of shutting it down to get a "real job". I'd dreamed of being a "Greeter" at Wal Mart; a great place to hide from the ruthless responsibilities of unruly cashless entrepreneurialism.

What drove me to this point?

Well... a very distant two years previous, on a Friday evening, at the McCarran Airport in Las Vegas, I was preparing to board a flight home after a weeklong convention, when I received a call from a stranger. This new voice was referred to me by a professor of Precision Ag at Washington State University. I met the professor at a trade show a few years earlier and since then we'd had several brainstorm sessions about technologies that farmers might use to manage chemical applications, save water, and use less power for their irrigation pumps; basic nerdy technical ag-data chit chat.

But, the call I received from Dave Nerpel that evening tripped a domino that fell hundreds that led to me presenting, in February of 2011, to the EPA, the results of "the work" begun from his call. At the end of my presentation, in front of God and 30 compliance officers, in his closing remarks, the EPA's Senior Advisor from Washington D.C. applauded the technology; "the work".

Afterwards, I was pulled to the side and received specific directions on how to proceed for EPA approval from an EPA Pesticide Programs representative. After which, I was told by industry and other government people that, "...that never happens."

The following Sunday, on that cold dark February morning, I lay awake in my two-room apartment and in those early morning hours when thoughts of doom would swirl I watched, hypnotically, the snow fall heavily outside my bedroom window and I wondered how was I to pull this off; I'm absolutely broke – did I mention destitute? Oh yes. Well, I was... And as I watched the large flakes of snow slowly fall, my mind had turned to skiing and dreaming of all the new snow at the Ridge needing to be skied, as I could watch from my window, throughout the night, the lights from the snow cats slowly grooming the ski trails atop the mountain. Well, I could not afford a $55 pass, so I retreated to reality and prayed for peace.

Matthew and Michael weren't with me that weekend, so I was alone. And, as I looked around at my surroundings, I thought, "I'm 56; what the hell am I doing here?" this is no place to bring my boys for the weekends! It wasn't quite Animal House, but I shared the bathroom down the hall with two neighbors who struggled with the concept of cleanliness. One's a cage fighter with a 5 and 2 record, a healing eye socket, and two day jobs. The other's a young and restless underachiever who would occasionally urinate near his car while enjoying a final smoke after a long night and day and night of binge drinking. I'd overhear him from my upstairs bedroom window as he'd swear at the earth with a drunken laugh; spelling his name in the snow, as he peed.

However, I cannot look back and complain, having had a roof over my head, good health, and food in the refrigerator. I'd made terrific mistakes in business that I cannot afford to repeat; I'd over spent, under-delivered, and feared I'd lost my touch and run out of time to build an estate for my daughter Samantha and the boys – and for me to never again be destitute.

I'd thought that if I'm not successful now, I soon will lose my business relationships, as they'd die or retire and ride off into the sunset; along with their memories of good business done with me and their invaluable purchasing influence. And in the far reaches of the back of my mind I feared I might grow old and die penniless, as did my father.

~

The hell I've created for myself had come from the constant search to develop and market new solutions to cure my client's pains and yet by solving specific technical problems I've earned the highest returns. The big problem has been that I haven't had a life-partner willing and able to reign in my poor spending habits; willing to live within an affordable lifestyle; a life lived well but economically, efficiently, materially to match earnings coupled with required savings, mandatory tax payments, and investment to grow the newest venture in business, to meet its potentials.

Any vision for a modest lifestyle that allowed the great ideas to grow to the point they repaid the investment and would feed our family was met with the reality that "no matter the amount of money I'd bring home, it was never enough." Money seemed to vanish in the constant need to prove our wealth, our worth; a concept I abhorred but a trap I willingly agreed to follow.

Besides, I love to start and grow companies even though to run a going concern is pure boredom to me without an exhilarating growth-path. I had become addicted to the chaos of the startup and the resulting highs of watching it come together and grow wildly. Without a cash cushion or strong commitment to live within our means in the feast and famine world of business development, the boy's mother and I together were fiscally unreasonable; unrescuable; irresponsible with the Gifts we'd received.

Finishing a project or building a business to its intended monetized conclusion before starting yet another and living within my means or, better, below my means in preparation for the uncertainties that are certain to occur are my top two least-favorite-faults. And the learning has proven constant, as these A.D.H.D enhanced and multi-generational viruses had eaten away at the means to financial stability that I've craved and that require a sound and daily inoculation of truth to avoid.

Truth had not been easily discerned through my thickened mind filled with misguided thoughts of pride in my abilities or pride in what I might own and show. Truth had been marred by my fears of loss and betrayal that attacked my good business sense and led me to care poorly for the money earned.

However, the Truth requested and accepted is the universal cure worth the pain to expose and from which to honor promises and to earn wealth. And if I might be un-owned by debt and establish a continuous cash-flow above my humbled lifestyle, my life-lesson will forever be learned and put into practice with the right life-partner of whom I could never have dreamed exists; so perfect; and yet she does.

CHAPTER 2

A Long Day

"Reach down your hand in your pocket
Pull out some hope for me..."

Rob Thomas

As the young waitress carefully refilled our coffee, my earnest "How's your day?" had apparently opened a door, long denied access, for her to discuss the important moments in her life, including the events that led to her first orgasm. Yes, this was easily much more sharing than I cared to reciprocate.

Is there such a thing as too much knowledge?

Regarding a stranger's carnal, I'd have to say, yes!

The point being; there is much more to the art of listening than conjuring logical associations in our minds; endowing a smart response. If our reason for listening is meant to be more meaningful than a polite interchange or filler-time between our amazing self-pronouncements, if our reason for listening is to have purpose; whether to entertain or be entertained, educate or be educated, or to more dramatically uncover the truth simmering below the surface; we must choose to be an active participant in the verbal exchange of life's antidotal perceptions.

Try not to drift into self-thought, stay Here/Now, and commit to an honest participation, as if another's soul-experience and whimsical or even a deficient gift of gab might unwrap a surprising answer to a gnawing problem; untrapped through even the briefest of honest dialogue. If the Truth truly is our mission, we must be unattached to personal affect and engage our hearts and minds to the credit of another's uniquely earned perspective.

Trust this: when we truly listen our mind, body, and spirit work well together to discern the Truth and, beyond human formulation, an appropriate response, whether in silence, humor, compassion, or remorse is an inspired response.

"Truth will ultimately prevail where there is pains to bring it to light."

George Washington

Yes, distilling the simplified narrowness of Truth from the broad perceptions of facts painted from our shallow visions of success pains our ego maddingly. Yet the Truth must eventually rise to the top of our combined awareness. And if we cooperate with the unobstructed unpainted flow of information, the truth rises without traumatic effort and possibly our better moments of peaceful resolutions garner new friendships. But as our thoughts generally seek to resolve personal trials, it can be agonizing to pay attention to non-verbal signals that might complete the story being shared by others. Often adrift in our thoughts, we're incognizant of the truth that rests somewhere within the delivery and our receipt of the spoken word.

Spiritual Logic

Remain vigilant with eye contact, as communication of thought may be delivered audibly, but much more is relayed visually and, from another's soul, learned through the center of her eye. To understand the rich flavor of the truth being expressed – beyond words – and to better understand and intimately know that which resides within another's soul, we must exit the confines of our self-made worlds and consciously choose to inhabit the moments we share with another, as if in a dance. Truly strive to hear the words spoken and listen closely to the tone in which they are spoken, but more importantly watch the way in which they are delivered.

While it may be impossible to determine if the voice over the phone is being sufficiently honest, non-verbal cues generally cannot lie. Watch for lack of natural eye contact, rapid blinking, or a distant look in the eyes when someone is pronouncing their brilliance, selling a financial product, or in defense of the President's claims requiring more moneys be budgeted to fight the frontless lines of the new wars. And be on the lookout for a slight smirk or stiffening of the upper lip, restless fidgeting; as these are a few of the body's response to an uneasy conscience.

By watching and listening closely to my clients' stories, in my better moments, I become an active participant in the dance; in a waltz for the truth. I've learned to listen patiently, actively, listening to those whom I am blessed to serve that I might peel back the layers of a client's perceptions of the pains they suffer in their chosen business. In this active free-form interview, I allow another to lead, as we maneuver between and around the natural obstacles of trust; that we might grant each other VIP status to closely held and sacred information that must be shared for the dance to continue with ease; at a polite and naturally comfortable pace.

There's a transition that occurs, however, in the dance where I must take the lead, boldly sometimes, to correct the course and to be of highest value to my clients. I must guide the interview from my knowledge base of past best and worst experiences or we miss an opportunity that may not repeat itself. So, as levels of trust are being determined, I patiently begin to set the scope, breadth, and depth of information transfer by asking general questions, and I listen with my eyes and ears; ask more specific questions, and listen, and watch and listen... hold it... hold it... wait for it... Now!

Ask the unaskable, and with humorously biting truth, I whisk in and take them off guard to find out if I really want to work with them; if we might enjoy the outcome of the investment of time with whom, when, and where we've been placed to serve.

However, it's impossible to fully understand the scope or the cause of the problems owners and managers perceive they must fix and the value of the fix, unless they are willing to openly share; honestly; unedited. This is only possible if we each come from a place of detached interest – earnest objectivity – I, being detached from the need to sell a pre-packaged fix – the client being detached from the need to negotiate me down to "my cost" or extract my learned recommendations "for free"; only to circumvent my work in an online search for the parts and pieces of the solution, now stolen.

However, a soulful hug may be achieved and natural barriers to doing business dropped to disarm our ego's defense systems and then and only then may we work; wholly. In this honored release of control, my clients have mindfully and spiritually approved me to ask frank and earnest questions regarding:

- Which current problems need fixing?
- Which fixes they've attempted?
- Previous attempts gone awry?
- Competitors they like and why or why not?
- And what would be the perfect outcome of a deployed solution?

~

I've been blessed and sometimes cursed with the ability to visualize – to see the video played – to be in the place a person exists, as they tell of their life experiences. It's more than me being in their shoes; it's me seeing through their eyes and feeling what they know. I am there, where they are and have been, as they speak of the pains and joys experienced in their business, as well as in their life.

To visualize their story in detail requires that I ask sometimes difficult questions to understand their intent, scope, and reasoning. And, in this dance, our questions and answers to one another come honestly and from a place of vested-interest, if not a legitimate concern for the other's welfare. By simply looking someone in the eye, loving who they are, and being with them in that specific moment in time, doors are opened that only minutes earlier were proudly barricaded shut; earned knowledge protected – cards habitually held close to the chest now lay on the table face up.

To consider the wellbeing of others, first; to be truly selfless in service; is to offer our sacred time and knowledge and character that wills success for a chosen client over self-gratification. In this fiduciary role, it is not possible to manipulate an outcome to an exclusive benefit or to the detriment of the client; we are brothers.

Greed and love cannot coexist in the same thought pattern; nor may deceit, larceny, or jealousy and love. Being relied upon to look after the "higher good" of my client, as I'd advertised I would, I've become an honored guest in their personal private lives. And there is so much to learn, so much that may be experienced vicariously through another's great and tragic experience and I sometimes cannot believe the amount of sensitive information shared; between courses.

The less we try to control the outcome the more we may receive in return. And in this attitude of brotherly love and unbridled service – I've landed on top of the Matterhorn in "Business-land;" reached Nirvana; Level 10; DEFCON4; I've earned a frick'n PhD in building relationships. But, none of those goals or esteemed degrees of success matter more to me than that of the lasting respect and friendships I've found in doing business; the rewards I most revere.

As part of the process of learning how best to serve my clients, that I might learn whether my offering is worthy of their time to investigate, I have an acid test that reveals how well I've listened and that tests the credibility of the presented solution. As well, it tests the client's engagement. If he or she says "Wow" in reply to a finessed move on the dance floor; the "Wow-Factor" tells me, we might be onto something of value. Especially important; if I can extract a "Wow" within sixty seconds from the time I've introduced a solution-concept, it's then that I've truly succeeded in untangling and simplifying the complexity of their pains and the moment proves we each are immersed in the conversation – and there's hope for a credible relief to their pain. Once a solution is accepted, the real work begins in my responsibility to perform, as advertised; in this holy and sacred dance.

∼

This became a serious problem for me in the summer of 2010, after the second season of field testing "the work" with farmers, crop consultants, system engineers, and programmers. As I explained the market opportunities to money-men – investor types, I began to hear

"Wow" from these folks, as well. And my shark-like instincts smelled blood in the water, so it was time to write the business plan and raise the money necessary to properly launch my newest ideas; never again would I run a business, underfunded.

Fortuitously, coincidentally, and serendipitously, all of which means that something good happened without me getting in the way; I could assemble an incredibly talented, experienced, and savvy group of businessmen to form an Advisory Board to help write and sell the business plan. Based on three years of market research and moderate sales projections a plan was devised and they, having in the past raised hundreds of millions of dollars between them, convinced me that to raise a few million dollars was "no big deal."

Finally, I would have enough money to grow the business and, in my eternal optimism and vivid dreams of unbridled success, within months we'd have hired top engineers and programmers; we'd have assembled a sophisticated sales support team. We'd have the world's best financial analysts at our beck and call; accountants would line up in single file each day to pick up their assigned truck-loads of money to reconcile. We'd assemble a crack staff of department heads readied to, at a moment's notice and with the precision of synchronized swimmers, deploy business processes required to fulfill the demand for our new and variant lines of ag-data products. And, due to what is sure to be a launch of universal success, I'd put hundreds of highly skilled well paid people to work and bring fame and notoriety to the city of Wenatchee (pronounced, wenatchee). And Mayor Johnson would march ahead of me, arms outstretched, with a broad smile and head held high as I followed, waving, sitting atop the back seat of a candy apple red 1959 Cadillac convertible, confetti flying, applauds and cheers abound; Bill Terry – Grand Marshall of the annual Apple Blossom parade.

Well, in another time on another planet, it just might've worked. Alas, in 2010, the usual Angel Investors remained in hiding from the market plunge of '08 and no large amounts of monies were raised; except that Denton Meier and George Buckner stepped up or I would've closed the company and retreated to sell a favorite product from a past-business-life. But the money did keep me afloat and gave new life to the business, but not quite enough to live-out an outlandish dream.

So, I was resolved to run the day to day business operations by myself. My hours were long and I slept very little to coerce time from each day to juggle the balls (promises) I'd tossed in the air. You'd be right to guess that I'd used my savings, available credit, and friends and family goodwill long ago. With an underdeveloped product, sales were slow and hard to come by.

Raising large sums of money or otherwise winning the lottery to stake a business hasn't worked for me in the past and I wouldn't recommend either as a primary strategy to finance a startup; once "Wow!" is fired in your direction and in rapid repetition. The mistakes I made in 2010 cost me greatly and many, many times all seemed hopeless. It got so bad that in September, I couldn't afford the bill for the cellular modem services transmitting data to our servers from the remote sensors on the farms.

It was terrible timing. Gathered just inside the building were several potential clients and industry executives waiting for my "Wow" filled presentation, while I nervously sat in my car with Verizon customer service to reestablish services for the modems shut off for non-payment. So, I called a friend who made a $400 payment on his card to get the modems back online.

Dusted off from the mental and emotional acrobatics, I landed on my feet in time to make the presentation, none the wiser to my cash-poor situation.

"Welcome to Wal Mart! Need a cart?"

Ahhh... I was seriously jealous for the life of the "Greeter".

Slow down now, I know you're thinking... but being a serial entrepreneur isn't as glamorous a lifestyle as it may appear.

There've been times I could feel my heart pound uncontrollably and my chest tighten from serious stress overload. I'd drive those long country highways between sales and service calls and think of how death might be a fair release from the immense financial burdens, client needs, and family obligations. I wondered is this why businessmen, under seemingly unbearable pressures such as these, might choose to disappear into a bottle of gin or the arms of an anonymous lover or, more dramatically, drive off a cliff and claim eternal peace rather than face another slew of creditor calls and spousal cross examinations of which there is no satisfying answer.

There were times when failure seemed inevitable and the price I paid far too great and I could just as soon be freed from the unendurable and the thought *did* cross my mind, if but for an instant, how I might just as soon be dead instead... a flip of the wrist and that'd be me impaled on the front of that fully-loaded Semi-truck coming my way. And, as I'd clung to the last knot at the end of the self-made rope and I'd become desperate and uncontrollably shaken, I'd be thrown another lifeline, if but only the nausea caused from such a selfish and stupid thing to consider; a healthy mind's suicide.

> "There is no situation... how desperate or seemingly benign, that God leaves us to face alone."
>
> Delores Dogood
> (from her short story, Shopping without a Cart
> Life before and after Fame)

Besides, I love life, I love my children. I have a wonderful daughter, Samantha and two great sons who keep me young. And I'm in pretty good shape for my age, whatever that means. I ski fast and run hard, have lots of friends including the two spiritually assigned to me that I may trust without reservation. I live in an amazing part of the world on the bench of the Cascade Mountains and along the mighty Columbia River and I'm confident that there's more to life than the extreme challenges delivered by self-inflicted poverty.

~

I did survive my self-made hell and continue to do so, but only as I remember that we're here to help one another and God's got out backs. In selfless service my fears disappear and, as I make a conscious choice to serve, I'm whole again.

We are equally-created and each is special in God's eyes and as I choose to trust in Him and remain open to His strength and courage; my darkest most non-negotiable problems vanish. His Love for each of us runs deeper than we may possibly imagine and, as we receive and express His Love, we are perfect; as He created us, in a perfect place, regardless of what we deem to be success or failure or as we face what we believe to be a life or death situation; in Him we are perfect.

If you have a hard time trusting this, I understand... I was a total skeptic, but for argument's sake, try to imagine these three things are true and believable:

- first, a higher power exists in the Universe and it's inseparable as is a loving father's heart to his children's – let's call this Good force God
- secondly, God is Love and His Love for each of us is real and without favorites
- finally, His Love cannot be earned, it's free of charge; let's call it, Grace.

Now, imagine that one aspect of His Love is forgiveness and another is knowledge of a path to dynamic Truth and either is accessible to each of us at any time; no matter what we've done…

… no matter…

Now imagine that the Truth for any moment in time comes from a deep historical well that we may visit unimpeded and the Truth from this well flows with no resistance from its Eternal source and there's lots of room for our neighbors and never is there a waiting line. As we reach for the bucket and drink the water in silence with no resistance from within, our souls are filled to overflowing and our mindal, emotional, and spiritual thirst for the truth, for this particular challenge, in this particular moment in time, is immediately satisfied.

Whether on a long walk or run, alone with our thoughts in the shower, or in quiet meditation and prayer, as we drink from this cup from this well of Eternal Knowledge and Love, we immediately see the world in a new light and our fears vanish in this light of understanding and knowledge. By His Grace, we've reached for Him out of desperation and/or gratitude and have surrendered our agendas and in this surrender, we receive more than we could've expected and now have a plan for the day. And we've been given the gift of courage and wisdom that guides us precisely to face the most difficult unexpected and life-defining challenges we thought we were under-qualified, ill-trained, or unworthy to conquer.

As when I semi-unexpectedly discovered that I had no access to data on the farms; I knew the modems were a few days away of being shut off, but please, not that day. For that day, I was scheduled to show off the technology at a seminar to industry experts and as these important people waited patiently for me, I sat alone outside in my car, seat tilted back, my eyes closed in prayer seeking an answer.

To relax, I took a deep breath to calm my mind and intuitively knew that I must dismiss the need to fix the problem. So, I let my mind's thinking processes hibernate. In stillness, God was given a doorway to get through the thickness of fear and doubt to instill in me His Truth. Here/Now, in stillness, His direction was made clear, as the thought came to me without thinking, the Truth was known in an instant; timelessly. In that Holy connection with Eternity, I'd been given the wisdom and courage to call a particular friend for help.

So, I picked up the phone and, within a few minutes, services were re-established and data again flowed. My friend gladly had done for me what I would have for him and a higher power knew exactly *who* I must call for help and gave me the necessary confidence, the will, and the choice of words.

By many accounts, I shouldn't be in business or alive to tell these stories and there's plenty of room for skepticism to my personal accounts of miracles or the existence of an ever-loving God. But, if we accept the idea that He may exist and that the un-provable is possible and that, if He does exist, He does so in our behalf, we're closer to discovering success, peace, and happiness in every aspect of life.

~

God never leaves our sides on this winding and sometimes belligerent road to earn a living and create an estate from that, which was once the rubble of past horrible decisions. And whether my business is to be wildly successful or not, the estate I speak of is not of material measure, rather of a far more lasting thing and one that is worth dying to protect: a fearless character of natural integrity selfishly fulfilled through selfless service to others.

Within God's mind, we are perfect, so why argue with Him?

In His replies to my prayers of salvation there is no need for me to be more than the person I am and, surrounded by His loving arms, I may honestly be the person He created and able to live fearlessly alive within this moment. And in this moment "resistance *is* futile." In the Here-Now, we are forgiven and resistance is not considered, as the truth is imminently known and a Divine Plan is set into motion. As we choose to accept His Plan, today in each Instant, we are brought closer to Him, as we make that conscious choice to ask a brother in need, "How, may I help?"

So, we succeed – together – in this Father and daughter/son relationship and today, as we commit the talent God has mapped into our DNA and apply His Wisdom through our unique personalities; we develop a God-forged character. And we succeed today in direct proportion to our Eternally directed and humanly followed actions, as we act faithfully to His Nudges and Bumps instantly, honestly, and lovingly. As we pray while in the midst of our trials, we hear His chimes and if we listen closely for His Genius connecting to ours; our genius hard-coded into us at birth, He directs us to the next step on our path to Safety, Truth, Wisdom, and Happiness everlasting. Regardless of the sins of yesterday and regardless of that which we are driven to accomplish before the moment passes, He never gives up on us and we are constantly given another chance to live happily-ever-after.

~

As I look back on all that had occurred in this millennium, most notably, 2010 and 2011 were disturbingly great years that I hope to never forget, nor repeat the stress fractures in entrepreneurial gaming. But, in the end, those years were more great than disturbing, as I'd landed a contract with a multinational irrigation-controls Company of which there is none more suited to develop my technologies and, coincidentally and eternally on purpose, is headquartered in Eugene just south of Portland, Oregon; a short day's drive from Wenatchee. Their president, Cecil Rock agreed to fund the design and engineering for "the work", to build inventories, and provide marketing; press releases, build trade-show booths, design collateral materials, and grant me access to 80 years of customer relationships to promote "the work".

Harvesting the fruits of goodwill requires unbearable patience, confidence, and trust in its unproven value, otherwise known as Faith. And once again I am reminded that these important relationships become friendships are my most treasured assets.

As I write this, it's just past five in the morning, once again, I'm alone with my thoughts and I realize how my life's changed since 2003. And that it's unrecognizable to that which so recently resembled hell; now, heaven. And what seems like forever ago and in another lifetime was only a short five years earlier, when on an atypical balmy January night in 2012 in Portland, Oregon, I met an atypical Sue.

After being matched on E-Harmony and having exchanged several emails and first conversations on the phone, we decided to meet in person. So, I made an excuse to do some work in the Eugene offices to meet her for dinner on my way through town; a short stop. I hadn't any high hopes, thinking I was too old in years to attract someone as young as me, but Sue proved me wrong. She's smart and witty; has an amazing smile, a pure heart; she's athletic, beautiful, and enjoys the adventures of living, in which she's certain a loving God is in charge to direct and clear a path.

The problem, of course, she lived in Portland and I wasn't ready for a serious relationship, let alone one at a long distance. So, I attempted to drive her away by completely being *me*...

... Yep! that should do it... she'd surely run from the inevitable madness from being in a relationship with a serial entrepreneur.

I figured that would solve the problem, so I let her have it; who I am, where I've been, and where I'm headed... even sent her the first few chapters of this book. Not that driving her off was what I really wanted, I simply had nothing to lose and she deserved to know the whole truth, best as I could explain. When we met on E-Harmony, in the essence of time and respect for her sanity, I prodded her to read my story.

Surprisingly, she didn't run. Rather, she revealed even more so the quality of the person Sue truly is. She explained that the first thing she liked about me was that I was unashamed in my honesty. In my search for the truth I appeared confident in the outcome God instills; my life's true journey revealed.

Sue and I clicked. Right away, we were enamored by each other and without hurry, we quickly fell madly in love with one another. We've been blessed to experience the kind of love that's written about in the classics; a love we waited our combined lifetimes to know; a love that's revealed in the deepest desire to learn and live the truth; those discoverable truths that lie in the silence of each moment; together. Apart, Sue and I are less than whole; together we seem Eternal.

Quite naturally, seven months later, a lifetime experienced, and Sue and I married. In September of 2012, in the back yard of the home she was raised, Nudged to marry sooner than later by her daughter, Kelci's, impending journey abroad. Seeing us together, my sister, Debi, went online and became a minister to perform the ceremony.

It was magical.

Debi and her husband Dave flew in from Sacramento, another sister Carmen came from Boston, Samantha and her fiancé Bryan flew in from Los Angeles, my mother and Dallas had moved to Portland from Tucson in July to be near Dallas' daughter, but since have moved back to Tucson for the sun. Sue's two daughters and mother and father and brothers put everything together, Matthew sang and played the guitar, Michael took great pictures, and Samantha and Sue's daughters Breona and Kelci became sisters and Matthew and Michael their new brothers. An amazing new family was formed, as a result of our Faith and steadfast belief that when we surrender our fears to God, He provides the answer.

Our world is changed forever, Sue's and mine; but God knows it has not. We're where He wants us to be and have been, for years.

Patrick's Gift

NOVEMBER 1981

My brother Patrick Joseph Terry and a few of us from work had locked up the little restaurant I managed, Gepetto's, during the ski bum portion of my life, and went out for a beer to unwind. We were toasting everything... Here's to beer, to Tampons, to the hockey-pucks who like watching hockey on TV. It was the height of youthful stupidity and if one of us raised a glass, it was to be a wise-ass and to mock the mundane mockable.

I don't remember who all was around that table with us that night, down at the Bongo Lounge, but we were having one of those simply stupid and great times that young adult idiots have after a long day at work. It was getting late, so we decided to break it up quickly and go to my house for late night ping pong battle. I grabbed a six-pack-to-go and walked out the front door as the rest of the party left out the back.

As the door closed behind me, I was shocked by the loud thunderous wine of a powerful motorcycle racing south on Highland Drive. There, right in front of me, my brother Patrick and Mike Archuleta were flying by, headed to God knows where…

The flight ended within a few thousand feet, though. The headlights of the El Camino were aiming directly at my brother; in the wrong lane facing north. Pat's break lights flashed bright red and off… He had no time to slow. The screech of his tires skidded on the asphalt for only a fraction of a second…

BOOM!

The explosive and absolute and decisive sound of the impact of a high-speed head on collision filled the cold November air and was immediately gone, yet it will never leave me.

Michael and Patrick were in a seemingly endless spread eagle summersault, like stick figures… they flew through the air some 15 feet straight up and over the car… everything was crushed.

My jaw dropped and time stopped… this didn't just happen, did it? My mind could not process the unmistakable death of my brother and Michael; and I turned away, threw my six-pack at the ground and sunk to my knees with my back to them. My eyes closed, head down, I knelt on the sidewalk… everything was happening in slow motion. My mind and body were numb to the surroundings. I heard nothing. The night was still and quiet and my thoughts were emptied in disbelief.

In a moment of timelessness, there came a rush of energy that filled my body from my back and engulfed me completely. The feeling of immense peace took me by surprise. How could I feel this calm and my mind be so absolutely quiet in the midst of such a traumatic and confusing moment in time? I Instantly had been filled with an energy I'd never known that came from deep within my being and from far, far away and I knew Instantly I was experiencing Eternity; Life beyond this material world; Heaven.

The peace I felt is indescribable. A hyper tingling sensation filled my entire body... every molecule of my being was alive and I was filled with a complete sense of knowing of the makings of the universe far beyond this planet, yet recognizable and amazingly comforting; ironically, joy. It was like walking through a door and entering a place where you've always wanted to be; a home you've known forever and forever sought to return.

I'd just witnessed that which we fear most, death, and I was OK with it; in that timeless moment, I knew Patrick was dead and at the same time, Patrick was still very much alive and he was doing better than all right. I knew he was in Heaven and he had just given me a sneak preview of what it's like to live beyond the need for a human body. I waited there alone on the sidewalk for the endless moment to pass, stood and walked back into the bar... called 911.

While it took several years afterward for me to accept and appreciate the existence of a loving and forgiving Father, God, I owe Pat a lot for that gift he gave me on that cold November night. He physically and spiritually touched me on his way from this world to the next and let me know it's OK, he's OK. From that instant, I've not again feared death.

I fear dying, but not death... for in that gifted moment in time I discovered that there is no such thing as "The End."

CHAPTER 3

"But Wait, There's More!"

"Amazing Grace, how sweet the sound
that saved a wretch like me....
I once was lost but now am found
twas blind, but now, I see."

John Newton

How does one find God?

For me, it wasn't magic, but close.

Try this.

Close your eyes and ask the unanswerable question, "Does God exist?" Ask it from your deepest desire for truth and, at that moment in time, when you're physically and emotionally open – desperate enough – beaten down enough – sincere enough and there's nothing left of your ego to hang up the process, God rushes in through the slightest crack in the opening to your soul and enlightens you; lifts you spiritually, emotionally, and physically. The eyes of your heart are now opened and you know it's Him that's saved you from yourself and your dire straits and you've discovered His Forgiveness and Love; unearned peace and hope; His Grace.

In time, the unprovable God is personally proven and you've been reborn.

For me, though, due to the thick layers of guilt, fears of oppression, and years of resentment that I'd built around my soul, it took enumerable attempts by God, as well as for me to finally be honest enough with myself, that I finally "got it"; that He exists.

In the best of times, things can always be better and most certainly in the worst. The fifteen years in a listless marriage with the boy's mother that led to a rescuing divorce wasn't my first experience in marital dismantling.

In October of 1986, Tami, my daughter Samantha's mother, and I ended our marriage. That year was the first of two "worst years of my life;" financially, the second being 2011. But, while the diseases that caused the awful pains were of a similar virus, the intensity of the symptoms and emotional recovery from each were vastly different.

The human ability to apply elegance to action, in the face of life's great challenges grows proportionally to our ability to emotionally absorb and master the suffering of socially- self- and environmentally-inflicted pain. As I'd mentioned in the Preface, by 1988, at the age of 33, through a series of miraculous discoveries, I began to understand that my ability to emotionally absorb and master calmness in the face of intense suffering is directly proportional to my ability to include God in the process. Until then, I'd planned to manage suffering solo. And, for Tami and me, without a habit of activating the God Protocol, we had no God to include as a Rescuer to solve our seemingly unsolvable problems.

Managing money was the unfixable unsolvable problem for Tami and me. Living a lifestyle a few classes ahead of our earnings is a pattern begun long ago; on credit. Young, and living a make-believe life in that "the party would never end", we were unappreciative of the need to battle to keep our family together. We didn't think marriage required that much work. And we assumed we were strong enough and talented enough to get through anything. Amid losing our home and everything we owned, we quickly began to lose faith in the illusory lifestyle we could no longer afford to maintain.

Being the King and the Queen of the Ball, these lines hit me real hard...

> "...they got an apartment with deep pile carpets
> and a couple of paintings from Sears,
> a big waterbed they bought with the bread
> they'd saved for a couple of years.
> They started to fight when the money got tight
> they just didn't count on the tears."
>
> Billy Joel
> Scenes from an Italian Restaurant

And Tami turned to her friends for relief, while I ignored the inevitable and by October, I called it quits on us and we separated.

Samantha was nearly three years old and, because I couldn't bear to be without her, I made arrangements to have her every weekend. Throughout the next two years I suffered the incredible pain and anguish from an incessant and self-punishing mindal-drone that would gnaw at the core of my existence.

"What good am I, now that I failed my family, so terribly?"

"I've lost what I've wanted most and now I'm the loser I never thought I'd be"

And without a relationship with a loving and forgiving God; my fragile, insecure, and destroyable self-esteem was ransacked by the certainty that I alone was to blame, that I was bad, that I was a failure, and there is no fix for my inherited money problems. I wallowed in shame and loneliness.

I had no God, nor did I approve of God; nor did I have an interest or desire to recognize His authority or existence. By that time, I'd lost touch with Him long ago and, as the pain and anguish from the divorce intensified; I became more accepting of my unworthiness and deserving of immense punishment and had grown comfortable in the illusion of my hellishly self-made lot in life. I was a sad lost child without a home or a vision of what a happy home might resemble.

~

By the year of my "great discovery", 1988, nearly two years after the divorce, to say I'd not yet recovered is a laughable understatement. My mind was torturing itself, tormented by "what ifs" and I'd yet to find the defining purpose for my life, except that every day I would wake up, shower, eat, and breathe.

By early spring, I'd moved to Park City, about 40 minutes from Salt Lake. At 7,000 feet elevation, surrounded by ski hills and mountain trails, the old mining town was a great place to exercise the demons from my soul. The room I rented overlooked the town's main street with all the happenings of a resort destination at my doorstep and above all, I could run the trails from out the back door to 10,800 foot peaks and in the winter ski home.

The cool morning mountain air and dead quiet offered me peace in the midst of the horrendous mental commotion and anxieties I'd self-imposed. But, there was no escape from the emotional and financial problems and my detailed visions of a failed life that would play over and over again in my mind; unwind to a place of peace and replay to draining agony. Refuge from my mind's over-thinking itself into an expected place in hell was found only in my sleep or as I'd fight for my life in the final hour of an incredibly painful trail run.

The trails of the Wasatch Front are rocky, twisting, and endless; through aspen and pine forests and carved from the mountainside, to reach the high meadows of wild flowers and sagebrush, above tree line. The lure was impossible to ignore. Sometimes I'd run for five straight hours, clear two passes and loop back and stumble the last few miles; absolutely physically and emotionally exhausted, dusty, hungry and dry, but nonetheless clear headed.

While running the trails, anxious thoughts appeared in my mind and vanished right away as I'd be pressed to maintain an upright position, scrambling down trails, meant to be hiked. The rocky trail tests your attention as roots will grab a toe and, if I'd be off fighting a battle in my mind, I'd soon be brought back to the "all important Now", that place in time I'd exited, or I'd be on my face or quite possibly thrown off a cliff.

So, either before or after work each day, I'd replace tormenting anxieties with constant exercise; exercise with a view. In natural surroundings, my thoughts turned to the beauty in the world and that, just maybe, I deserved to be free of negative thoughts; although I couldn't begin to forgive myself for my actions.

As a bonus, in my escape from hell through difficult and challenging exercise, my will could push my body through the pain; push beyond exhaustion; in the process, massive amounts of endorphins are injected; nature's pain killer; next to adrenaline, dopamine, beer, wine, and chocolate; my drug of choice. Endorphins provide the mind the illusion that the body is in no pain while muscles are being torn and ripped apart under the stress of endless hill climbs and speedy quad-punishing descents, as muscles cannibalize themselves for fuel, once the fat and glycogen stores are spent. My eye sockets kept barely the fat to be able to hold my eyes in place.

Time alone with my thoughts and the experience of surviving endless trail runs was the perfect therapy required to organize thought; process and compartmentalize issues; if not only to endure my punishing insanity. However, my peace was not to last. Once I was cleaned up and fed, shortly my mind would begin to churn the problems over and over again and again. Those negative thoughts had become a part of who I was, as I'd be haunted by the incessant destructive self-talk. It was debilitating.

Physically exhausted, yet mentally and emotionally alert to my inner turmoil, it would take hours to get to sleep at night. I could hardly look forward to bed, as I'd slowly count backwards from 100 to zero to get my brain to stop working on "the fix" for my problems. Over the months, a simple countdown quit working, so I raised the bar to begin the countdown from 1000, and when that quit working, if I made a mistake and took my focus off the shape of the number, as I counted it down to zero, I'd punish myself and begin the countdown again from a thousand.

Crazy is a good word to describe where it is I was going.

~

Interesting guy... Ian. Don't recall his last name, met him down at Cicero's, a club at the top of Main Street in Park City. I being 33 and he about 60 years old I considered him the Sage. He had long stringy gray hair, and a wry yet serene smile. He dressed down, way down, but he was quite wealthy. On his business card, he had two phone numbers, one in Park City and the other in Bali. What struck me interesting, though, were the words on the back of his card.

"Don't let the sound of your own wheels drive you crazy!"

The Eagles

Just what I needed to hear, but what could I do about it? I was jealous for his demeanor. I'd lived in emotional misery for so long and was so confused about life and who I was and what was to become of me that I'd *almost* begin to pray for direction; seriously... I nearly prayed to a Higher Being of which I'd abandoned long ago. I couldn't imagine that by a prayer I could somehow be lifted of my every issue and my problems could magically be resolved.

First off, it sounds ridiculous to pray!

And at that point in my life, the thought of resorting to prayer was, well... it was beneath me. Prayer was for the weak and those who needed to escape the realities of life by giving their problems to some abstract being they called God.

I was young and tough and who is this, or what is this God anyway? And why trust God when the world is so screwed up? Look at what He created; a cancerous growing mass of strange and greedy power-hungry people stealing from and killing one another. And to kill in the name of God, the irony, I will never understand. Besides, I can handle anything, I can fix any problem... "bring it on!"

And I don't need a Church to tell me how to live. Church is for goodie-goodies and phonies who need a stage for the show, to show how good they are. Church is for those brought up in a religion and are just too lazy to explore a different path or those so insecure that they need a place to belong and Churches can't say no to them. Forget it. That wasn't for me; I had it figured out... really, I did!

Spiritual Logic

~

Despite my self-reliance and proud determination to handle things on my own, it was during that summer of insanity that a completely unexpected awakening began to take place in my soul. Ironically, an awaking rooted in the stories of one who might be the world's most famous agnostic, Benjamin Franklin. I took the summer of '88 to slowly and carefully read his 800-page autobiography; enthralled by the details of his story; each phrase had a rich meaning, so, as I read, I studied with intrigue and couldn't go a day without reaching a new facet that could change my life in conclusion; once adhered.

I was amazed by this man's ability to inspect the world with a child's intrigue, recognize wisdom in nature, and connect with our world's leading minds. What interested me about his story was his desire to act on his instincts filtered through character traits he'd developed through industrious and honorable work. I credit his book and story with igniting my search to develop and claim my good character and instill in me the determination to live a life based on high moral values, social responsibility, and right action. While I'm sure he might have been overly generous in this self-flattering memoir, I appreciate his willingness to share his story with such great detail and absorbable prose.

That summer of reading about his life instilled in me an image of a life of possibilities and success and he showed me a model to follow that leads to the accomplishment of great things; an image of what might be achieved through a virtuous life, lived well. These are his 13 virtues as written in the book:

Order
    Let all your things have their places.

Resolution
    Resolve to perform what you ought; perform without fail what you resolve.

Industry
    Lose no time; be always employed in something useful; cut off all unnecessary actions.

Frugality

Make no expense but to do good to others or yourself; i.e., waste nothing.

Justice
Wrong none by doing injury or through passive omission benefit from another's loss.

Moderation
Avoid extremes; forbear resenting injuries so much as you think they deserve.

Sincerity
Use no hurtful deceit; think innocently and justly, and, if you speak, speak accordingly.

Tranquility
Be not disturbed at trifles or at accidents common or unavoidable.

Temperance
Eat not to dullness; drink not to elevation.

Silence
Speak not but what may benefit others or yourself; avoid trifling conversation.

Cleanliness
Tolerate no uncleanliness in body, clothes, or habitation.

Chastity
Rarely use venery but for health or offspring, never to dullness, weakness, or the injury of your own or another's peace or reputation.

Humility
Imitate Jesus and Socrates.

Humility, which he was prodded to include by his friends, was not his greatest strength. But, by practicing each of these 13 virtues, one at a time, every day one week at a time, as he recommended, my mind was beginning to focus on being a better, more successful person that I'd hoped for my entire life I could become.

And it started with a single step to bring order to my life. Making my bed each morning was something I could control; a simple, yet conscious decision I could make each day to establish order. "I will make my bed" was my first decision of the day. An accomplishment, the importance of which, made by that single powerful decision to make my bed each morning and relate this as a defining act speaks to just how screwed up I was.

~

Not being one to give up on going into business, that fall I ventured into a plan with five of my Cable TV comrades, to form a Cable TV auditing company; looking for people illegally connected. We had a sure-fire business plan, so we pooled some money together and I was elected to fly to Minneapolis to represent our group and meet with a company that could help us launch the new business.

This trip changed my life.

It was on this fortuitous business trip that I discovered God and I'll forever remember the time and the place, but never understand why me, why then, and why not everyone?

On Thursday afternoon, October 27th, 1988, Tom Behr and John Poulos picked me up at the Minneapolis airport in their company Bentley. I couldn't believe how well these guys were doing; how successful they appeared. John was wearing some kind of dead animal fur coat that reached the ground and, oddly, it didn't look too terrible on him, for the way he carried himself.

I knew John in Salt Lake and he'd developed great marketing concepts, but had yet to hit his stride. We drove to their offices and I presented our group's business case and as they explained their business model, I knew there was no match. But not being one to give up easy, I floundered in every attempt to align our forces. We simply weren't connecting on any, but superficial levels.

That evening, as planned, I stayed at John's home with him and his family. His wife, Jane, and I had gone to school together, so it was easy to leave our briefcases at the door and have a nice dinner together. Later, in the living room with a glass of wine, we talked about our families and how important they were to us. We spoke about our children. I remember telling Tom about my daughter Samantha and how I couldn't imagine working for their Company; too much travel; living on the road. There was no way I'd leave Sam for an extended period of time. I'd placed a tremendous burden on myself for breaking up our family and, since the divorce; I had eagerly spent every weekend with her. I would not let her down one more time by working so far away.

That's all it took.

Out of the blue, Tom looks at John and says, "He needs to meet Leni!" John smiled and agreed. The energy in the room picked up and they had my attention.

"Who's Leni?"

Tom got on the phone and, without answering me, as he waited for Leni to pick up, asked me, "When does your flight leave tomorrow?" Speaking to Leni, now, he set up a time for us to meet, hung up and smiled. I obviously had no choice but to meet Leni, no explanation, and subject changed…

There's no script for this kind of a thing, but everyone I've known who's shared their experience with me, nods and gets it. It's an awakening, a new beginning, being "Born Again". But, for me it was absolute and I know that sometime between 11:00 AM and noon on that Friday morning October 28, 1988, at the town home of Leni Behr; I found that God exists and He loves me even when I couldn't.

The best I can describe it is that during our meeting, which began with an unusually comfortable "prayer of protection", Leni began telling me things about me and about whom it is that I am and what I can accomplish with the gifts that I've been given.

And I believed her.

As she spoke to me, everything was spot on and I began to believe in her Source. In this fully trusting moment, I found a deep inner sense of peace with what she had described. As she spoke it, I knew it. She was reading my book out loud to me and I was hearing it read for the first time.

During this brief encounter, I realized I wasn't alone; we are not alone. God knows each of us intimately, He has a plan for each of us, He forgives us without price and before we ask, He gifts us with an answer, with His love; a love so grand that it's beyond our ability to comprehend.

To this very day, I can't help but choke a little every time I hear...

> "He saved a wretch like me.
> I once was lost but now am found
> twas blind, but now I see."

Wow!

So, that's what being "Born again" is about.

I was a new person. I don't know any other way to describe it; my old self had died and I was born anew. I'd had a life altering, eye opening experience and I was filled with an energy I'd never – ever known. So much was becoming clear to me so quickly that I couldn't hold it in; I needed to run out and unleash it onto the world.

"There is a God!"

"He loves me!"

"He forgives me!"

> "Hello, Bedford Falls. Hello, you old Building and Loan!"
>
> Jimmy Stewart
> from It's a Wonderful Life

I was Home again. God had become real.

And He needs nothing from me to be accepted by Him. He actually wants me... you and me to succeed and for us to share in the amazing life He knows we are capable of leading. I could feel it all around me. "I was forgiven, loved, brand new and not alone." Try to imagine the reprieve I felt from the hell I'd endured for so, so many months; so many years.

I was weightless.

~

Poor Carmen… my sister had no idea of what was about to hit her. She lives in Boston and, for the second leg of the trip; I was to stay with her and her husband Jimmy and my brother from another mother, Rich Albert. Needless to say, that first night in Boston was one of my favorite nights; ever. I had more energy than I'd had in years, my mind was hyper-clear about everything and I made a terrifically grand spastic spectacle of myself trying to explain to her and my friends what I, now, knew. But, I don't remember trying to go to sleep that night. I must have quit counting.

So, I'm a little slow, it took 33 years for me to "get it" but I couldn't believe what a very cool thing it is to have such a loving relationship with a supportive God. He immediately became my top priority, learning about Him, discovering who I am and deciding to live my life – incredible – with Him; and at no cost; without a hitch. I didn't have to become anybody else, I didn't have to join any church or pay any dues. All that I had to do is be me, be a loving son, be appreciative of His Love for me, and take a small step forward every day to hug Him back and make an honest attempt to hold Him close, in everything I do; hang on tight; He's got me.

Back in Salt Lake, the following week, at a Mexican restaurant with John Jenkins, one of my Cable TV comrades, I shared the story of my "awakening". In the excitement, he cut me off and asked, in a kind, but direct tone, "Bill, what do you want?" And without blinking, I surprised myself, as two words fell from my mouth, "The truth." He smiled and said, "OK, I can go for that." My search had begun and an endless array of miracles was about to unfold in my brand-new life.

CHAPTER 4

A California Mission

"California isn't a place; it's a way of life."

Nancy Reagan
(paraphrased)

After that first meeting with Leni, in October of 1988, I was like a child in a new home; exploring every nook and cranny; searching the world with eager curiosity for the truth about God, Angels, and Saints. I explored what had, for so very long, gone unexplored; my relationship with God. And with my mind and eyes pried open from a long spiritual slumber, I read ravenously all that I could about God and Spirit. New understandings arrived daily and I began to appreciate the beauty in this living tapestry woven by the laws of the spiritual and material worlds.

I'd receive a newly discovered wisdom as a gift; fascinated by the depth of Eternal reason, I'd embrace it, yet I'd be left with many more unanswered questions. The more I learned and continue to learn, the more I realize just how much I don't know, as well as, how little I know that is worth arguing to insist that I do.

Embracing my new "life in the spirit", fully, I studied organized religions' role in our spiritual growth. I studied Taoism, Buddhism, Hinduism, New Age-ism, Protestant Reforms, Mormonism, Unity, Evangelical Christianity, but surprisingly I circled back to the one religion I could not understand its seemingly strict and ancient ritualism and critical stance on progressive growth with a loving God; Catholicism. Through this great and fantastic journey I determined that most religions have two basic similarities; a love and devotion to God (or whatever the Creator or Universal Force might be called) and the mission to treat our neighbor as we would like to be treated and to do so beyond color, age, gender, or ability.

And despite what the Catholic Church leadership or the Vatican may pronounce, until Pope Francis came along, nearly every major religion shares one basic flaw, a flaw that has led to the most horrific wars and desecration of life; the belief that theirs is the one and only true pathway to salvation and the rest of us are or should be damned and will most certainly go to hell for our blasphemous and inappropriate methods of worship and praise.

We may be a truly insane people, for as smart as we are.

Even as a spiritual-newborn, I couldn't fathom the idea of joining a church. I believed there to be no solace found, for my mind's many troubles, in worship with others. I needed time to explore, unobserved, un-judged; my relationship with God. I wasn't ready to experience a group connection, especially among those whom I believed were intoxicated by the Kool-Aid served by institutional religions. My perception of the grand purpose for organized religion was in a serious flux, having grown up in the Mormon State of Utah; Land of Zion; I being a gentile; an Altar Boy; with no seat at the table.

My understanding in the God/man relationship/experience is that it's a daily challenge that must be met, unobstructed by pride of specialness or by fear of not being accepted by one of man's seemingly superior belief systems formed into a named Religion. God has no favorite son, no favorite Religion, no favorite way of being loved or honored... God is Love, uncontrolled, and unconditional.

So, I kept my learning to myself and prayed; prayed and meditated, a lot.

And I found the ever-elusive peacefulness and profound security and confidence in life, finally, in the easy connection with God through unstructured prayer. So, I've learned the moment by moment value in prayer and how easy it is to talk with God, as if He were here with me, right here.

And why not?

He is right here with me, with you, with them (no matter who "they" are).

At that time, I had the freedom in my schedule to meditate deeply for hours each morning and I journaled my findings and did so, in the safety of privacy untouched by others profound learning. Perfectly timed, Leni had taught me a meditation that guided me to be released from my downward ratcheting thoughts and that could help open my mind and spirit to connect with the Spirit of Truth within and the Father of all; everything of which we are a piece and part. She taught me how to prepare my mind to listen for His powerful voice of wisdom and truth; that breathless voice that can be heard within the mind; a voice without sound; a loving voice of truth beyond the mind's concoction.

It's a freebee we each have; His guidance. And when we choose to take a time-out from our daily routines and our rush to hurry; stop our overworked minds from sampling too many inputs and conniving self-satisfying outputs, when we stop and listen, we hear His Thought and receive the gift of His Truth, as it presents itself; Now.

Unobstructed by self, this Eternal and freely disclosed Thought is His Will. It is His uniquely personalized Will for us, for this precise moment in time; times 7.3 billion; give or take a few hundred million of our brothers and sisters here on earth.

He can do anything and we don't have to figure it out – nor might we!

And in this uniquely gifted Thought driven by Love; combined with the totality of each of His divergent and unique and universally-connected Thoughts for each of us; He creates for us a myriad of unrecognized and seemingly disassociated materialized miracles, instantaneously, to keep this planet's inhabitants mostly moving forward toward His giant Will for our combined happiness; His outcome being perfected.

And we move more quickly in His direction when we take the time; for an instant; to stop thinking, become still, trust in His Thought, and allow that Original Thought to bloom from within and allow it to become completely who we are in this single solitary moment; then the next and the next... simple! But this simple act is insanely difficult to act upon while in the throes of disbelief and striving to make our selfish wants and manufactured needs become real; by every metrics.

Yet, in these quiet moments of stillness a clear vision and purpose for the new day emerges; a Truth for the day beyond confusion, frustrations, fears, or personal needs to create safety and security for our families and friends. The truth for this day, instilled from Eternity's ultimate creative Thought, is a free Gift we mustn't ignore the value of its import.

His Thought, freely gifted, inspires ingenuity and goes by the names Intuition and Genius and we realize there is no coincidence, there is no such thing as luck, nor is an outcome left to chance. We are loved by Him mutually and individually and He wants for our happiness; especially and equally.

~

About Leni; I remember her presence more than her face; beautiful from the inside out. She had an aura of kindness and knowingness about her; a calm reassuring woman. She taught me well in our brief encounter as she explained the importance of unclenching the mind, especially a mind as busy and troubled as was mine. But first, quiet the body; envision every muscle relaxed, as that of a cat lying on a hot porch in the summertime sun. And as you reach to pick it up, sliding your hands palms up under its body and its head and hind legs fall limp, its warm body wraps 'round your hands; imagine it's you; fully relaxed from head to toe.

Next, envision a spiritual master being present, sitting with you. She chose Jesus. Focus on His loving eyes and stop any thoughts of pain and need; no guilt or need to hurry. That's when you're ready to connect with God and He's been invited to work on the depths of your psyche and cleanse your soul.

She began the "guided tour" of my eternal soul with her "Prayer of Protection". The prayer, she said, was to protect me/us from ourselves more than from any outside source. So, here's how it goes:

"God"

(breathe...)

"Thank you Father for all that you are doing for me, for my family, for all whom I love and who come into my life. I ask for Your protection during this time we have together that Your thought becomes mine and that You protect me from fear and regret and from outside pressures or negative thoughts of other's that might disturb me and lead me away from You. Replace my fears with your love."

Now, imagine you're lying in a high mountain meadow near a calm clear lake, with not a ripple, and the breeze is slight and the air fresh, small white clouds float effortlessly in a deep blue summer sky...

Pause and breathe...

Now a disturbing thought passes by and the clouds become darker and the wind picks up. The water is now choppy and turning to white caps, as the storms in your life disturb your soul and angers you for disrupting the peace and beauty of the day. The storm is your featureless fears bundled into a troubling and sometimes terrifying experience.

Now focus on your breath and the imagine yourself filled with the strength and the courage of God's Wisdom and Love; unaffected by each thought arising from a fear that naturally crosses your mind; unaware of your surrounding's noise; unmoved by self-made pressures; life goes on around you unnoticed, unaffected. In stillness, allow yourself to become less; become nothing; become a part of everything and the lake is once again, as it's meant to be; calm peaceful; as are you.

Deep breath...

If you feel any tension, allow it and breathe through it and relax your shoulders and eyes; no weight on your shoulders, you've handed it all to God.

Now, envision a column of bright white light entering your body through the top of your head downward to fill the heart and as it connects with the Eternal Inner Light within your heart it fills your chest and it glows and time stops as God's purest Energy and Love for you and us is pondered; without hurry.

Now connected with Eternity, focus on this light glowing brightly in your heart and see it swell and grow to fill your entire body as it shoots down each leg through your feet and out your toes. As the light shoots up the back of your neck and over the top of your head to fill each muscle of your face, your eyes relax and jaw releases. The light travels from your heart up and across your shoulders and down your arms through your hands and finger tips and out; untrapped.

As brilliant white light travels through your body, every muscle has released ancestral, current, and unknown fossilized tension and you melt in God's loving-warmth.

Lay still, present, relaxed with God; aglow in His Eternal presence, safe in His arms; there is no darkness allowed, no shadow or hint of grey; completely brilliantly aglow... fully energized within Him. Take time and allow the light to take over every corner. Every dark spot is filled with light and you slowly brighten, more so than the moment before; slowly you brighten with no resistance or need to consider a reason or limit.

There is no past. There is no future. Stop and contemplate, this Eternal Now where God resides in whole.

Spiritual Logic

Now, as God's light shines from your body it fills a surrounding bubble, six feet in all directions, and this bubble is your aura of life energy, which is now filled with this bright white light and instantly there is no regret or fear. All that is, ever was, and ever will be, exists right Here and right Now. Instantly, as your body and mind is emptied of stresses and fears and self-doubt, God fills it full with His Love.

Envision the light now fills and surrounds the room and every molecule is lit; harmonized.

Pause... the light fills the building. Pause, give thanks and bless the space... the city... state ... country... Pause at each to consider loved ones, friends, coworkers, and allow loving thoughts to surround each and see each filled with this same light.

Now imagine the world, every country without border, friends and family abroad, the poor, the homeless, the suffering; our world family. Now see the leaders in business, institution, church, and government filled with this same loving light. Take as much or as little time as you're able or would like; hold conscious attention at each step; no pressure to perform; be easy on yourself, as is God.

The world is now filled with and surrounded in light... Next, the Universe and all that is, is covered, surrounded, and filled with this bright white light that is pure, absolute, true, loving, and all of which God is. And all that is, is in the hands of God; aglow.

(Breathe... smile, relax in His arms)

Protected in God's loving light; pray that only love exists in this day's thoughts and that all other thoughts are dismissed without resistance; released from the need to control or fix. Now, listen quietly in stillness.

Open to God's truth and without want, released from ego's agenda, you may love all that is, just as God loves us. In stillness, give God all that is required of you, all that you fear, need, want, and all that must be done. In this true and honest moment, give up everything important and pray for the courage and brilliance to do His Will; only. Trust that His Will for you and us is greater than our imaginations and that He loves us, each, more than we may know.

We are safe in His arms surrounded in His light; filled with His Love.

Breathe… quietly listen to a breathless still thought that is His… ask your questions and enjoy a private conversation with the Creator of all that exists… and give thanks for His comfort in this safe place and time.

You good?

OK, snap out of it and get to work!

~

Over time, the physical vibration experienced in this connection may become frightening. But, as the energy is allowed to flow, you'll learn to relax within it and more easily embrace it. You might feel you could levitate; go ahead; why not, if the ceiling's high enough.

In this Eternal connection, the vibration is merely a result of a release from the illusions we've created for our lives and the vibration is our body's natural connection to the Eternal that lies alive within and with the whole of God's surrounding Love. In these purely honest moments, we begin to understand that we're worthy of this completeness and it's OK to be connected absolutely with God.

And when His thought is heard, feel free to laugh or cry as this is a safe and healing place and our personal connection with His Love is precisely what He wants. In meditation, to this day, I may experience the precise sensation that I had when my brother Patrick was killed, as he left this world for the next. The mind's emptiness and God's readiness to fill the vacuum is His promise fulfilled. He rushes in with this gift; a Holy connection with the mind of Creation; of Eternal love and forgiveness. It must have been pure love; the sensation Patrick filled me with when his body was killed.

This period of awakening was an incredible time in my life; with answers to the unanswerable, at my fingertips. And I had a lot of help. As exciting as discovering personal proof of the improvable God, Leni introduced me to the reality of our loving Guardian Angels. These beings are as real as are we, as necessary to our survival as the air we breathe; neither may we see, but in absence we suffer unnecessarily and may perish helplessly.

Leni spoke of Angels in "a matter of fact" terms, that they are assigned to us at birth to protect, connect, and guide us throughout our journeys on this planet. She also spoke of a plan that is written for each of us and she read to me my road map and gave me a vision of the possibilities in life that I'm capable of achieving and the tools we each have at our disposal to uncover the truth for the day. No matter the difficulty of the situation or confrontation faced, I now had the tools to understand and tap into the courage required to speak and act with honor and integrity; but only because of this free Gift I've found in the intimate moments in stillness; which connects us to the Almighty's Eternal and loving Mind.

~

Fresh from my amazing cross country, mind altering, business trip I'd been freed from the turmoil of a hyper-guilty mind and distressed soul and with the newfound clarity and ability to forgive myself; I once again began to accept that I could lead a deservedly happy and productive life. So, the decision to leave Utah was easy, although the courage to do so was not without a Higher backing. I was on a mission and now had access to the knowledge of what I must do. This Knowledge came from a source I could trust, beyond the manipulative selfish-mind I'd mistakenly honored for my entire life. I now had a connection to the Highest Source, not mine but mine to access; the Source I could trust beyond myself.

From this inner knowingness, I knew what I had to do and that Samantha would be better if I were better. So, I went to work for John and Tom and hit the road. The first stop was Reno, Nevada for the first two months in the winter of 1989; then off to California. Since childhood, I'd wanted to live on the beach, especially in Southern California. So, when an opening came up to work a contract in Los Angeles, I jumped at the chance. It seemed that I'd been rewarded for following the direction to dedicate my life to follow God; from knowledge and understandings gained by meditation; my first stop in L.A. was the marina apartments on Tahiti Drive in Marina Del Rey.

The melodic near and distant sounds of the marina – the muffled bells and restless riggings of the sail boats docked, the smell and feel of the briny ocean air, the majestic palms, and the aromas of the gardens and flowering trees. It was precisely where I needed to be; a place I could prepare my soul for the craziness of fulfilling the contracts in the Los Angeles marketplace.

Fascinated, I'd been thrust into an amazing racial mix of bustling humanity; it was new, big, and would have been overwhelming had it not been for the support of true men of faith; Tom and John and of my new-found relationship with God. I could not have planned a better jump from the perceived safety of normalcy in Utah to the open and varied attitudes and lifestyles of Southern California.

Moderation in all things is important. By the time, I'd made it to California, after a few months of practicing these extended meditations on the mountaintop in Park City, I found myself walking in the clouds to the point I couldn't be real. I saw life in living color and all things had a reason, there's a bigger plan – relax, be a part of it – the Universe is not against us; it's cool.

Well, I soon was reminded that everything isn't always cool and when people hurt they don't appreciate, what appeared to be, my ambivalent happy-happy wonderland attitude. So, I had to learn, quickly, to keep one foot on the ground, to be real, and to sincerely understand and appreciate the seriousness of another's pain and personal struggles. How else might I well serve another, wholly?

~

Before I could reach a place in my development that I could think of another's plight and how might I help, I had to clean up my personal troubles; clear my troubled slate. Early in my spiritual awakening, I'd made what I thought to be a major discovery to discern the answers received in stillness, to correct wrong thinking, and guide me correctly.

I'd pray thoughtfully to cleanse my being of negativity and stop the wheels in my mind from churning and, in stillness, be able to listen without expectation; I'd get an answer in the form of a solid, yet quiet and breathless "yes" or "no". To receive an answer so vividly was exciting. But, I had to question the answer with reason, as my mind would take over and an earthly rationale gives its answer based on merit and experience.

These second-thoughts, I learned are my ego's directives based on fear of loss or of how to protect the ideals I firmly held, owned, or felt the need to control.

I began to realize that my ego has its own agenda, which is 180 degrees from that of God's. My Ego's desires and directions are filtered through my history, my wants, my story, and in reaction to my deeply imbedded fears. Its mission is to construct a person of its own; a person who is far better than the weak and frail being God created; with all of its perceived imperfections.

The little guy on my shoulder that speaks into one ear that justifies greed, retaliation, or whatever it is I am selling or trying to get away with... that's my ego. In time, I learned better to recognize just how much I wrestle with my ego and had begun to make critical moment by moment choices – to tap into the mind of God or go about business as usual and follow the herd mentality.

And as I took note of the outcome of my decisions, as I listened to one direction over the other, I discovered that the very first Thought, the Initiating Thought, is undeniable Truth; revealed.

Admit how many times you've said, "I should have gone with my first thought" and regretted not doing so. Well, I learned right away to take that quite literally. I found through trial and error that that first thought is God's answer, He does not hesitate, He knows the question before it's asked, and once we make the decision to ask, His thought is instilled; it is presented.

However, I found that I wasn't very good at determining that first thought. It's not as easy as it sounds. Our minds work so very quickly especially when we're in trouble and must react quickly to outwit a personal attack or defer realities' pain or when we overthink the solution to a problem and, because we're intelligent and sentient beings that've been proven to be right before, we're certain that we are right and must defend our well thought solutions.

Excited, but confused by the prospect of access to this Eternally Right Information, I found it quite difficult to distinguish which directives (thoughts) are mine from those of God's whispers. Quickly... which thought is it? From the multitudes of thoughts and counter-thoughts on any given subject: Which is mine? Which is God's?

Practice, practice, practice...

While God's thought on any given subject or answer to a prayer is my first and Initiating Thought, I also learned to trust the outcome of acting upon it and my Faith grew with each conquest of fear replaced with its natural counter; Love. As I would commit myself to act on His Thoughts, my life became a series of miracles. Miracles show and have showed themselves in succession and soon became expected. And I began to ask often and always, no matter the dimension, I'd stop, pray and act on the First Thought. The First Thought is right; right on many dimensions that we may not be able to perceive. The more I practiced listening, the more success I've had at living; the more trust I'm able to put into God's Plan ahead of mine and the less I've cared if I am right and you are wrong.

Once comfortable with the Word received and if it's more than His imprinted feeling or a simple "Yes" or "No", the next step is to write it down; the single word heard and another will surely follow. I began writing these thoughts on paper just after arriving home from meeting Leni. As I'd write what I heard in stillness, some words I would need to look up their meaning, nonetheless, the words began to form a sentence. If I stayed out of the way and allowed the message to appear, in whole, regardless of how absurd or wrong I thought the word selection, the message clarified and made perfect sense. One sentence finished then the next and little by little, as I learned to listen with patience, in earnest, and without agenda; a complete direction, admonition, or assurance was received; revealed.

Sound crazy?

Well, it might be, so here's the acid test for lunacy:

Does the message guide us to better serve God's Will or does it massage the truth to help us protect ambitious claims of authority, to change or control others, or to form the world to fit our imagines of greatness?

Don't forget the lesson Lucifer didn't learn; there's room for only one God, one true Source and Center of Creation in this Universe. Another test; God's voice is not audible. It is a distinctive voice, yes; recognizable and just, but it won't jolt you from the chair as if mom hollered your name. The exception is discerned as He speaks through the thoughtful voice of a kind stranger or a child's simple honesty that questions well held static thinking.

And God may speak to us in a single word from a friend not afraid to be honest as he questions self-diagnosed ills, or we might hear God's Word by the wisdom of a passing Angel that tells us we are loved.

Acknowledge that the words received are from the First Source and you'll be enamored by the process, as you discover the answers to life's toughest questions originating in those quiet still moments in meditation. If practiced in the morning, you'll receive direction for the day and be instilled an answer to questions yet to be asked and later in the day your response has been preprogrammed and you may smile as the words flow easily from your lips unobstructed by ego; as if you've heard those words before; and you have.

Smile, it's OK.

That's how it works for me, but be careful with this new ability / super power! If you begin to take credit for this "special" connection with the Creator of all things seen and unseen and begin to think yourself unique and special and deserved of honor and praise…

"Enjoy Hell."

Lino Rulli
The Catholic Guy

Pride of ownership destroys the connection and we find ourselves hanging over the abyss alone and our words have no meaning and our actions are once again based on fear and rightfully ignored by those who discern well and we are not trusted, nor ought we to be. Life becomes empty and our accomplishments are without reward, as all roads lead to nowhere and we suffer because of our selfishness and pride and once again we are the naked fool holding an empty bucket; once filled to overflowing with the results of honest Truth-seeking.

~

Some might think His constant guidance interference, but I've found that the payoff is obvious and my abilities more pronounced since I formally agreed to this relationship. Yeah, it was a real formal negotiation; He said, "Follow me." I said, "OK!" and He said, "Good!" That was it. I was easily hooked, yet I know that the "Course in Miracles" is an eternal project of which there is no advanced-degree offered except from its messages we might live life fully alive and know happiness received from its Source. Within Him, we are free to be active participants in His Holy acts of love and everything good may be accomplished.

Our mission in this "Holy Instant" is to explore the world, enjoy life, and conquer evil. That doesn't mean God singles us out and loves us more than others or that we're somehow "special or chosen" and life just became easier. Become an active participant in life within Him and He gives us more challenging work to do.

With grand experiences of His love and forgiveness, the truth is understood and accepted as knowledge and we are more able to endure more pain than we think we must. There is an Eternal constant, though, as we must endure the pain caused by our minds and bodies being stretched beyond our comforts and previously held self-limitations, as we are formed into Beings others might model to improve their life stations, and as we each commit to do our part to achieve greatness for the whole of humankind of which we are created as one body; selflessly – we discover joy.

A Spiritual String Theory

JUNE, 1989
Sunset Blvd
Pacific Palisades, CA

Have you ever rolled out of bed in the morning and stubbed your toe on the frame, then dropped the same thing repeatedly to the point you wonder, "Is this going to be one of those days?" Most days aren't that way, but when they are, you'd have to consider crawling back into bed to start over. In reality, that may be what God's telling us to do.

On the other hand…

I'm in my Jeep Cherokee, pulling out of my neighborhood and onto Sunset Blvd. and the light's green. I make a left turn and I'm on my way to Downey; some forty-five minutes to the office. Same thing happens every day that week; the light at the busy intersection is either green when I get there or, when I arrive, I don't have to stop as it changes to yellow. Sometimes, well before I'd get to the intersection, the light goes green or it stays green longer than usual and I have no urge to hurry to make it through, or it changes to green as I arrive even without another car tripping the sensor.

I begin to wonder what's going on. And this happens all summer long to the point, where if by some odd chance, the light's red or changes to yellow and I must stop I'd reflect on what I've done differently that morning. What am I doing to cause the Universe to fall apart?

Without fail, I'd find that I had misplaced motives. For some reason, I allowed fear or pride to rule me and I'd begun my day self-interested and accepted my ego's plan to protect or control certain situations. In this quick introspection, I'd locate the "spiritual virus", pray for help to quarantine and heal it and make the appropriate change in attitude and the lights are green again... and, yes, nobody gets hurt.

Really... amazing miracle, huh!

Except that no one was cured from a life-threatening illness and I didn't see Mother Mary's face in the traffic control lights... just these simple reminders from God that I'm in His flow and that I'm coming from the right place in my heart; don't worry, all is well.

Believing in "no such thing as a coincidence", I'm determined to pray every day for God to make the lights red or otherwise force me to slam the brakes on my race to success based on selfish motives. I pray that I falter when I try to convince another to follow my dream when the dream is mine alone. I pray that God throws a bomb into anything I think I must do that takes me away from serving others and doing His Will.

And amazing things happen, easily, all day long... or within seconds of me losing my mind. But, great things mostly occur without me knowing the details of the miracles staged behind the scene, the string of happenings that specifically influence and go to create the great moment in time that I, right Now, am able to experience, Here.

CHAPTER 5

The Nature of God

"Everything that is done in the world is done by hope."

Martin Luther

From wandering darkness to enlightenment, we have infinite viewpoints from which to make judgments of God's salvation and how He affects the simplest details of our every breath. Our personal stories encapsulate broad arrays of immense difficulties in understanding His Love or ability to accept the truth of our self-made struggles and coincidental successes. And individualized definitions of God's Will and in which form must we worship Him varies dramatically even within the same tribes.

The bigger question for most of us is the fact of His existence; the primary unanswerable; unprovable question: Does God exist?

Yet, once satisfied to any degree in the affirmative, the eternally endless questions arise in our heart's thoughtfulness and go mostly unasked for fear of challenging and finding well learned or cultural beliefs to be wrong and being ostracized by the clan for not believing. But, are the unasked unanswerable?

- What does God look like and where does He live?
- Did He create us in His own image; really?
- How do we love an unprovable mystical God?
- Are we a product of chance and is Darwin right?
- Or does God love a Big Bang as much as any other man-like creature?
- Is the temptation to sin merely a challenge to overcome to prove ourselves worthy of His Love and admittance into Heaven?
- If He created us and loves us so much, why does He allow such horrible things to happen to us; to the world?
- And if God is Love and only Love, how do you explain the existence of evil in the world He created?

Every 30 minutes the worst of this world's happenings are repeated for public display on the 24-hour Cable News channels; 24-hours of the ratings-driven horror shows called News, not necessarily Journalism, where images of the worst of the worst are hammered into our collective consciousness; "brought to you by Colgate!"

We've become addicted to the hour of News programming and tune-in from the comfort of our living rooms, jaws ajar, in witness of the most horrific acts of devastation and murder; the most insane slayings of truth the "news producers" can report, formulate, or sensationalize. And we're enamored by the human train wreck, the twisted views of the distortions of God's highest intention that we love one another and care gratefully for the planet on which we were given to enjoy its nature, resources, and beauty.

In fairness, we usually get an occasional breath of fresh air with 5 of every 30 minutes of News programming to illustrate the world is mostly good and filled with mostly good people doing mostly good things for one another.

But, if God is alive and Ultimately Powerful why would he allow these horrible things to take place? In my search for "The Truth" after my great discovery, I stumbled on to the Urantia Book and studied it for several years. Following are excerpts that offer reasonable explanation to the unknowable nature of God.

"God may only be good, and his goodness is so great and real that it cannot contain the small and unreal things of evil. God is so positively good that there is absolutely no place in Him for the negative evil. Evil is a human misstep; the immature choice and the unthinking attempt to shortcut the processes of living by those who resist goodness, reject beauty, and are disloyal to His evidential truth. Evil is the sour thinking of immaturity or the disruptive and distorted doings of ignorance."

I take this to mean that the potential for sin and evil lay within each of us, if we allow it by our laziness or indifference to the natural processes of living truthfully. And without sane and vigorous attempts being made to question traditional beliefs long held unquestionable, a spiritually-warped belief may cancer into socially accepted insanity and the Holocaust occurs, borders are rushed, whole races of people are annihilated.

The results of evil are inevitably dark, which follow the rejection of light. Evil is dark, selfish, and untrue, and when consciously embraced and accepted as the Way, it becomes iniquity and hopelessness is the result. The passive inability to alter one self's personal ignorance by laziness or indifference begets intolerance, anger, wrath, envy, vengeance, prejudice, inequity, war...

"Our Father in Heaven, by handing us the power to choose between truth and lies, created the potential for the negative of the positive way of light and life. But, the horrifying outcomes of evil do not exist until the moment a decision is made to choose that way of life. Such evils later become sin by the knowing and deliberate choice of willful and rebellious creatures, such as we may choose to be from time to time. Our Father in heaven loves us so deeply, He allows us every choice to live our lives and therefore He permits the good and the evil to go along together until the end of life, just as nature allows the wheat and the weeds to grow side by side until the harvest."

He does not destroy the weeds for us, yet God delivers us from ourselves with His immense and endless Love. He provides us knowledge, a boost of strength, clearness of mind, and courage to grow stronger within His light and with each passing experience, our abilities are ever so slightly honed to better "fight the good fight" in earnest belief and growing Faith in His Love and His most positive outcomes of the direction we travel, today.

So, if God is Love and only Love and He truly is on our side in the fight against evil; our darkest fears of abandonment and loss; what are we to think when an overly zealous preacher shouts from the pulpit, "Happily hand your sinful life over to a Wrathful, Angry, and Jealous God, for He will bless you?" Shouldn't that go against everything we want to appreciate of a loving Father in Heaven?

~

The world is filled with good and evil, but evil and desperation are not brought on by a God who is seeking vengeance on us for the bad we might have done or are about to do. No! God does not desire to harm us or punish us into submission to become more respectful of Him. Is it possible that God would choose to "lose it" and display anger when a thoughtless son or daughter chooses not to honor or otherwise obey His Bumps? I'd like to think God has things more under control, self-realized and all that… Why would he lower Himself to such a savage and human emotion? Could you imagine a God that lost His cool because He was afraid of losing your devotion to Him?

God, afraid?

Saddened yes, but never afraid.

But, a human viewpoint might reckon that if God experiences love, joy, happiness, sorrow, and sadness with and for His children that it's only logical He'd be capable of anger, as well; especially when He's bombarded by every vicious thought, envy radicalized, and of our ludicrous and sometimes iniquitous behavior. If this makes God angry, it must certainly transform to wrath especially when His spiritually-insane children attempt to justify sin with superficial acts of kindness or blatant disregard for life. How could we possibly expect Him to meekly standby as we flagrantly demonstrate our indiscriminate and oh-so evil actions towards one another? And if He's angry, what good is anger without a little "plague and pestilence" to expend the energy of His exasperated patience? You know… it's not healthy to hold it in!

The problem, however, with anger turned to wrath is that on all levels wrath is vengeance and vengeance is sin. God does not sin. If anything, He is compassion and wholly approachable. So, why would God begin the process of discipline by considering such an undesirable human emotion as is anger? It's a misconception. The truth is, God is above vengeance and He completely understands us and loves us deeply, regardless of our ignorance. He's love and only love; devoid of fear, impatience, or disgust, which all or in part begets anger. His attributes are beyond our human comprehension, as fear and anger or fear of anger are two emotions we have fully learned to accept, as natural results of human conflict.

~

If you're a father and a loving daughter drifts away from the loving guidance you so freely offer and she chooses to go it alone, would you smite her and cast your anger down upon her, only to make matters worse? Even if you were angry with her, would you add to her disappointing life by further casting down upon her any form of jeopardy that you might consider due such a thoughtless daughter?

Or would you be forever understanding and compassionate for the dilemmas she encounters on the lonely path of selfishness (self-enforced entitlements, masked insecurities, and need for instant social and self-gratification). As a loving father who knows we each must be free to come and go as we please from the over-care of a loving parent, wouldn't you look out for her safety and, at the same time, allow her to make mistakes that will surely teach her sound lessons; yet spare her harm? A loving father will subtly influence his daughter without interfering with her free-will in hope that the learning takes hold and resentment is minimized. The hope being that someday she realizes her faults, accepts and understands forgiveness, and has corrected her life's course, on her own will-power. And with any luck, in the end, she might appreciate the loving hand that was *always* there for her to grab hold.

Our Father in Heaven guides His lost sheep with a loving supportive message not by throwing down bolts of lightning and instilling fear of His vengeance for our wrong doing. Nor will He plant land mines just off the path He paved for us, that we might step on when we shirk our duty to thoroughly please Him and…

Boom!

Wouldn't that be evil? Planting booby traps to foster compliance is evil, if not unlawful. So why would God resort to these measures? Sure, He allows us to choose our path, but He only has compassion and love for us when we make a mess of things and drift off course. He is and always will be a loving Father and He does amazing things for us daily. He gladly reaches for our hand when we make even the slightest gesture to move in His direction, to ask for His help when we're lost and dismayed. So, when we falter and find ourselves precariously balancing on a dangerous precipice and we don't know which way to turn…

Reach for Him!

HOWEVER

Since the days I discovered God's unquestioning love for me, for you, and them (you know… the weird ones) I've come to understand a healthy "Fear of God". An insane phrase, but when I exchanged "Fear" for "Respect", the concept of fearing God made sense. This thought process was part of a natural evolution in my constantly growing relationship with an amazingly loving God. The fear that I deeply cherish (weird, huh?) is that I might someday consciously choose to abandon my relationship with Him.

This is twofold. First, I fear that I begin to take credit for my success; success that I experience only because our loving Father has led me to the opportunity and given me the talents to fulfill His Will. I fear losing my connection with Him and the connections of those whom He's led me to serve. God is ultimately and eternally well-connected and my success is His, in reality wholly His. The point being, I fear that I become prideful, insistent that I'm in control – I'm in charge, it is me – Bill the Great One who made this cool thing happen, accomplished that amazing feat, or made this incredible statement of truth. So, I fear that I forget whose success it actually is. I fear that I take ownership of the good that happens all around me and that I whimsically ignore the opportunity to thank Him.

On the flipside, I fear that I will choose to turn away, become exhausted of the journey and take even one day off and that day becomes a week and maybe a sabbatical, from which I may never return.

And I lose my ambition and desire to search and fulfill God's plan of service to those whom He loves (in service to them, yes, the weird ones; those people; anybody who's not me; yes, those them who in my heart, I truly do care about). I fear I give up on the dream too soon and the "city of gold" that I'd for so many years been in search, that may lay just around the next bend, is abandoned without praying to God for stamina to reach it and appreciate its whole reward. I fear that I take time out from my commitment to "stay in the moment" with Him and He takes the biz-op that provides my financial security to the next available player and I'm out of the Game.

And in those times that I disappear and ignore His Grace, my greatest fears come to life and all hell breaks loose and nothing is correct. I fear being OK with excessive struggle of which my ambivalence has caused and that I live my day justified in a life of toil and disappointment. "I'm only human and life can be harsh" and my struggle is constant and failure is expected and under these circumstances I smile and lie, in response to a greeting and say, "I'm doing great!" And this image is the mask I wear as my dreams once again are tarnished and buried in the muck of inner toil; possibly despair.

I fear that I once again am accustomed to the financial struggles of my young adult life and I retire early and retreat into a life I've decided cannot coexist with God. I fear that I might come to believe that that's all there is to life and, out of habit, I become happily ignorant of a better Way that may exist within the walls of my life. I fear becoming comfortable in the pain and forget there's a choice of a more vibrant life lived in a joint venture with God that overcomes apparently severe and insurmountable trials or the mundane servitude to man; the daily grind.

I've really come to fear God the more I've come to know and love Him. I fear missing God, making that conscious choice to live without God in my life, but even for a day, an hour, a moment. I fear that I become lazy and abandon God's Plan in place of mine and I'll soon be the cause of unnecessary suffering to my friends, family, and business associates, because of this prideful decision. And when I do make that bad choice to go it alone, I fear that I go one step further as I struggle in the anguish I've created for myself. I fear that I will do that great human thing and blame anyone and everyone for my hardship and in so doing, make things exponentially worse. And it will have been God's fault; and I am angry with Him for smiting me. And I will say, "Thanks O Great and Mighty One for leaving me when I most needed you. I thought you loved me. I've been good, I've done everything you've asked of me, yet look at what happened... What's next????? Just kill me why don't you!"

And the self-prophesized drama unfolds...

Imagine hearing those words from a friend or from a son or daughter. Try putting yourself in God's shoes for a moment. Where is it written that He promises us an easy life? We blew it in the Garden and shouldn't expect life to be one blissful moment after the next filled with charm and glory; pretty ponies to ride all day in the warm breezy sunshine with fluffy clouds floating by in the otherwise clear blue sky. It'd be nice, but adversity and intuitive-ambition to overcome problems drive growth and I'm thankful to God for the role my so-called enemies might play in my life as well as my friends and family when they have the courage to be honest; speak the tough words I must hear that are beyond the noise of my defenses.

*** Level Three Metaphor Alert***

If the captain of a ship on the open seas sails day by day, year after year on fairly calm waters, how valued is he to his crew or his country when that great and dangerous storm unexpectedly hits? He's not yet experienced such a challenge and his directions to his crew are mere guesswork; untried. He's spoiled by calm seas and you might even hear him complain about the foul weather when the ship begins to roll and yaw... the crew ought to want to toss 'im off.

The storms in life test our mettle and prepare us for far greater challenges we know not we are capable to manage. And the day we retire or no longer desire to learn or fail to face the storms life presents is the day our ship is sure to be damaged during the next great wind or worse it is moored off shore, mothballed, never to sail again.

~

One of the greatest lessons my newborn-self learned early is that God knows our limits and fully loves us regardless of our weaknesses and denials of greatness. We have strengths today we did not own yesterday and talents we've never completely unleashed, as we might fear an outcome that is beyond our experience and seemingly out of our control. We have strength not realized until the day comes when we're required to pull ourselves together in a time of crisis. And when we find ourselves in a wreck of emotion we pray to God for help. He listens before we speak and instills in us the courage to seek the truth and accept and correct our lost ways. He sends His army of Angels to our side to assure that we arrive safely at our destination.

And we arrive alive, although maybe not in this world... But when we awaken, we've made it through yet another terrible and possibly horrifying storm. A little tattered and broken spiritually and emotionally, we are made better somehow by the process. The storms we survive take us to new lands and we arrive at a place to heal and prepare for the next journey; there's always a next.

"Kites rise highest against the wind - not with it"

Sir Winston Churchill

On the other hand, the next time you easily experience a strange ability to foresee a need and instinctively act to supply the answer or become extraordinarily calm in a very stressful situation or discover unusual patience as you intently listen as she explains her point of view or as she stretches herself to better understand your concerns or needs – either way, a war is avoided. Bookmark that moment; you've just experienced a moment in the Heart of God. These are the miracles in life that simply happen when we deliver ourselves to God.

And this is what I fear losing, this is my fear of God; fear of my conscious separation due to laziness or exhaustion, or worse; the expectation of creator-status that comes from an overly exaggerated view of my self-importance. In this separation, I fear the subsequent disastrous outcomes that living the "Life of Bill" entails. My fear of God is my fear of being "Bill-reliant", pridefully driven by my ambition for greatness, of proving my high opinion of myself, and living those precarious moments alone, without God.

So, my prayer for the day is simple:

Father, Jesus, Holy Spirit, and all of you angels who've been here with me and my family and my friends, clients, and coworkers throughout; thank you for all that you're doing and have done for us in our lives to get us Here safely. God, today, I pray that I am doing Your Will and I pray for the strength, courage, and fortitude to reach for Your loving arms in times of difficulty and need and in happiness and joy; and I remember to thank You for either and all. And I pray to give up all that I think I must own and control and I hand my fears of loss to You, today, as I seek peace in this place in Heaven on earth that you've given me to reside. I surrender all that I am to You, to do with me as You will. So that I may offer Your Hope and Peace as I walk and speak with Your confidence and as I brush away negativity I do so with the question, "is this a God thought?" And my heart's immediately returned to the right place; to Your mind and within Your zest for life; reassured. Thank you Father, I love You Lord.

As I strive to be inside the mind of God and attempt to do His Will and realize that today His Will may be mine, well, that's when I do have everything I want in life and everything big and small goes my way. Maybe not how I'd like it or expect it, but God answers our prayers in His own mysterious ways. When we begin to look at God as our eternally loving Father, we discover a Being that is lovingly supportive, for no reason. When "Shit Happens" and terrible things do happen or we fear they might; we may realize that in non-resistance there's no smell to endure and we may quietly and quickly reach to Him and He'll guide us to safety. He's always at our side, as a loving father is forever willing and ready to leap into action when a son or daughter calls sincerely for help.

Needless to say, over the past several years I've come to know a more loving and understanding God; the One who is eternally loving. God does not know anger nor does He lie in wait to cast down His wrath on unthinking dopes like us. God is incomprehensible Love and nothing less. And when my son or daughter reaches to me for help or gives me credit for helping them through a situation with a thank you, I am pleased beyond words. One can only imagine God's joy, as we likewise seek to include Him in our lives or as we bring others nearer to Him by example or words or through sweat or thoughtfulness we reach to help a brother or sister in need, and for this one and single moment in time in which we praise Him, acknowledge His handiwork, and we give Him thanks; and He is ever more fulfilled by our happiness and safety achieved.

Snowbirdima — A Snow Miracle

Samantha and me on Saddle Rock – 2005

The death of my brother Pat brought Samantha's mother, Tami, and me together. Tami and I'd become great friends while working at Gepetto's Restaurant, in Holladay, Utah, and I was more than mildly infatuated with her... We married in the summer of 1981 and had our stunningly beautiful red headed baby girl, Samantha, in '83.

Now, let's fast forward to February 12, 1998, and Sam's in 9th grade, living with her mother. It's around six o'clock, on a snowy Thursday evening, and I get a Bump. This seemed to be an unusually weird Bump, directing me to go against fatherly common sense... to go way against the norm and my values; but not really.

I was Bumped to call Samantha and ask her to skip school to go skiing with me in the morning; Friday – Test Day.

What a bad dad, right?

But, I could see the reasoning. The snow storms had been dumping foot upon foot of light dry powder all week and friends were flying into town for the long President's day ski-weekend. I'd planned to take the day off and ski, anyway, but when I checked the weather report, the granddaddy of storms was on its way and the Lake Effect would triple its impact... the perfect storm. No more thinking... I knew what I had to do.

So, I said a quick prayer to make sure I'm not being impulsively stupid. I'd never taken Sam out of school to go play, especially on a test day... and especially for a non-emergency. But it kind of was an emergency to a skier. And when I got the Bump again, "clearance from tower", I gave her a call and explained, "Sam... this is really important... I want you to take your time and think about this." "I want you to skip school tomorrow so we can ... (dramatic pause) ... go skiing."

"What! I can't do that," she insisted.

I went on to explain about how everybody's coming in and a perfect storm's going to hit tomorrow. I told her to take some time and think about it, talk to her mom, and call me back.

It only took a few minutes before the phone rang. "OK. Pick me up at 11:00 so I can finish my big tests."

It was a little later than I'd hoped, but I was surprised she would break from the norm...

"Great!" ... she laughed and we got down to the details.

When I walked into her school office, dressed in ski gear and asked for Samantha Terry, I never felt so comfortable about doing something so seemingly wrong. I was completely unashamed standing in front of the office ladies waiting for Samantha, to take her out of classes, to have what would be the most incredible day of skiing I would remember.

The snow was really coming down. Ours was the fourth to the last vehicle the Salt Lake County Sheriff officer allowed up Little Cottonwood Canyon. I watched in my rearview mirror as he shut the road down. There were cars sliding back and forth struggling to get up the canyon as we passed them; rental cars, I'm sure. With just a hint of smug, in our four-wheel drive Jeep Grand Cherokee we charged up one of the steepest canyon roads in America to make it to Snowbird ski resort just before noon. Surprisingly, the parking lot was relatively empty. The intense storm must have scared off all but the die-hard of skiers.

Spiritual Logic

We never caught up with our friends. Probably because we were too busy enjoying the experience, but the snow was dumping so hard and everyone so well covered in gear; you couldn't recognize 'em anyway. It was waist deep for me and well above Sam's and it was falling so hard that the tracks from our runs were covered, in several new inches of new feather-light powder, by the time we made the next run.

Utah powder is so light and dry a snowball cannot be made from it; it will not compress, it simply falls apart in your hands and blows away into thin air. So, when it's deep enough, as you ski through it, it caves in on itself, plus the snow was falling so heavily. Every run was fresh, all but untracked, like it hadn't been skied.

In this perfect storm, the air is still and giant flakes fall at a steady rate and as you ski through it and deep within it, the snow flies up into your face and over your head and quite literally you'd like a snorkel to breathe, at times. As we rode the lift there is a quiet in the air; sound does not echo, it's deadened, absorbed in the depth of the falling snow. The mind's stillness is broken by the occasional crack of a dead tree's branch giving way under the weight of a season of snow. Or you might hear the distant laugh, hoot, or holler of another skier who's not obliged to contain the excitement of the moment as he flies through the snow unobstructed by resistance.

Standing in the short line to get back on the Gad 2 lift, I smiled as Samantha skied towards me covered in snow. Bundled in ski gear, only the tip of her nose and lips were exposed to air. She came to a stop, her eyes shined brightly through her goggles. Her broad smile full of braces and the snow that covered her upper lip is an image eternally burned into my memory and was the absolute reason for the day.

Weeks later, while riding the Blue Tram, I overheard other skiers tell of that day to their friends; for months afterwards, as well. It's truly amazing that when we live inside God's plan, going against the norm of what our ego has determined so absolutely important to fulfill the day, breaking with comfortable habit, and living fully within this moment in time is exactly what God wants for us and living life fully is the reward we receive for trusting in His Way; not by my planning, unfiltered truth, and completely lived well.

CHAPTER 6

So... What About Jesus?

"... test all things and hold fast to that which is good"

Thessalonians 5:21

If, $He = mc^2$

And $He = Jesus$

Then, $Jesus = mc^2$

Easy as π!

I think this is really exciting... But what if, for some strange reason, you can't accept the associations and mathematical assumptions; the logical basis of my newly founded religion:

The Church of Speed of Light of Saturday Nights?

Then what?

Will I think less of you?

Maybe!

But, upon further review and in your defense, as with most religious associational absolutes or absolute absurdities, hewn through time with good intentioned pulpit-pounding to get our attention; a gross misinterpretation of fact may morph into a false belief; an appealing story worth sharing door-to-door. And as often happens in the overzealous attempts to prove the story, well-crafted tales and fables become hardened beliefs and begin to trump the Truth.

However, from a newcomer's perspective, what if the carefully inspected "absolute" makes sense when linked to personal observations and treasured experiences and that which appears absurd to the outsider might actually have important meanings with, possibly, a spiritually-factual, if not personally-factual basis of truth?

What then?

At the age of 16, I wasn't nearly ready for "the truth-search". I believed all religions to be absurd. And I quite proudly left the Catholic Church; unquestioned, unquestioning. I don't remember what it was precisely that turned me away; just quit going to Mass. It happens a lot to young Catholics, in the absence of a strong youth program to keep us together during the crazy teen-years. I was left to work out the bugs of growing up facilitated by an adolescent brain and no healthy male role model – virtually fatherless.

Here's the formula, if they ask.

the Hope in Entrepreneurialism

Imaturity^2 multiplied by Experience$^\circ$ = Trouble^3

By the time I had my tightly unpryable eyes pried opened at the age of 33 I'd lost much of my youthful relationship with Jesus and when it finally hits me that God has a place and time for me, I wasn't looking for Jesus I was simply trying to piece my life back together. Developing a closeness to Jesus wasn't my first spiritual interest, Him being so "over marketed" so to speak; Jesus this and Jesus that on bumper stickers and T-shirts.

And the motto, "Jesus Saves" didn't make sense to me. "Saves me from what?" I'd decided that God the Father Himself had saved me and thought He'd done a real nice job of it. So, I considered God the Father the real spiritual-muscle and had conjured sound arguments against reaching up to Jesus and praying in His name, even after my great epiphany in Minnesota.

Emphatically opposed to the idea of Jesus' role of God, so much so, I'd hear the name Jesus praised and I'd shudder in disbelief that people really buy-off on Jesus-worship.

My argument was simple:

While Jesus may have been the son of God on earth and He did amazing things while here, why pray to Jesus when He, Himself, prayed to His Father in Heaven and taught us to do so, likewise. Praying to Jesus didn't make sense when I could go right to the source of all that is Good, skip the middleman, and go right to the top.

And the thought of including Jesus in my life became less probable the more I relied upon God the Father to answer my prayers for daily direction. In fact, downplaying Jesus' role had become a campaign of mine, as my life was filled with incredible daily spiritual experiences by the "Gifts of the Holy Spirit" exploding within my being; back in my noobie-to-God days in California. The Holy Trinity is a mystery, of which I'd experienced a closeness with two of the three parts and had begun to develop very real relationships, but had zero understanding of the need for the third; Jesus Christ, the Lord.

"The Lord of what?" was my problem; my question; my angst. And it troubled my soul to the point I prayed for an answer that would reward my questioning spirit; of Jesus' reality; His duality? And in that prayer, I promised God I'd honor the results of my search, whichever way it went.

~

Over the next several years of study, I got what I prayed for, but not in a traditional sense... The answer came to me as simplified as is the equation, $E=mc^2$, is the simple five symbol solution to the complexity of Einstein's Theory of Relativity. But like his theory, I questioned everything to block its reality until it became real; real without question; a belief had been formed.

The formation of a belief is a process of theorization, experimentation, discovery, examination, and forming relationships that fit perceived benefits. But, the formation of my belief, that the invisible scientifically-unprovable Jesus existed as God on earth and understanding His humanity and Divinity is truly personal and unexplainable; it is purely experiential.

For me it's profound, like describing the color blue to one who is colorblind, I can see it, but cannot explain what makes it not red or why it's my favorite color. And I can't offer cliché or superficial descriptors; my relationship with Jesus has become real and continues to grow, yet I continue to question it; too deep of a relationship too amazing are the possibilities.

Living a life fulfilled with Him is an hourly, if not moment by moment, decision to speak, be, and do, as would He. Otherwise, I'll become a Sunday Christian with an empty smile thinking I'm doing the world a favor by joining the Christian Club; praising and singing loud, worshiping hard, and on Monday I'd be back to feeding the dragons of pride and fear rather than asking for and believing in His help to slay them.

And while I cannot "Drink the Kool-Aid" served by the Bible Thumpers and the absoluteness in the written story, with my many years of study and personal questioning and proof through experience, I've dropped my Jesus resistance and, today, better understand Him; who He was and is. And, at least for me, I've learned to appreciate the man Jesus and have a much better understanding, acceptance, appreciation, and love for Him as the third person of divinity as the Creator Jesus. I've found a personal acceptance of His dual nature; His duality; of which I couldn't understand until I'd experienced His enduring love; personally.

His duality is puzzling, as I'm not sure where the separation is; or must there be.

~

So, my relationship, today, with Jesus, while its reality seems uncertain at times, is unforced and on the contrary I seek to know Him better and include Him more in my thoughts, as each day grows me further from my old self to the new one He knows I am to become and forever becoming.

His Eternal Divinity and Love for each of us, once "absurd" to me, is now a mystery resolving in my heart, mind, and soul. And Today, His love for me is a treasured journey's answer that I begin the day in prayer for His inclusion to understand.

And I've learned to pray for the wisdom not to know too much, so that I might peel back layers of Jesus church-learning to find the Truth in Him and the journey seems to have no end. We're each valued in His heart and have varying beliefs and understandings of His existence. But, if you can resolve or predict that you might resolve that Jesus is "The Word become flesh" 2000 years ago, today, you'll begin to move with more elegance in the midst of turmoil and miracles will begin to be the answered prayers to struggles faced.

Today, I'm listening when He speaks to my heart and when I drop my resistance, which still occurs, His voice and poise is mine to share, as my will becomes His, my life rolls evenly and does not sputter; it shakes but does not collapse. In the present moments with Jesus' light shining on my footsteps I live more freely as the person He Created me to be and, when I'm True, I might be blessed to act as His surrogate; just by getting out of the way and simply doing good.

He reaches for us before we ask and in our quest to find peace, success, and happiness; He strikes directly at the problems we create in this world run by "the crazies" and He gives us the Answer that disconnects us from our insanity and that of our cousins and friends and He does so without brokering a deal or making us crawl.

But when He came to earth, did He really come to "Save us" did He "Pay the ultimate price to resolve an ancestral Debt" and, if so, are we really "saved"? Are we honestly less prideful, less vain, more loving and caring, less sinful, and less fearful than our brothers and sisters of 2000 plus years ago?

Or did Jesus simply come to better understand us and our struggle, personally; at ground level. Or did He just want to show us a model of which to aspire and to know greatness and humility in the midst of insanity? And in that process, He saves us?

~

Try to imagine, from His perspective, as He walked, lived, and breathed as a man – Creator – on earth; why and what He might have endured of our spiritual blindness. He experienced our spiritual ignorance in its grand nakedness – face to face. What might He have hoped to gain by enduring an enjoined savage plight?

In the grand scheme of things, He was willing to give up what must have been a pretty cool gig in Heaven as the Son of God-the-Father; Son of the First Source and Center of Thought. He is and was absolutely connected to the heavenly Creator as Jesus the Creator and been endowed the ability to be at one with His Father the first Father of all fathers.

Visualize being in His mind, for a moment, as He observed from Heaven His every child's every thought and move, as He knows the intentions of our hearts' yearnings for Truth derailed by fear. We battled and continue to battle with worldly ambitions for wealth, safety, and security; frustrating His Words' revealed through His many prophets' dispatch. And as our Creator (Father and Brother), could He stand by any longer, as His spiritually blind children continued, in their self-righteous Specialness, to lead others in worship of a "wrathful and vengeful God" with a favored Will for a chosen few?

What's a Creator to do?

It appears that He chose to take a sabbatical from Creating worlds, as the Father's Will would have Him so do and He was birthed by a young mother Mary, in a lowly manger in Bethlehem; no fanfare; just cried, as would we, when His warm wet body met the chilled night air. The Creator of the Universe and beyond chose to enter our world, an infant; scared, yet known from above as the Creator – heralded baby Jesus.

He must have known it'd be worth the trouble to live amongst us. But why come at such a backward time and land; no cell service, Facebook or Twitter, or Satellite TV and Radio to rapidly spread the Good News?

He chose to travel on foot and speak with us one by one sharing the Truth: The infallibility of God the Father's Love, Goodness, and Forgiveness and that it all comes without a price – free to all His children.

His beloved children would witness God's Grace, first hand. He loved us deeply even in our backwards smallness and He stayed on message – God the Father loves us and forgives us and He asks us to do likewise to one another. And He drove this message right up to the moment He was executed a heretic and breathed His last breath.

Ironic... God a heretic.

And so the story goes, Jesus chose to join the suffering and live completely a human life, the son of Joseph and Mary; Jesus. At some point, probably at a young age, He suspected His Divinity and the struggle of living on earth would include maintaining humanness with a "Big Secret". Always alert to exposing His Divinity, He must have struggled to remain the observer – not the fixer – as His human-self explored the world; a boy becoming a man.

And think for a moment that; God on earth was raised by an earthly family in a religion taught by the most learned elders of Nazareth; a truth formulated and manipulated by man's best interpretations of the prophet's message handed down the ages.

By this experience, though, He learned how we learn, how we smell; see; hear; feel; work; play; sweat; smile; struggle... He grew up working alongside His earthly father and brothers and sisters; He interacted with us; amongst us; as one of us. How extremely difficult it must have been to endure our closed minded, strange, and obscure religious and social behaviors, and in the days of payment for God's forgiveness and animal sacrifice for future benefit.

Compassion and eternal patience must have been His earliest lessons learned.

In the 21st century, we may think we've come a long way, but He must be saddened by our continued reasoning to go to war; nation against nation, brother against brother, on the battlefield and in our homes; in the name of God.

~

Now, imagine being in the shoes of our brothers and sisters, 2000 years ago, as they met Him, spoke with Him, loved Him, and struggled to know and understand Him. Think of how incredible it'd be to stand next to Him and feel His enormous ever expansive Love and to look into His eyes filled with Eternal Wisdom and be able to ask any question worthy of explanation and receive God's Truth revealed. And how incredibly difficult it must have been to follow this God/man and how frightened they must have been to witness the many odd and miraculous things that He did and amazing Teachings and especially as He began to proclaim His divinity; absolutely; publicly.

"I am He!"

I'd freak-out... "Sweet baby Jesus... He said it again."

As much as I might have fully understood and believed His proclamation, I wouldn't want to have been the cause of a revolution; threatening my personal safety.
True "delusionals" have said those exact words in our lifetime – proclaiming to be The Word or the Chosen Son of God? His Apostles might have thought He'd be branded as "one of those crazies" as He boldly stood before the establishment and declared that He Himself indeed was the long-awaited Messiah.
Jesus is our Savior! Yes, OK, but I can't honestly say that I'd have had the courage to stick by Him even after witnessing mind blowing miracles and experiencing His tender unquestioning love for every man women and child He met.
I see myself standing next to Him as He fearlessly, clearly, and unmistakably proclaimed that which I know to be true and my mind races with multiple routes of escape. How do we explain His claims, when the Pharisees will surely persecute us for following Him, as He continues to make such bold and seemingly blasphemous pronouncements?
First, Jesus hadn't given us the ammunition expected to fend off His accusers. He failed to take the politically relevant leadership role, as was for generations prophesied. The long-awaited Messiah would arrive to rid Israel of its oppressors, yet Jesus made no attempt to lift a finger against Rome or convince Caesar to free Israel from its stern rule. And the Messiah was expected to answer the critical problems of living on earth with Heavenly rewards for "The Chosen People" easing life's burdens with overflowing abundance for their undying commitment to

Yahweh while suffering enslavement and injustice at the hands of their conquerors.

Instead, Jesus walked the countryside… homeless… poor… albeit in good cheer. He must have appeared quite the lunatic, to the establishment, calling himself the "Son of Man", as He mysteriously appeared in one place or another and disappeared for months at a time to return with some ridiculous story about fasting in the desert and battling Satan. And then He'd go on a miracle-making-spree where He'd cure the incurable, walk on water, feed thousands with only a few fish and loaves of bread and He'd teach us about our Father in Heaven's unconditional Love and the importance of doing His Will; above and ahead of man's. He taught us to love all of God's children, even those we so easily discard as unfit or too sinful or too sick, too crazy, too Gentile, too ignorant, too poor, too young, or too female.

What kind of Messiah is this who sits and eats with the sinners, the publicans, the tax collectors, the prostitutes?

As a disciple, I would have questioned His fearlessness and non-resistance to public ridicule … we know many left, one denied Him three times, and one betrayed Him horribly.

The politics of the day and the rule of Pharisaical Law imposed extreme and strict compliance to "religious" tradition in fear of God's retribution. Jesus' disciples and Apostles faced the risk of retribution and stood at His side, nonetheless. John the Baptist faithfully paved a path in an ill-rewarded mission to usher in the new age of Jesus, as he prepared the minds and souls of men and women with his incessant message, "Repent, for the Kingdom of Heaven is near." The youngest Apostle, John Zebedee, fearlessly stood by Jesus' side during the public trials that led to the crucifixion. And His mother Mary and Mary Magdalene and the rest of the men and women who witnessed His execution would boldly ask for the body of Jesus to prepare Him for burial and not be denied. They remained true to their newly discovered truths and well-formed beliefs, in the face of overwhelming public hatred towards them; personally.

They watched helplessly, as their beloved rabboni, brother, son, and God was betrayed by His own creation. Imagine their stalwart dedication to stand by Him in the face of like retribution for outwardly loving and following Him. These early followers, willing to give up their lives for

Him, deserve our honor and thanks. They selflessly served a newly forming Christian community and carried the message of Hope to the ends of the earth and they knew not where this journey would lead, yet they worked fearlessly alive in Christ's message.

~

No one can know the depth and breadth of Jesus' sufferings and sadness in living with us nor may we know the natural serenity He slipped into, by His joy in living with an immense love for us. But, we may know that He absolutely understands our human fears and trials; first hand. And we might surmise that by the experience of living the human life on earth, He is forever more understanding and experientially more compassionate for every simple and astonishing screwy thing we do and say.

Not being one to leave us alone, He asks us to invite Him into our lives; to talk with Him and ask for help in every detail, every chore, and every honorable stand we attempt to take. By His every moment experienced in life, He's been better prepared to help us unscrew our minds from the earth and make the way True for our lives; fulfilled in Eternity. He is our Brother and our Father – human and divine – and He gladly shows us the way to peace and happiness and finally, the way Home.

And because of His duality; that He lived amongst us and experienced hell and heaven on earth alongside us; His compassion for our prayerful requests to be saved must be more easily appreciated, but only by His personal recognition and memory of human suffering and relief by salvation through vigilant prayer to our loving Father for His Connection – disconnecting us from the fears the world initiates. As a loving Father Brother and Friend, He promised to answer every sincere request that no prayer goes unanswered. So, ask!

~

Twenty years before I married Sue, the woman that solves the female puzzle of my life, I'd reentered my old faith community at St Vincent's Catholic Church in Salt Lake City. Knowing love today, however, I am not welcome at the table of Communion in the Catholic Church, being remarried; happily, or not, the hitch made it unacceptable for me to take Communion. More to the point, at the time I returned to the Catholic Church in 1991, to help Samantha prepare for First Communion, I personally couldn't understand the teaching about the Holy Eucharist, in any way.

The Host is the body of Jesus? The wine... His blood?

Wait... what does that mean?

Not that being a longtime vegetarian mattered but the concept was absurd to me... Jesus' flesh and blood?

The "mystery" is challenging for at least a third of all Catholics and the totality of the balance of mankind, as well. So, I squirmed in my seat when our priest would exhort, "If you don't believe that the Holy Eucharist is truly Jesus body and that the wine literally becomes His blood... well... you're not a Catholic."

"Absurd" on many levels; a crazy belief; how is this possible?

And why is it necessary to define membership of the Catholic Church by the belief in this mystical action taking place in preparation, by the priest, of the sacrament of Holy Communion; that it be so rigidly enforced; "the bread and wine is the Body and Blood"? Jesus also asked that the bread and wine be taken "in remembrance of me." So, why is it a deal breaker to the Vatican if not adhered to, in full belief, you ain't Catholic? Jesus taught us that "When two or more are gathered there am I among you" and if Jesus lives within us as the Spirit of Truth, why must the host and wine also be Him, that when partaken I'm somehow in a more absolute communion than was I capable just minutes prior?

Every year in the springtime, Catholics celebrate a mass dedicated to teaching on the Eucharist. In 2007, five years before meeting Sue and while regularly attending mass at St. Joseph's in Wenatchee, as Father Tom gave his standard homily, "if you don't believe this ... then you're not a Catholic." I prayed for an answer to the question I was sure I'd long ago surmised correctly the answer.

I'd intellectually contrived a solution that justified my ability to remain a good Catholic and I'd been absolutely happy with it and was doing just fine for many years. I'd reverently take Communion as an outward sign that I am decidedly and publicly a disciple of Jesus. I'd rise from the pews and walk up the aisle, hold out my hand, and accept Jesus

– every week – with love and respect; "in remembrance." And that's just got to be good enough, because I didn't get it otherwise.

However, during that particular mass I was moved to pray for a final understanding. Is this really You in the bread? Is this actually Your blood in the cup?

Throughout the Homily, I heard no answer... Fr. Tom continued with His pronouncements...

I prayed and... nothing... OK, I'll just walk up and take Communion as per usual, I thought. And as I took the Host from Fr. Tom, when handed to me, he said, "The body of Christ." I was reverent, bowed my head, took the host and said, "Amen." I ate it, did the sign of the cross; still no word, no miracle, no eye-popping epiphany – no spirit buzz.

As I took a step towards the Eucharistic minister holding the cup of wine, she stood smiling, and as she handed me the cup and said, "The Blood of Christ." I prayed for an answer... and in that small breathless voice... I heard,

"What do you want it to be?"

And I instantly got it. My eyes watered, I smiled, took the cup, and said, "Amen."

I had answered Him.

"You."

I wiped a tear and left communion with an answer; maybe not yours, but mine.

Now, the mystery is resolved for me; the terribly absurd has become my comforting belief, so much so, I might go door to door with the message, or one day write about it... a new, enlightened theology struck me dumb. However, arguing theology, if not the physics, immediately became a non-issue. My relationship with Jesus was instantly made more complete and opposing views not worth the energy of debate. The end result of my search is clear to me.

It's not about who wants to control what or whether debating with others how the Catholic Church has cornered the Jesus market; Jesus locked in the Sacristy until Communion-time every day. None of these things matter, as it became simplified in this one single and simple question.

"What do you want it to be?"

I want it to be You, Jesus, and that powerful thought completes the miracle of the sacrament; my prayer answered by His Thought; our Communion. And what the Catholic Church wants is totally up to it. What you want is totally up to you. It's really simple, Jesus isn't asking for much, nor is He making it difficult. He wants us to believe only that which we are capable, in this moment, and He leaves it to us to include Him or not and He loves us as we are, regardless of our ability to understand Him or of our desire to know and follow Him.

~

Yes, I'd accepted Jesus as God revealed on earth. And yet I hadn't resolved the need for salvation, in my mind; why must Jesus have been crucified for our sins; in payment of sorts? If God loves us each beyond our ability to know, what issues does Salvation solve that isn't cured by that constant act of Love and Forgiveness?

In the summer of 2016, while listening to my friend and pastor Andy Dayton, at the Church of the Nazarene in Leavenworth, Washington, he spoke of the meaning of Jesus' Salvation. Andy speaks from the Spirit of Truth like few I've heard and with a passion for precision in discernment that makes him stop dead in his tracks as he feels himself drift to pontificate from his humanness. He's an amazing gift to our faith community and, that day, he puzzled me with the question of Salvation.

So, while listening to Andy speak about this thing called Salvation, I sat in the pew and prayed... once again asking for an answer to a significant issue I've had in the Jesus story; told by every missionary. A question I could not answer, "Do you accept Jesus as your Lord and Savior?"

My Lord, Yes!

Savior? Not sure what that means... again, "Save me from what?" I believe in Him, but continue to sin, so how is accepting Jesus as my Savior different than accepting His Guidance and Love? How does that help me in mine and His relationship?

So, I prayed, "Did Your dying on the Cross 'Save me'? Does the spilling of Your blood in sacrifice for my sins, mean I'm cleared of sin?" "Did You pay a price that had gone unpaid, somehow spiritually making good on a debt, cleared by You, in our behalf?"

The answer came as clear as always, "Yes." And more, "What do you think I was doing up there (on that cross)?" Clear as if He were sitting next to me, I heard Him speak and was immediately certain of Salvation, by my Faith in His Word. Not sure I understand fully the impact of His death for me, but an unsolvable mystery is solved in my mind and soul, by His Word to me, personally; Now, I'm certain that He did die for us, you, and me. We're clear; by His Sacrifice!

~

With uncertainties now made certain, today, whether the Truth about Jesus or God or the Holy Spirit is shared by a Rainbow Gathering hippy type or a mascara gone-wild beehive hair-sprayed Preacherette or a loud and obnoxious Bible Thump'n witness-yeller; I can receive the message all the same. If I close my eyes and ignore the circus, I can hear the clear voice of Jesus. His voice may be their voice of hope and love that He urges to fall from their lips to be heard by those familiar to them; not necessarily for all. And while some may need to be yelled at to be reminded of what they believe, if Jesus were here today teaching us from these pulpits, what would He preach to us? Would he be talking about Himself and His miracle working, as is the message taught by many of these great preachers? Or would He rely on His performance of public miracles to prove He is God on earth? Or would His miracle working simply be a part of His nature and possibly an unfortunate distraction for those of us with such little faith, as we require more; we who need proof?

Or would He simply say:

"Follow me."

He might tell us great stories of how others had followed Him and He'd ask us to do so, as well; follow Him on the path to the Truth to share His Love with our brothers and sisters.

He might ask us to be incessant, patient, and hopeful in prayer to our Father in Heaven and to:

"Fear not."

And He might remind us that He's always at our sides, to help us develop into that person He created us to be, that He'll guide us safely along that, sometimes, frightening path our Father has so carefully mapped for us. He'd tell us that we're not alone, we're each a beloved member of a greater community of believers, a critical person in a church of brothers and sisters; all and each, sons and daughters of an ever-loving Father.

The stories of the miracles of Jesus' life and of His death on the Cross are not the message He came to deliver. Rather, the message being delivered in the manner in which He lived, as He lived with us and amongst us; a human, Divine. In the face of ignorance, hatred, and evil; He showed tenacious loyalty to His Father's mission; by His fearless honesty, kindness, compassion, and unbending Love.

And His story might be wasted, as words are just letters on a page, unless we choose to act upon them, as would He; Now; Here. By resisting the temptation to investigate the saltier side of life and, instead, choose to pray for strength, a pathway is cleared for His messages to be heard and Hope is our salvation. We are repreived from Hell, as the Gift of His Guidance and our willingness to listen and to act upon the Gift extinguishes fears that hammer at our souls. And His only request of us, in return for the loving guidance that leads us from Hell into Nirvana is that we:

"Love one another."

The answer to the complexities of living on earth are His mission directives; spelled out in less than three words; simplified as is $E=mc^2$ the answer to the universal problems of the romantic scientist; and with infinitely Eternal implications; He wants for our happiness.

"Love one another."

Problem solved! Sort of...

Coincidence, is there really such a thing?

SEPTEMBER 1995

Wasatch 100 Mile
Endurance Run

For a little background, in 1993, I received a grant from the Utah State Office of Education and KUED, University of Utah's public television, to produce a set of exercise videos for elementary grade students called

"Kids on the Move". The videos were produced for 4th and 5th graders to get them a quick workout next to their desk; get 'em up and jump'n in a structured workout; improve cardiovascular and endurance; and to model healthy lifestyles.

As students reach their learning limits and glaze into unconsciousness or unrest, the teacher pops a VHS tape into the VCR and off they'd go; arms and legs moving / flailing, choreographed to strengthen core muscles, increase cardiovascular, and stimulate their brains. Energized physically and attitudinally, fog cleared, they're ready, as they ever will be, to absorb more of the curriculum.

With grant moneys in hand, I bought my first PC with a screaming Intel 486 with 140MB HDD. Using my favorite Lotus' AMI-PRO word processing software, I began scripting the program. And by the spring of 1994 I had assembled a terrific staff of health and fitness professionals who volunteered to define the lesson plan content and choreograph the exercises. We produced the videos at KUED studios, with their crack production staff and ended up with a pretty good product. Now we were ready for a pilot study and needed a few teachers to test the program.

Scott Hess, the State Physical Education specialist referred me to several who might be interested, but told me, "No matter what you do, you've got to get Cindy Andrus on board. She'll be a great resource for you." So, I did and she was. With her help and others, we tested the program against a control group and found a 400% improvement in "Pacer Test" results, compared to children that used the videos over the 10-week trial.

Not that I was trying to compete with the kids, but I wasn't doing so badly myself... getting in shape, that is. At 39 years, old, I was in the best physical condition of my life; lifting weights 3 days a week, running 30 to 40 miles of the Wasatch Mountain's trails each week, skiing at Alta and Snowbird 20+ days each season, rollerblading... it was a great time in my life.

In 1994, I ran four marathons; Las Vegas, St. George, Deseret News, and Boston. I'm not real fast; never able to break the 3-hour mark, but I always had had a goal for races and had much more energized and ambitious training with that goal in mind. So, what's the goal for 1995? I'd reached my limit of road races, as trail running had become my new obsession.

During the hell years of 1986 and '87, Brent Hale and Rob Koch, two of my closest friends, introduced me to mountain trail running;

which sounded crazy, back then. But, there are hundreds of miles of trails that dissect the Wasatch Range, overlooking Salt Lake City. At our doorstep, we'd run these long and twisting trails, following creek beds through the forests, cut through rocky faces, that lead to jagged ridgetops and peaks at nearly 10,000 foot elevations. Salt Lake never looks so good, as it does from the views above it and from far away; especially at sunset looking down and across the City as its lights slowly brighten, the sun falling behind the Great Salt Lake to the west and beyond the distant salt flats and Great Basin Desert into Nevada, where it apparently explodes; for the brilliant colors set off.

Beginning in the winter of '86, Brent and Rob were determined to torture me on these steep trails leading to the top of Mount Olympus; a trail that's usually cleared of the winter's snows earliest, but we'd run on the snow packed trails, regardless. So, they'd lead the way up this gnarly single track and rocky trail and patiently wait for me. As I'd push to keep up, Rob would slow and stick with me for a while then pick up his pace and run ahead and double back to get me. By summer, on the upper mountain trails, we'd repeat this routine for hours.

Rob has a great sense of humor and an enviable way of telling stories. It was said that if you asked him the time he'd tell you how the clock was made and it'd be interesting. His stories were told in great detail, humorously and all who'd listen were captivated. For the fact that I could hardly breathe running, I'd gladly give him the floor. He'd be talking about this or that and his voice would get more and more distant as he'd disappear from sight around a bend in the trail. I'd work to keep up with my eyes intensely focused on the trail, not to trip on a rock or root or slip off the side of the mountain, and I'd hear him coming down the trail, the sound of small rocks kicked by the tread of his New Balance 1300's, and together again, he'd ask what I heard last and continue his story from there. He patiently worked with me to get me up to speed over the summer and by winter we'd explored most trails and now had our favorites; loops that cleared several passes and took three to five hours to run.

Always, though, the most amazing thing to me was that in 1983, Brent had run the "Wasatch 100". I couldn't understand how or why a person would want to run one hundred miles over these same trails and be able to do it in less than 28 hours. Brent is a story teller, as well, and when we'd run, he'd talk about the day and the night and the following day of that 100-mile run. He'd run a lot of races by that time in his life and I'd say that he's more mentally tough than physically. He finished a marathon in under 2:40. That's an incredible feat; running 26.2 miles at an average pace of 6 minutes and 45 seconds per mile. Get on a treadmill and do that for one mile; amazing how his mind pushed his body beyond its training; for that long.

As per usual, Brent tackled the 100 on his own terms. "I just wanted to put as much distance as I could between me and the pack in the first 50 miles and then I'd drag myself in for the rest." And when he finished The 100, arm in arm with a chemist friend he'd spent the last 30 miles running with, he did so sharing fourth place. The stories of that run filled with pain, extreme suffering, delirium, and the elation of completing it had intrigued me for years. But a 100 miler was not for me; I'd thought.

~

By 1994, however, after having finished my goals in marathons; a 3:24 Boston and "owning" the Wasatch trail system; Brent, that Christmas, gave me a sport watch with an altimeter. It was then that I made up my mind to run the 1995 Wasatch 100. "100 Miles of Heaven and Hell" is how it's advertised. And it is. All but a few miles of asphalt are run on single track trails and old mining roads. The run has an incessant rhythm of climbs and descents; 24,033' climb and a 23,523' accumulated descent along the 36-hour limit course.

Web sites were uncommon in 1995; determined to run it, I hunted down the race organizers the old-fashioned way. Brent had a phone number of a guy he thought knew someone on the race committee. He gave me Grizz's number; Bob, I think was his real name. As it turned out, Grizz was on the "Hundred Committee" and could direct me to registration. Being run mostly on Forest Service trails, the Service limited the number of runners, so the Committee is particular regarding applicants' ability and desire; desire to train for the event and complete the course; not on an ego-powered whim requiring a rescue.

My call to Grizz went something like this.

"Hi, I'm looking for Grizz."

"That's me," a rough and grizzly like voice growled through the phone.

He was good.

Spiritual Logic

"I'd like to run the hundred," I said.

Grizz paused (dramatically) and said, "First, I gotta ask you a question."

"Ok, shoot."

Paused again and in his best Grizz grrrr, he asks, "Are you CRAZY?"

After a few words about the trails I liked and how I'd been training over the years, he opened up and shared like experiences and told me I really needed to talk to Cindy. "She's the person who'll make the decision and get you an application if there's room."

Well, it was Cindy Andrus, the teacher who I'd just met three days earlier regarding the "Kids on the Move" videos. Out of all the teachers in all the schools and all the people who could have been the first to step-up and help me launch the videos, she was also the one I needed to convince that I was capable and deserving of one of the few slots available to run that year's "100". She welcomed me with open arms and helped incredibly with my training.

That fall, I completed the Wasatch 100; a life-defining victory.

Coincidence… is there really such a thing?

If we believe that coincidence and serendipity are simply expressions of chance… that's OK, but if we might consider that there's more to it, we might recognize Karma or Providence and that doing good with "no thought of return" is a means God may choose to connect us with the people that help us get where we need to be. And, in our most private successes, we find that we smile for no outwardly apparent reason as we see the smartness in God's plan and that coincidence is Him in action; and connections that happen for no apparent reason might appear to be coincidence, but are simply His way of getting things done in answer to our prayers.

CHAPTER 7

A Case for Miracles

"There are only two ways to live your life.
One is as though nothing is a miracle.
The other is as though everything is a miracle."

Albert Einstein

Like a kid jumping from the roof of the garage with a towel wrapped 'round his neck trying to fly like Superman, we make similarly insane attempts at defying natural laws in our, supposed, adult lives. Universally, cause and effect do not relate to one another consistently; temporally and spatially. So, when our ego's designs seem to defy gravity, we might think we are genetically gifted, especially skilled, or of a chosen spiritually-blessed lineage; only to find that the slow-cook recipe for disaster-cake simply takes time to bake.

When we escape injury, incarceration, or death unscathed and somehow think we're special, we've added yet another layer of grime to our ego's design of who it's concocted that we must be or are destined to become. We might have driven home a little "buzzed" and arrived safely or made bold and terrible mistakes in business or in "extreme recreation" and we've survived. But, how do we muster the gall to take life and freedom for granted; so cavalierly; so smugly? The most of us are mostly alive, healthy, and living free of bondage and the others, well... they were not quite so lucky.

We've witnessed their demise; their untimely dismissal, paralyzing injury, or death. And we're momentarily moved to rethink consequence, but, soon, we habitually choose to live beyond the boundaries of common sense; tempted by the alluring chance for thrill and we ignore the negative possible outcomes of our actions. Thinking ourselves invincible, our reckless behavior skirts the edge of doom and we survive another incident and the thought that we're more "gifted" or "special" or, better yet, "specially gifted" is refueled. So, we raise our glasses, tip our hats, and toast the poor bastard who fell in our place.

We live in precarious times for soul development in a world filled with a myriad of distractions designed to provide instant gratification or quick escapes from a busy over committed and, at times, visibly chaotic life. If we live to tell the story of our escape, of our lessons learned, we may be emboldened by God to break the patterns of greed, selfishness, and excesses in entertainment, but that takes an awakening commitment to live relatively monk-like existences, or does it?

I'm not bored. On the contrary, I find that living a more simplified lifestyle of "the earthly-content", joining the "spiritually-guided adventurers" provides me a full plate of living in exploration of the Way of miracles.

But, I, you, and we vacillate between natural and supernatural forces – to enforce our God-given prerogatives to live within His designed adventure or to barter away the goodness and greatness we were born to become in fear that it won't happen as promised. And, when once, we might have served as a mentor to another we, instead, have chosen to explore the grey areas if not the edge of darkness; seeking a shortcut to financial and emotional happiness. And if others are to follow, we become the devil in their hell.

This glittery winding road to material aspiration-satisfaction and instantaneous-gratification justification, at whatever the moral cost, eventually results in the implosion of our dreams and we lose our footing, the party ends, and we live deep within a question mark; confused.

Why me?

In the process of instantaneous-gratification justification, we've become relatively tarnished goods among those stalwart and refined characters whom we greatly admire and respect; those who've chosen to be patient within God's Plan. And when our mannequin busts, we might make matters worse in flimsy attempts to hide our addictions or, out of shame, we make openly juvenile displays of oratory to justify our imperfect reasoning and the ruckus begins in our souls that cannot be hidden from those whom we love; those who know us far too well; know us too intimately to let us get away with the lie we adamantly perpetrate and defend as truth. They know the edge of truth we've crossed and so eloquently spread, as if butter on toast; and we are ever more defensive of the lie and, if we continue, someday, we lose their trust in all things.

What a clever and thoughtful God to have entrusted us with "free will" to choose to make such fools of ourselves as we attempt to justify these character debasing and embarrassing false pathways to success and happiness. Yet, He is not amused. He knows the pain we attempt to hide as we seek a quick dopamine or adrenaline rush through our chosen material, physical, and emotional excesses. Jesus feels our sorrow, He knows our fears intimately, and He wants for our salvation.

Each action, whether selfish or selfless, affects the world. And our words are extremely powerful. Words may launch us into war or heal a once raw and open wound. We are given the choice, moment by moment, to take a more loving, compassionate, and ethical path to success; choose a higher purpose for each action and word... or not.

We know right from wrong and Jesus leaves us to our own devices, but He didn't leave us alone. He's given us Guardian Angels and a host of Saints and Heavenly Beings to clear away ancient overgrowth haphazardly strewn across our pathway home. He's even given us a piece of Himself; the Spirit of Truth; that resides within our hearts and minds that connects us with Him; His Truth for the moment; Instantly.

This brilliant Eternal connection to His Mind and Truth exhibits itself to the world through the gifts of conscience, discernment, intuition, goodness, and love of which we may choose to honor and display, as we choose to live within *this* single and particular-moment in time; where He is and always has been, and will continue to be. He's blessed us with a visceral desire to choose to be with Him and know the truth He has for us, yet He's given us the choice to ignore the knowledge of a higher good and to choose otherwise.

~

Acting, otherwise, guided by selfishness, pride, and fear, we hope the human mistake is soon forgotten, overlooked, or magically forgiven by those they affect. However, the strategically and untactfully selfish-option taken, procrastinated conflict, or blasting remark *is* of consequence and inhibits or delays the growth of our souls and of those we love, in the many human-relationship-worlds in which we inhabit.

Even the best amongst us sin. We are human and our desired blockades to temptation wear thin under our earthly pressures to over-perform or out-acquire, overpromise, excessively celebrate, snuggle anonymously, and otherwise accept the false securities of the world; our due; our earned pleasures. And even when we're at our best and *do* comply with the Truth we're meant to be, it's not always as simple as rejecting the world and following our Inner Goodness.

To be rescued from our comfortable attachments and excesses, we must choose, moment by moment, to make the conscious decision to honor the goodness born within us and step aside and allow God to work His many miracles through us. Living our lives clothed by this Faith, we must choose Instantly, without fanfare, to act decisively, balanced by trust in His Love we act precariously on the edge of becoming His Plan realized or we might succumb to the bombardment of uncomfortable scrutiny by those who won't try, for fear of failure.

And they jealously spit, "No you can't! No one can." As the naysayers often live within a self-restricted vision, an earthly-vision that blinds God's vision that lay dormant in lackadaisical neutral or backwards status in the far reaches of their once vibrant ambition.

Yes, we may choose to ignore "the herd" that choose to stray into the dark; without our endorsement. When they say "Come on. Join us!" We might choose to say, "No thank you very much." For in that fleeting moment of relative enlightenment, we're unaffected by the herd mentality and we seem odd. We safely surrender a chance for fun and excitement to that trusted better Place designed for us by our Lord; to plan a project or fulfill a commitment or act selflessly in the spirit of service. And we share a quiet moment with God and experience nothing less than timelessness; truth, beauty, and goodness.

Becoming safely addicted to the highs found in selfless service, we are unaffected by the orneriness of others who will not venture beyond the perceived safety of the known, of the comfort of that which has "always" worked. From a progressive perspective, determined to follow the God-driven adventure, we recognize a brothers' boredom with the sameness of life that leads him to explore fulfillment of primal desires for uninterrupted entertainment. The shortcut-cures for boredom, as well as greed, are on display in our society's demand for excesses in the extreme valueless adventures sought beyond reason or kindness; the worldly lies that, daily, tempt our inner goodness to stray. But, who amongst us is innocent?

The Progressives who over-progresses?

The Main-stayers who over-resist natural growth?

~

While living in California; distraction's paradise; and with a new arsenal of discovered hopefulness and abilities to forgive and love; as I learned of this fascinating relationship with an ever-loving God, I found myself blessed with the determination to include Him in every part of my new-found life. I made that difficult decision to seek His presence in all things and to make my intentions known to my soul that I am here, today, to grow ever more close to Him to repay Him for saving such a total screw-up as I had allowed myself to become.

Accepting His forgiveness and forgiving myself was the first step; then and only then might I learn to be me, to appreciate me, and to freely express who I am – honestly, fairly, and justly; without owning mine or the worlds limitations set. And it became my mission to make conscious attempts at simple acts of selfless kindness and mercy, to share unscripted unfiltered honesty with friends and acquaintances.

Being alive in the moment unlocks the humor so blatantly pasted on the face of the absurd.

And every day I'm ever more able to be me, more wholly who I am and, as a nice byproduct, I'm becoming more likeable to me. The struggle survived I'm strengthened, another fear abased, and another day lived wholly one Holy Instant lived at a time; I may forgive myself as does Jesus, as I move to the next exhibit and hurdle of Faith.

We each have a time and place to begin to understand our value to the world, in our simple roles to serve. Each of God's customized Plans has a signature line for His endorsement and a line for ours, as we choose to sell-off or hand-off everything we think we need and, instead, agree to His terms. Life on earth is mine, yours, and ours and a masterpiece in the making and our selfish aspirations are as disturbing, spiritually, as is graffiti desecrating a work of art.

Yet, His Way is filled with excitement, lasting joy, and is of great consequence, as we learn the value of unpaid service to others; which, ironically, feeds us with dopamine and adrenaline and the resulting peace that once we would have paid cash for the experiential-contraband that "Stays in Las Vegas."

But, humans vacillate between selfish pleasure seeking and the rewards found in honest work or by anonymously helping someone in desperate need or in rescuing a sister in immediate danger. And even the most depraved amongst us might display fearless strength and courage in the face of the great unknown risk to his life and limb, in an attempt to rescue a stranger in need; whom he at one time might have slaughtered for the loose change in his pocket.

~

What do we really, really know about our brothers and sisters' hell survived, love rejected, inadequacies accepted, or family infused shame known from the moment of birth that makes them who they appear to be?

What we do know, however, is that every imaginable good and great thing that occurs in this world is achieved by selfless acts of courage; if not, valor. And, "in *the* moment of truth," our heroes have followed their hearts, ignored their fears, and abandoned their manmade dreams of honor and glory. And we know that instant success doesn't come overnight.

We're not privy to the internal agony that led great men and women to an unselfish intention and superhuman spirit that conquered their fears and shown in brilliance. They, those we respect who seem to be most successful in life, like us, live one day at a time; one decision at a time. One moment in their lives follows the next, just as with us, and we may join them in accepting a Higher agenda in service without a campaign for acclaim or reward, although our reward is great, fulfilling, and is the results of our Heavenly Brother Jesus's infused and Will-directed Power.

Jesus wants for our success and loves us beyond our ability to know and waits patiently for us to approach Him to repair every glitch in our character that potentially leads to lonely and deeply painful outcomes. But, how does He do this without blatantly interfering in our lives; without taking charge as an overbearing father might a misguided son or daughter. Of course, we'd "flee with our hair on fire" resentful of any attempt to be saved by a father's veto of our seemingly well thought plans, backslash, schemes.

Jesus is understanding and wants us to freely come to Him, when in need. But, when we ignore Him for too long, the Holy Spirit guides us with a gentle BUMP to knock us out of our selfishness and makes it uncomfortable to continue down a self-serving path. The Heavenly BUMP reminds us to rethink our motives and, if we're lucky, it softens us a little around the edges that were so sharp to cut another. These BUMPS are physical and emotional communications that show themselves in God's miracles revealed.

In 1989, on a sunny summer Saturday afternoon, I was standing in the checkout line at Vons grocers, down by Pacific Coast Highway where Sunset Blvd. meets the ocean. And I'm grabbing a few things for the week when I overhear a man talking to his lady friend and he casually says to her, "You're beautiful." That was it. That was all I heard. Yet I remember, clearly, it being so natural and unpretentious. He wasn't trying to get her into their favorite position; he was simply letting her know, kindly, what he thought of her. And it was great to hear it and to witness how easily she received the compliment; with an appreciative smile. She held herself well. She did not look down or become dishonestly embarrassed by a compliment she knew full well she deserved. She was, in fact, beautiful! Not a word spoken, she replied only with her being – eye to eye – in silent honest gratitude, that moment they shared was eternal and simple.

It was how he said it and the honesty in which she received the compliment that meant so much to me, more than the words he spoke.

Spiritual Logic

It made me think about being real and that I needn't try so hard to make things right or to be a perfectly right person in this imperfect and quite often perfectly imperfect world. Rather, it made me think about how easy it is to see things for what they are and to appreciate where we are and appreciate the many BUMPS that might seem to hurt, but have led me here and placed me with whom it is I share my life; today.

The point being; God sometimes speaks to us through others; through words of those who pass by on our hectic mental roadways. Maybe they're Angels, but I'm sure mostly they're not; they may just be sitting-in for one.

In contrast to the simple word in passing and food for thought, God's Angels have literally touched me to save my life. I was out late on a Saturday night at The Baked Potato, a jazz club in Hollywood. I'd enjoyed dining alone and a few drinks, great music and friendly acquaintance. On the drive home, later than I'd liked, I was heading west on the 10 Freeway and entered the tunnel as it curves into the Pacific Coast Highway in Santa Monica… near the beach and pier.

I was very tired, somewhat intoxicated, buzzed, and drifting into sleep when a hand touches mine and turns the wheel to wake me and save me from a crash into the center lane barrier. I felt the gentle touch, as it turned the wheel and woke me, but did not startle me into an overcorrection. It was firm enough to let me know its reality and that it had saved my life. My Guardian Angel was being fairly blunt, just then, that while I was being a total dumbass for driving buzzed, I'd more work to do and it was not yet "my time"

And the Angels in my life and God's Inspiration guides me to make bold, if not sensible, business and personal decisions that have led me to safety and security. In the process of living "in love of service," I've succeeded by following His Bumps and developed that fearless, courageous, wise, understanding, and loving character that is becoming wholly desirous to serve God and my brothers and sisters without accepting the tides of loss and success as my lot or reward… they simply just are.

OK, that's a mouthful. In practice, it's more an affirmation of what I aspire than it is reality. I constantly screw up and lead the way rather than follow His subtle Nudges that would have led to the easier, safer, more productive way.

~

The great lessons in life ultimately will teach us not to take ourselves and our grandnessness too seriously, still, we must be accountable for our actions, take responsibility, be thankful, and admit when we're wrong; to grow-up emotionally and spiritually. And when we screw-up, as each of us will today, remember to trust in God's good Outcome and the healing quickens when we admit we're spiritual-infants.

So, be willing to admit you're wrong and laugh at yourself for your simple-mindedness; your human forgetfulness. And your reward is Instantly felt in your newer attained ability to remain cool as others freak-out or as you enjoy your career while others complain and you'll crack a joke by surprise and smile more often, more naturally; just shy of appearing stupid or insane or insanely stupid – you'll be cool.

So, pray for sanity; to be sane in the face of insane opposition. Pray for the Bumps, for the miracles that guide you to be where He knows you're safe; to guide you wholly to that Holy Place and Time that is Now.

"God… What do You want me to do today and what will You have me say? Where is Your Here? When is Your Now? What is Your Truth?

In this request and relinquishment, you're freed of the lie and needn't carry the weight forever you've thought yours to bear alone; He gladly takes the weight and makes your unsolvable problems His problems solved; through you; through your friends; through your loved ones; through your rightful associates.

Jesus gladly helps us, just as we would be moved to rescue an overwhelmed son or daughter silently or outwardly screaming for comfort or peace or safety; a son or daughter who needs our help to stay on course and get through the hell *they've* created. Just as He waits for our submission and emptiness, those who need our help must only ask and even before their lips begin to move, we respond with the power of love, we strengthen them as we act in their behalf, as does Jesus for His children; pre-Instantly!

But, with all the work we must do to cleanse ourselves of our past badness that would lead to future hells, where do we begin the scrubbing; what must we do differently to succeed? Simple, remember there's no hurrying the process, simply make the decision that the Truth is truly what you want and that in service to others you'll fulfill God's highest Truth. In this search for the ultimate Truth, know that Grace is immediate and has always been here to partake.

And as you reach for the branch of Truth, be willing to abandon a human or material relationship that might have made perfect sense a year ago, as relying on what's worked before is a common error and proof of our human reluctance to explore beyond previously held safety zones. Try not to think too hard, your path has been paved by an Eternally progressive and unconventional Creator; just trust Him and commit to be determined in your quest for Truth. And take a single step towards selflessness through the love of Jesus' Thought.

Simple!

In this commitment, with humility and with confidence in a magnanimous outcome, delay your need for instant gratification and empty the bowels of your selfish desires; flush your needs and wants from your mind; and take one single step towards His loving Way. Trust that He's got your every need registered and He's preparing you to take delivery with a single step towards Him. A single step is the only thing any of us is capable of doing; in this one single day. And one life made a little better, today, becomes a marker for others lost to follow.

The key is to know that no matter what we've done or have failed to do, we are worthy of forgiveness and of living in a home filled with peace and happiness. And while our pasts soulful-irritations may not be undone or unfelt or easily forgiven, we've been given another breath to breathe and another singular moment in time in which to create and to live life fully alive; truthfully; honestly; miraculously. And He loves us deeply and forgives us; pre-Instantly.

Follow Blindly; Begin a Journey by Leaving

SEPTEMBER 1995

What a wild September that was, in 1995; an emotionally bipolar month. I'd run and finished the Wasatch 100 miler, married the boy's mom on the 23rd, flown to Tahiti for our honeymoon on the 25th, and twice, as I answered the phone, was asked, and never since, "Are you sitting down?"

The Thursday before the 100, Rich Albert (my brother, born of another mother) called to explain that the pain he was experiencing in his lower back, from the mountain bike fall, was in actuality cancer eating his kidney... for a year and a half, it would spread uncontrolled. This made no sense. Rich was an incredible athlete, strong agile and lean; a super healthy lifestyle, a happy disposition, and his limitless love for life and people should have immunized him from every known disease.

His wry smile should have belonged to his grandchildren's fondest memories.

Spiritual Logic

Within a week, I received the second "Are you sitting down?" call.

This, from the VP of Operations for the company I was entrusted to manage its South West U.S. Region operations. He briefly explained the decision to shut down our regional office in Utah and consolidate it with the Portland, Oregon operation. I was tasked with winding down and transferring operations and, more troubling, laying off 20 people and their families. I was instructed to have the office shut down and floors swept by the Friday before the wedding.

With all that was being asked of me and that was unfolding; all that was falling apart, beginning, and ending; I was at peace. I was riding a magnificent rollercoaster cut down to a manageable size by my Faith in God's Goodness; you'd have heard no fear-induced screams or beaten whimpers; as I imbued my being with a peaceful coexistence, compassion, and confidence in our God's sure outcome for all; through a constant search for Truth in meditation and prayers at every turn.

And that month, I was surrounded by His Angels as much, or more so, than at any other time in my life. I could feel their loving breath on my neck with the warmth of their wings around my soul and I had a peace about me that was unearned, yet knowledge of a positive outcome that got me through each day of that month and onward to the rest of my life in a manner in which I cannot claim was "all me".

From years of rigorous training in the Universe's advance courses in "Defeat Management" and "Advanced Eternal-Trust Logic", I had received a diploma from the Spiritual Logic Prep School and was Instantly put on the fast-track program in Eternal-life studies.

I'm grateful for the trials, though, for much of my life, as I know it today, was put into motion that month: The impending loss of a great friend to cancer; a marriage that led to the birth of my two incredible sons Matthew and Michael; and my career path changed dramatically. By closing the office, I was Bumped to create a new position for myself at the Company more fitting to the re-structuring.

However, by the following summer of '96, after a year at work within the confines of the new business structure, while in a breakfast meeting in Portland, with my good friend and business-associate Dino Delello and our new boss, I spoke candidly of the business. Shooting from the hip in a free flow conversation sometimes creates awkward and reality-check moments. I told them (to the shock and awe of Dino) "I wasn't long for the business."

I continued that I believed the position I'd created was no longer useful to the company and while paid well in a relatively cush' job, 30 days prior, I'd written a memo to the President of the company explaining that the position I, along with eight other district managers filled, had become a redundant layer of management and no longer fueled the growth of the organization.

Dino knew I had no other job lined up and he disapproved of how I'd abruptly verbalized my plans to leave the company, without discussion and without a safety net. To top it off, Tere was 7 months pregnant with Matthew and we were looking for a bigger place to live where she could comfortably nest. Yet, I was cool; un-panicked. I was absolutely sure of what I was doing and, at the same time, completely in the dark as to how it was to play out. What I'd done was easy for me; I went with the Bump from God-only-knows-where-it-initiates and lived faithfully by the guidance of His loving direction; as per usual.

Insane? You'll see.

After breakfast, Dino grabbed his jaw from the floor and we walked the hotel corridors to his room. We discussed what options I might explore and in our discussion, he remembered that one of our salesmen had been approached by a guy from Los Angeles who owned a large burglar alarm company. The man thought our products might be a perfect fit for his sales teams to broaden their offering. Dino's a great guy, quick thinker, and a man of action, so he picked up the phone, right then and there, and set up a meeting in Salt Lake for the following month, a time when this guy would be in town again.

The meeting happened to be set for the very day after my second, yet failed attempt to complete the Wasatch 100. So, I was bound to be in prime form... well, sort of... I could barely walk, having made 50 of the 100 only two days prior.

Terry Cattermole was the gentleman's name and he was charismatic as he was intelligent; some would say, too smart for his own good; able to charm his way through life. He, his attorney, and I had a great business lunch that ultimately ended in a partnership being formed with me and four extremely talented men in the industry; an industry foreign to me but a great fit for my marketing approach. So, I received shares and full authority to run the Company as I desired. I named it, USAlarm, wrote the business-plan, and hired and trained the management team and Terry wrote a few checks and went fishing in Montana.

Nevertheless, two weeks before Matthew was born, we were in business and within six months it was the fifth largest dealership of its kind in the United States, with sales over $450,000 per month. I'd tripled my income and earned shares in a very lucrative dealership by listening and moving with the Bumps and Nudges, instead of fearfully bumping back and gett'n fat in a cush' job that would have ultimately spoiled my creative juices.

I'm here to say thanks to Jesus for the Bumps that haven't killed me, and for two close friends who've gone to Heaven before me. Tragically, nearly four months from the day Dino had set up the meeting, he died. Dino collapsed in a parking lot; his failing kidneys quit on him. And as he lay next to his car, as people gathered around him, he held on to consciousness for a few moments longer waiting for his wife, Misty, to come home from work. He stubbornly held on to life to say goodbye; before letting go... he really did love her.

And five months later, in the spring of '97, weakened and starved from a year and a half of cancer running wild, eating the last living organs of his digestive system; my good friend Rich Albert left.

Thank you both for inspiring me to think bigger than my self-made limits and for showing me what solid preparation, joyful kindness, an infectious smile, hard work, and a positive attitude can do to warm up a room, build friendships in business, and create an atmosphere in our workplace that puts service to others first and foremost; affording us to explore the world, with vigor.

A special thanks to my brother Rich. Thank you for your friendship and teaching me to never give up on living. Even in his final months, he insisted he could learn to play the saxophone. One sunny afternoon, that spring in the living room of his and Georgeanne's home at the mouth of Big Cottonwood Canyon in Salt Lake, he sat me down for his first recital. He looked me in the eye, smiled, and worked up a breath he'd hold to play a single solitary note; to exhaustion. The light in his eyes and the accomplished smile on his face, I will always remember and cherish. That well-toned note held for only a few seconds exemplified the courage and spirit that explained Rich; who he was; who he is.

CHAPTER 8

Our Battle with Perfection

*"The first and the best victory
is to conquer self."*

Plato

In my quest to live what I believe to be a perfect life, a life of financial stability and enviable happiness, I've been forced to confront the demons in my nature that conspire to distort visions of success and avoid failure. These demons have gnawed at the roots of my financial wellbeing since my young adult life. They've caused aguishly sleepless nights, as I'd lay awake for hours in perspiring, sometimes gut-wrenching worry about money; the habitual question being, "Where's the money coming from to pay for _____?"

I wasn't born with these demons; they've been hatched from failed aspirations of a lifestyle I'm certain I deserved; the lifestyle of the rich and famous, and of our wealthy friends and neighbors to which, at times, I've paid with my good credit to participate.

Those demons of pride and vanity and their unruly offsprings, namely, greed and envy (all of which are birthed by fear – lacking love) have covertly sabotaged every attempt I've made at sustainable success, as I've built and operated over a dozen Companies. Each with what I believed to be a solid plan and each, I knew, would fulfill my financial quest to lead "the good life"; the life of sickening wealth and global fame; once and for all, I'd live the life I am certain is mine to own.

As you might guess, the first of these required exorcisms is the one I like to call "I know, I know, I know!" You cannot tell me anything new, because, in fact, I know! It's my visceral need to be right and to prove that I'm right, clever, and smart. And I can do anything and everything quickly, smartly, and, of course, do it right! Being "right", I'll be appreciated for my intelligence and, of course, for never being wrong – more easily relied upon so others might lazily follow.

So, I'm right; right?

The next, I like to call "Step aside, here's how you do it!" otherwise known as, my need for things to be done my way; the perfect way; the "right" way. So, now you've learned how to do it right; precisely the way I did it, because I've taught you, perfectly taught you, now, the world is a much better safer and more wonderful place in which to live.

Right?

However, for me to expect others to perform perfectly perfect, I must be perfect, as well and; while my ideas are almost always perfect, but not quite, only mostly; I push myself to over-perform to fulfill my self-determined goals of staggering wealth and fame. Compounding insanity with insane expectations, in my perfect world, I firmly believe I have the right to insist on rightness, fairness, honesty, and for things to be done in a manner in which I've declared right and correct; if not, compassionately socially consciously progressive; from my most intelligent and superior point of view, that is.

Well... the earth has to and has had to cave in for me to begin to think otherwise; that I might be wrong about anything important, by which I'm certain I am not; not wrong, that is... But, while these lessons hurt terribly, it did not immediately and has not completely taken hold. So, my life has had to be shook up again and again-again and again... and again... Finally, my thick skull being worn through and the light of reality finding its way through the thinned structure, with the darkness of insanity illumined, I've been abruptly corrected; agonizingly, at times, again and again.

And it's taking me a lifetime to learn the importance of these simple lessons in Pride-Control and Truth-Acceptance and to not beat myself up, as I forget the lesson and screw-up, again-again. These lessons, I know now, are Gifts that I must accept the difficulty to learn, sink in, and adhere. Yet to break the cycle and need to relearn, I must recognize that it's OK to be happy with myself, despite my inherent weaknesses and release control to correct the issues in my being, to Jesus.

He wants to take my weaknesses and fears; my sins. It's the Gift of His Salvation-Promise – Grace.

So, my weaknesses, I give to Jesus to correct and the trust discovered in the lessons brings me closer to Him – as He proves Himself to me at every step along the path – every moment of the journey Home. And when I give myself up to Him, I give Him an opening to free me of self-doubt and strengthen me to grow to be a better man; a better me; less the mess.

~

And I'm, daily, discovering the value of me being my own me and the importance of appreciating you being your own you and that there's distinct beauty in the natural diversity of thought and of race and religion and opinion and that there's no perfect way to be; as we're imperfect beings by so many standards; except God's.

God has no sense of humor when it comes to creating humans; there is no "perfect" or "normal" human accepting that He's created each of us individually uniquely perfect; to express His love uniquely. Yet, we have a vision of the perfect human and strive to rid ourselves of the imperfections and that we might surpass ours and others' expectations and meet or beat every arbitrary human standard never matchable or beatable.

And, without lifting a finger to change who we are, we are perfect in His eyes and, in any given moment, we might be a perfect expression of His compassion, understanding, and futility overcome. It's up to us to choose son-ship and prove this lesson right that we might abdicate the poisoness thoughts of comparison to fruitful thoughts of a higher purpose and realization and appreciation of His Grace. And we discover peace within ourselves; simply by being kind to our brothers and sisters, in humble service, unconsciously broadcasting earned-wisdom and Eternally sponsored acts of courage by consciously living in this singular moment; Here-Now; without fanfare or need for congratulation or accolade.

~

Smile, for there is no perfect way to be you or to express yourself or to complete a task, nor can there be (or is it may?). By agreeing with this spiritually pragmatic view, after a lifetime of wins and losses and some very devastating mishaps, when I needed answers to prove that my superior point of view was right; when it mostly was not; God opened a portal in my heart and mind for me to listen to another, Higher, point of view; when, before, I had agreed with myself, so profusely, that I could not, nor, need not.

Failed projects, mishandled opportunities, embarrassing proclamations of self-learned wisdom – ambition tattered, I more easily listen.

Don't we all?

The answer is No.

Sometimes we flail inelegantly for a very long time, but in the end, we "get it".

Thankfully, one day I really did "Get it". That day, I was awakened with a big stick that knocked the poor-me and the shame of a mistaken identity out of my soul... And I found myself naked in The Garden and it was there, in The Garden, naked, that I also realized that we each (not just I) have moments of incredible genius and that each one of us is capable of great performances. As well, I recognized that we each act horribly, at times (not just I). So, there is no perfection that may be known absolutely and, there is no sample of brilliance worth fighting to control. I've recognized that my human vision of perfection is simply a self-projected collage of my most grandiose images, pieced together from a lifetime of fortune hunting and of modeling the wealth and free-living lives of others; imagined perfect. And I sometimes wince from those many haunting memories of a selfish and proud boy vying for manhood filled with riches and stardom (as seen on TV).

Remember the time you _____ and then you and your friends _____ and you were so embarrassed; you tried to cover it up, but knew immediately… Oh, crap! "We're busted."

You either did or said something that could not be undone or unspoken and, even today, years later, you cringe to think of what a total and complete dork you were. Once we've agreed that we really blew it and decide to fess-up to our mistakes, we find that self-forgiveness is the most difficult thing, but key to repairing the damage. And when we've made that "adult" decision to be respectfully accountable for our mistakes, we may also determine that "That" will never happen again.

"Be grateful for this breath; it's yours to endure, if not, to cherish. Listen closely, there is an answer."

Delores Dogood
(first Tweeted January 24, 2014)

So, we change how we do things and become more careful; at times, maybe too careful. Careful is good, right? But there's a happy balance that may be sought, as too careful might restrict our core goodness and we second guess God's choice of our words and plans and we procrastinate making the important decisions for fear of being wrong – traveling the unknown road God has cut for us to travel.

And determined to be well understood and reduce the chance of social-media-tized embarrassment, in our "overly-conscious carefulness", we may appear to be happy and joyfully nice; but in this prolonged procrastination, of facing God's Truth, we are internally and uncomfortably coy and we skirt the difficult Truths that must eventually be explored and communicated and we shove our gifts in a hole and miss the chance to endure the ultimate pain – "the lessons" – as they present themselves in the spiritually logically precise moment in time in which we've been best prepared to learn or relearn.

And we find that our finest learning is freely alive in the "Here-Now," detached from our fears or need to prove our worth, our most direct and intimate path to success that simply just is — it is alive within us, expressed Now.

~

Notice the discomfort in your being when you drift away from "This Moment" to scurry to defend your actions, protect your brilliance, or dodge self-constructed shame. Notice how your smile becomes cardboard and your eyes drift into the nether world; where lies attempt to hide; and you disappear from the magic of the moment into an illusion.

In the process of maintaining the lie; the illusion; and trying to be more wonderful than whom it is that you are you've lost the chance to be a unique addition to the world. Leaving the Here/Now to invent, defend, or maintain this counterfeit being you're no longer amazing. You've replaced the amazing Thought that God created with your limited version and you've become unreal and uncomfortably plastic and, ironically, more than odd; less believable and less lovable; unable to exude the inner peace and greatness you were hoping to advertise that you've fully and completely mastered.

And you're not alone. We all do this to some degree, from moment to moment, as do I; lie. My ego controller-self and chief antagonist to inner peace is the main instigator of the wars begun against God's best creation of me, as well as those good souls who've innocently followed the selfishly designed lead I've created. This ego-created self, let's call it Bill, not that Bill is quirky and enjoys writing in third person; it's my name.

Now, understand that Bill is a self-developed character sculpted, from an early age, by a rich imagination and wild visions of life as he thinks it must be and has developed his image from a compilation of heroes he's admired; with a pinch of greed and envy of and for that, all so elusive, "good life".

That being achieved, Bill's ego should be able to get it right, whatever "right" is, as Bill's been thoughtfully created and imaginatively honed by a really great guy; Bill. And Bill is a hard worker, so Bill can do it, if anyone can. And handing control of my life to my ego-self doesn't mean Bill's lazy by any means. If anything, it means Bill's willing to work overtime to create and maintain an image worthy of admiration; the great mirage-achieved reality.

However, the energy spent to protect the lies about our lives is wasted; about whom we think we must be and the fantasies of perfection we think we must fulfill. I, for one, have allowed my ego to drive my decisions, determine my values, decide what to wear, how to project my words and works, and how best I might make it very clear to everyone just how great and valuable Bill is to the world.

~

Thankfully, in the process of exorcising my demons, I realized I'd been living a lie. For so many years, I'd thought so highly of myself when I'd succeeded and self-effacing in defeat, when suddenly I realized I was merely acting out an exaggerated view of my self-importance. And my overly developed pride (is there any other kind?) had accepted the lie, by which I've been well-imprisoned.

The lie:

Relative success proves my worth, relatively and, therefore, my ability to be happy; relatively. And failure, well, failure is bad. It exposes my well-disguised weaknesses; whether of hereditary or environmental formation, shameful weaknesses, nonetheless. So, as failure seems to spotlight my self-deemed ineptness and marks me as a wrong person; it also proves to the world and to myself that my fears are real, that I'm faulty and therefore, imperfect and incapable of long-term happiness and, worse, of no enviable value to the world.

While it's natural to outwardly celebrate, smile cheerfully, after-party, and share our joy openly with the world when we win, failure proves that our weaknesses and faults are real and damaging. In our failures, we fear we have become the person people should want to avoid, so to retain a powerful image and we might respond to failure with outward displays of disappointment, even anger, as a public display of self-punishment for having screwed up so badly; for having let everyone down.

In our defeat, it's entirely acceptable to swear and tantrum openly, as our roles command us, ironically, to prove we are men – big pissed off men, yes! – men, still in control – men, still powerful; a childish ceremony, but we are, in fact, manly men that will not "go down without a fight" and, most certainly, we are *not* born to lose. Now, go ahead, just for fun, throw your clipboard at the ground, curse, and storm off the field; blabbering self-effacies.

The reality:

If we allow ourselves to accept that we are wrong, mostly, and consider the possibility that another's point of view is credible, we may also accept that both success and failure are facts of life and that each is necessary for personal growth. And the experience of failure and success, if relatively appreciated, begets evolved wisdom; relatively.

So, whether we deem a disagreement as conflict, stalemate, or an educational opportunity or we judge a marketing plan by its immediate results, as a success or a failure; either must be appreciated from the learning received. And the payoff is found by the brutally earned morsel of wisdom that serves to improve our judgment in future and similar situations; that we might avoid the pains equally associated with success and failure and that we might suffer hardship with less drama and more manageable tribulation.

~

So, is it reasonable to expect that we humbly celebrate success or accept the loss and failures in our lives only with appreciation of the knowledge gained? That our leaning serves as a vaccine for the ills of our failures and that it be such a difficult pill to swallow?

If failure's medicine were meant to benefit our lives or livelihood, why do our falls from grace and public defeats (our reactions to the medicine) feel so terrible, like a punch in the chest; a kick in the teeth; a blow below the belt?

And, why so many cliché's?

Is it just that it's early and I'm tired and there's two feet of snow to shovel outside, when I'm done with my tea?

Yes, is the answer and I just got lazy.

And yes, we're emotional creatures and sometimes it's just OK to get anxious when we feel rushed or get pissed off when someone is driving in the wrong lane forcing us off the road. Anger is an important part of our nature in reaction to unfair and possibly evilly intended interactions.

Anger increases the adrenaline vital to powering our instinctive mental and physical acrobatics required in our seemingly spontaneously choreographed efforts to save a life or strengthen our resolve to enforce goodness in the battles against injustice and pride; preventing the liars from stealing our peace.

But, in the absence of evil, we must be honest with ourselves and with those around us who are simply doing their best to survive and persist. When confronted with discomfort, annoyances, or incidental failures we must remain appreciative of the new layers of Wisdom earned from the extremely difficult challenges met in the process of living on earth – growing our Faith.

Know these three Truths:

1. The payoff for agreeing to take your part in this earthly growth process is Wisdom earned – that we may more elegantly navigate all levels of discomfort and trial – literal or imagined – and through prayer-initiated miracles we might appreciate, with less resistance, the human and Angelic assistance that improves our lot in life and keeps our families safe from evil-initiated harm.

2. While nobody is perfect and there is no perfect way to do anything, as long as we're evolving emotionally and spiritually, admit we're usually wrong, and remain a sponge for learning; our relative Wisdom increases.

3. And we may more easily accept and appreciate the fact that struggle and change is a natural constant of living on earth and the inner peace earned is our summary reward for the risks taken, the greatest of all risks, to publicly and unashamedly be our imperfect selves and to act immediately on the unconventional and sometimes quite odd actions the Spiritual Bumps and Nudges directs us to endorse.

Spiritual Logic

"Most people think they know what they are good at.
They are usually wrong.

More often, people know what they are not good at
and even then, more people are wrong than right.

And yet, a person can perform only from strength.

One cannot build performance on weaknesses
let alone on something one cannot do at all."

Dr. Peter Drucker
(from his book, Managing Oneself)

    The instant I accepted this concept as my new reality; I conquered my need to fix my weaknesses and began to focus on honing my skills and improving on my God-given strengths. I no longer desire to maintain the façade of who Bill thinks he is; more easily surrendering my version of a perfect Bill to God. And a long and torturous healing process is beginning to take hold in my soul and psyche to rid myself of my self-defined me; my demons are being exorcised.

    And I'm slowly losing the desire to condemn myself and others for our messy upbringings, for our hereditary prejudices, and illogically derived decisions that lack basis in fact; for our imperfections; our personal lies. I'm reluctantly learning patience, as well; to hold my criticisms of others in witness to the most intolerable acts of stupidity that, before, I'd found much too painful to restrain correction or remain silent and of which not to poke fun; at; about; and of. And, as important to perfection, I've learned the value of not ending a sentence with a preposition…

"Ending a sentence with a preposition is something up
with which I will not put."

Winston Churchill

~

OK, besides our constant drive to free ourselves of our deepest fears and needs to be constantly right, we might want to lighten up a little! Wouldn't you agree?

We take ourselves and our predetermined portrayal of ourselves and ever important "to do lists" much too seriously and, at times, our egos rear their ugly heads as we think ourselves and our personal agendas so time-sensitive that we passively or overtly dismiss another's point of view or we ignore an injustice in our hurry to accomplish or in our hurry to meet our projected business targets we forget to enjoy the journey and we ignore the beauty that exists within the moment.

So, stop! Relax, have a little fun, smile, accept happiness, and take time to visit with a stranger or to be patiently respectful of another's just cause or expressed pain; it'll only hurt for a minute, and then go back to being insanely focused on whatever's worth all the stress in proving right and correct. It's OK...

Surprisingly, though, it's not that difficult to stop the wheels in our heads from taking charge and criticizing, condemning, or complaining and, instead, respectfully staying out of another's business. When I realize that I'm no better than they, you, or others; in my own special ways, I can more easily keep my mouth shut and smile.

With this newfound clarity and appreciation for the power of "minding my own business" or "non-resistance" or "non-cooperation" with evil, as Gandhi referred to it, I may actualize the thought that I am wrong, mostly and that I might fight evil, simply by not cooperating with it. And that goes for *my* horrific attitudes and agendas, as well; not cooperating with my wrong thinking, my internal negative and bad thoughts that could easily cancer into great fear, then evil if adhered to, at, for, or from.

Wow!

Another epiphany! I decided that not only am I not perfect; not perfectly perfect from every perspective; I, also, needn't be right, always. And it's not absolutely necessary for me to believe in nor must I cooperate with mine or any other person's negativity or controlling evil. In the same breath, I must be comfortable admitting my failures, as I recognize their frequency and that I may live honorably, without fear of permanent shame, as we're all wrong... and we're more wrong when we shade the truth or condemn another's failure or accept the wrong being applied, in our cooperation with it.

By not cooperating with lies, I might be released from prison and freed to be me and more happily accept me and others for whom it is that we are; without trying to fix, criticize, or condemn another's perceived failures or weaknesses exposed; as we're all idiots in-waiting to be exposed on Twitter.

From an Eternal and Heavenly perspective, though, we're cosmic toddlers tripping over toys, bouncing off the padded walls in our cells, and making insane judgments upon one another, as well as ourselves. Take notice as we bang our sippy-cups on the table or pound our chests like a Silverback Guerilla to get "our way" and our feelings get hurt when things don't go just right; the way we've been admonished they should. It's really a great show to watch, objectively, from afar; as it plays itself out, constantly, in our living rooms, on Cable News, and in our board rooms.

~

The truth, however, may be found in each instance, as we realize that God created each of us to experience life well, individually and socially, and to simply love one another fully, in the process. And I propose that when we see a brother fighting for what he's certain is his share of the American Pie, we might take a step back and realize; we're all just doing the best we can to live in safety and comfort. It's just that some fear losing to a greater degree than do others; we each fear losing, though. Before pointing out a wrong, keep in mind, we are imperfect temporal beings, with varying degrees of spiritual consciousness, born with free will, but each on our own path and without an original thought; except that thought which is God's.

So, who are we to judge another when the smartest amongst us may not be the most intelligent, simply the one who knows how to use the intelligence s/he has been given or, as equally important, the one who knows when to shut up and listen?

Our roles fulfilled, God has expressed His love to the world through our beings, through these incredibly diverse personalities, as we've co-experienced life in non-resistance to, but in cooperation with His Thought. From this stand that the "Truth in any moment is not to think but to love one another and to serve selflessly", fulfillment or protection of *our* personal wants and needs is no longer our main priority and surprisingly, our needs are met. From this surety and conscious surrender, His Genius is unleashed and we may serve others more selflessly and we fearlessly glide through conflict with His Strength and Confidence and we may be more compassionate and forgiving of others as we recognize ourselves in the most condemnable human and fearful defects of others.

Today, in this Here/Now, we may choose the ultimate path to peace, which is to serve others; first. With a selfless attitude, we may serve without thoughts of reward or need to prove our worth. And we need no thing, and paralyzing fears are extinguished; we ignore our self-made defects and there is nothing more perfect than living within this emptiness of our true-selves, as we accept whom it is God created us to be; filled to overflowing with God's Love; directed by His Thought.

From years of failing to do so, as my energy becomes consciously focused on another's wellbeing; "Bam!" I'm fair game for the truth to enter my thoughts and I'm no longer weighted by failure-drag and success-dread and relief is known.

By choosing to act selflessly and determined to live honestly in service to others, we live in harmony with the truth served to us in this Holy Instant and we relinquish self-consciousness and are on fire in search of the deeper meanings found in this now Holy relationship with one another. And Now and only Here, we have instantaneous courage to act, Spiritually-Guided action that requires no earthly approval and we shine automatically as God shines automatically, through us.

So, be yourself and be that better than anyone you think you must be and be respectful and loving of others and pray you don't become overly self-enamored, self-absorbed, and overflowing with pride when you've done extremely well and been proportionally well-rewarded for doing only that which you were born to do well – be you.

~

And what does this have to do with finding Hope in Entrepreneurialism and the Game of Money?

Everything!

My best ideas being dismissed to the point of slander or supported with a pat on the head or parade in my honor, my ability to be who I am, as well as my ability to perform unconsciously; fearlessly; courageously in behalf of my clients is crippled when I weigh my business decisions on another's opinion of my worth or in those selfish moments, as I connive to prove that I hold the Golden Key to the truth.

Each day, I must be reminded of my mission to remain in a constant search for Truth in service to my clients and to do so with zero regard for how it might build my earthly empire. In this painful release of want for high-reward and my need to control outcomes, I've found that earnings will care for themselves. We ultimately get what we deserve and we somehow survive. Yes… whether we ban or embrace arrogance, stupidity, or larceny; we get what we deserve.

> "… You can't always get what you want
> But if you try some time, you find
> You get what you need…"
>
> Mick Jagger and Keith Richards

So, to be successful, I constantly pray for the strength and courage to give up control of what I think I want and need and I pray that my fearful self will go away; far away; really far; so very far, far away that I can't tell you how far…

Letting go of my agenda, I am able to allow God to work through others, as well as myself to help Him get what He wants; instead. And when I'm doing well at that one simple and most terrifying thing, letting go, I've become aware of those subtle moments in time when my clients and I've decided it's safe to go to work in one another's behalf and we've taken a seat on the same side of the negotiating table in a spontaneous ad hoc, yet spiritually pre-arranged, Holy partnership.

At this point, my role in developing and deploying a brilliantly simply solution is simplified, as I'm able to work for a client from a spiritually logical basis and we may now stand aside and allow God to put the right people, vendors, and technologies together to solve problems now clarified – important to all.

And from what might appear to be serendipity or insane brilliance or Forrest Gumpian dumb luck, today, I am blessed to have built relationships with many gifted and talented "experts", each a flawed and wrong person, but each doing the best we might to employ technologies in agriculture – saving water and growing healthier foods to better sustain and improve the quality of our lives on this amazing blue dot, in space, called earth.

CHAPTER 9

The Board of Directors

"Live as if you were to die tomorrow.
Learn as if you were to live forever."

Mahatma Gandhi

Spiritual Logic

Carmen Ortiz Vega Bigelow, my mother; a strong Puerto Rican woman of deep ancestral Catholic faith and stubborn in her love for God and belief in His guidance; raised seven children with little financial help or family leadership from dad.

She is adamant in her devotion to St. Jude for she had reached to him with no choice but to pray for his intercession, almost daily, when we had little or no food and were threatened with evictions. Her soul was constantly harassed by fear; for our health and safety and she prayed constantly, hourly, that God provide relief.

In times of thanksgiving I would see her cry alone in the solitude she sought, which was impossible to find in a chaotic home with so many immature but growing characters; with our endless needs for food, comfort, medical attention, education, and entertainment; all of which the supply weighed squarely on her shoulders.

In the most recent twenty-five years, though, she's received her earthly reward for her devotion to family and God and her selfless sabbatical from romance; and she found her love, Dallas Bigelow; an incredibly loving and kind man with a sense of humor that loads the Spanish Armada of laughter canons for an explosion the neighbors have had to bear the brunt. Dallas and she have been one another's eternal answer to the mortally unsolvable question and found a partner with whom to grow old and continue the adventure far beyond this earthly plane.

Back in the day, mom worked at the Utah State Department of Commerce and for over twenty-five years helped businesses set up shop; file corporate documents, issue DBA's (the name for a company – Doing Business As), etc. So, when I was a kid, 23 or so, and decided to go into business, she showed me how to set up the corporation and, within minutes, I owned my first Company!

How cool is that?

I'd crawl out from under the supervision of fools and could go to work for myself... I became the "top dog" and answer to no one.

Well, irony has a great way of sticking its nose in our greatest plans involving leisurely money-counting. It really should have worked. We had a great idea, Scott Garrett and I, to produce and broker music jingles (catchy songs) for radio commercials, for small town radio stations, and

Gemini Productions was formed. We were free to take the business we had learned and to grow it into our very own production house. That first and final summer of business netted us a grand total of $800. The summer of 1978 ground slowly; three long months of travel, meetings, and waiting for the phone to ring.

And since that experiment, I've started and run a dozen companies. I've named them, developed product, designed marketing and sales strategies, hired and trained hundreds of sales and marketing people; start-up after start-up… to open and close, succeed and fail, and when lucky enough I'd sell my shares to start another.

Forming a business is simple. But the fascinating thing to me is that in forming a corporation I'd given birth to a living entity; I'd had a baby. If the age of a company might be related as are dog-years to human (1:7); Gemini Productions didn't make it to pre-school. In fact, most companies don't make it through adolescence (2½ years). Keep in mind, a company is more than a metaphorical life form; it is an entity with legal rights and many of the same protections as does a "Citizens United" Supreme Court Ruling attempt to unrulily justify.

Although it can't bleed, a Company may be bled. It can't marry and have children, but it may merge with another or spin-off divisions to create new entities. It can't vote but it may hire a lobbyist to influence public policy, and in many respects the baby has legal rights respected without border; globally; where Governments have little leverage to battle against their financial backers (cowardly politicians refuse to bite the hand that feeds them).

However, the Company may grow to harness the strength and power of many men and women; many intelligent, savvy, and imaginative persons each striving to thrive within the structure, yet each accountable to management and shareholders for their purpose and productivity.

~

Now, let's take a step back and take a look at our lives here on earth.

Who am I?

What am I doing with my life?

What we're doing, where we're going, and why we're here might be easier inspected objectively as if our person were incorporated; a legal entity.

Let's call this galactically ginormous metaphoric-entity – Me, Inc.

How differently might we treat things if we had shareholders to account to for our productivity, for our public image, for maintaining share values, debt to earnings ratios, etc.? And what about our mission… our unique selling proposition or our reason for being… what's the purpose of our formation? And what exactly is our long-term business plan? What would we say are our core strengths and weaknesses? What about a partner? Who might we marry to offset the weaknesses and magnify our strengths; inspire positive energy, enthusiasm, and unlock charisma, as Sue has done for me?

And what exactly is our exit strategy? How do we cash out? What happens when the Company dissolves; ashes to ash, dust to dust? What precisely is it about our character that we might take with us to the next fantastic venture, beyond this life, when we retire these clumsy bodies to the dirt of the earth?

~

Yes, one day we'll be flat on our backs; a final sigh; the simplistic natural exhaust of our last breath. Surprised by this new and final experience on earth, it'd be a shame to have not shared our love completely with the ones who needed it or to have left something vitally important left undone or to have left a trail of lies behind – to be uncovered by those whose love and respect we cherish and to whom we have desired to be remembered most favorably if not honorably.

As time stops, in that final moment prior to the release of our spirit into the hands of God, besides being scared to death, do we really want our thoughts marred by shame or regret?

If we live our lives as if each day were the final, with every choice, action, and word fused to kindness, honor, and duty; our accounts naturally attract order and we naturally surrender all that is worldly to the world from which it came. In that final moment of our dying breath, weightless of earthly burden, once defining ambitions of being loved by all, meeting our obligations, or amassing earthly treasures and experiencing worldly comforts is brought meaningless.

Death assured our mind reluctantly makes its final earthly decision to give up its body, to slip away into unconsciousness, and... our body lifeless, our spirit-mind instantaneously becomes a seamless being of the whole of creation not separate pieces sewn, as we had for so long held strongly guarded beliefs. Our self-willed material specialness, now, has no meaning and there is no value greater than that of meeting God; experiencing the might of His Love.

Humbled by the inevitability of this ultimate and finite action, realizing that death may occur at any time, we may be led safely into an infinite adventure with God while breathing earth's air; alive. Far from dead, alive today, we may respond fearless to the rumors that an over-stimulated mind concocts of loss, lack, and attack; simple daily distractions comparative to the snatching of our lives by accident or fate or the slow demise of our once good health.

If we knew that God was to "call us home" today, filtered through our powerful "OK, let's do this *death* thing!" attitude, what shame or regret would we disguise for fear of being found out? Whose opinion would we fear reprisal for discussing the previously non-discussable "elephant in the room"?

If this single breath drawn is truly one of 3600 of our final breaths, besides fear of the great unknown, precisely what would we want to think about that is more vital than experiencing truth, treating others with respect, and insisting others treat us likewise; to the death?

So, if there's an embarrassment we've hidden in the closet, get it out in the open today and surprise everyone with honest evaluations and unarguable common sense; without agenda except that the truth must prevail. Freely accept or expose the truth of past mistakes and bad endeavors sought; much as an elderly and long-retired Congressman might as s/he clears the slate of regrettable pushed-legislation; s/he now, has nothing to lose with no political influence to attract or peddle; clandestine lobbying contracts and speaking engagements, long ago, unrequested.

Fearless, in the face of the fires of hell, our overworked minds are emptied and the Truth may be lived and the road out of hell is surprisingly easier to navigate an exit than it was strongly rumored. Jesus carries us to His destination. But, as you're reading this, time is ticking, and with little time left – get to work. Do not leave a responsibility ignored or undone, today. Grab that ugly useless object of obsession tucked away under the shorts in the chest of drawers of your soul and run it to the trash. Sanitize, by a short prayer and new belief, that smelly little goopy thing under the sink in the kitchens of your mind that cooks up wildly selfish schemes of glory and physical gratifications. And don't forget to clear the cookies from the search engines of your ambitions' that point to a wild online to on-street search.

Decide to make a change in your desires and just "behave"; really. Your last day will come, so choose, Here and Now, to take a single step forward to repair and prepare your legacy for an honestly respectful tribute by the many who love you, that they may easily speak well of your life; without disguising their courteous recollections with a fault-disclosing smirk.

Do it today and live this day fresh with the vigor of a pure soul; forgiven, new and unleashed of its gnarly and somewhat socially twisted indiscretions; freed from infestations of ego's need for greatness and superiority and the natural response loaded with fear. Drop what you've been doing and be Great in this Holy Now; this Holy instant in time that Jesus completes a father's greatest desire for His child; alive within your being; forgiven, forgiving, loving, and loved.

Washed, purified, and ready to enter the world a cleansed spirit; purified mind and sanctified body; we know who we are.

Or do we?

Whether it's our home or the neighborhood in which we live, the car we drive, the clothes we wear, how we speak, with whom we associate, where we vacation, the toys we possess, or the degree we hang on the wall, our titles, professions, elected positions, businesses named and built, or even the amount of money and drudgingly acquired assets we donate to charities; for the most part, we acquiesce spiritually to the world of the material and consciously or unconsciously judge and rank approval of the performance of others and are likewise judged in some degree with bias to our favor and success-formulas.

We judge and are judged, and our choices in how to respond and react fashions us; unveils our character and enlists parallel actions from those who surround us.

~

If not to create a better world and succeed in living and to do so more peacefully and with more creative vigor than our counterparts or those who've unselfishly cleared a path for us to travel, what is the purpose of our ambitions in life and for forming Me, Inc? Did God create Bill Terry merely to have him build an estate for succeeding generations to benefit or for Bill to control more of the world's resources than the next guy? Is our innate desire to improve earthly conditions merely a competition with our ancestors; can the need to grow and improve on things become a distraction taking focus from building relationships within the family; or is it a classical instinct God implants in each of us to be a healthy addition to the world condition; selflessly, one experience, one transaction, or project happily completed at a time?

> "Last night my wife said,
> 'Poor boy when you're dead
> the only thing you take is your soul.'"
>
> John Lennon
> The Ballad of John and Yoko

    In our search for ultimate success, we experience value-conflicts between pride of ownership, fulfilling pleasure, and creating long-term happiness. To inflict defeat may be pleasurable as we witness its impact on the jerk down the hall or the other side of the world, but that form of success is a false god and is of no lasting consequence to the enrichment of peace or development of either's soul. There are many "riches that cannot be stored" and building friendships, sharing compassion, and growing good character are three we may choose to value above all else; these are the bounties that make the effort in playing The Game of Money well worth it, to acquire.

    The end of The Game is not won by the money totaled. Remember, the end is the character we have formed in this lifetime that is resilient to the negative impetuses of envy, distrust, and pride.

~

    So, let's get back to treating our person as if it were a Company with assets and liabilities, with a P & L, balance sheet, etc. What if we or our spouse is hyper-focused on increased earnings each year and competing with the Jones's and owning more things is better and even more is best? When times get tough and downward market pressures determine that cut backs are in order, do wives lay-off husbands, do partnerships dissolve? Yes, I guess sometimes they do. For when the amount of incremental net cash has become our measuring tool for success, stagnant growth must mean it's time for a change... One spouse might say to the other, "I've got some bad news... this is as tough for me as it is for you... but we just have to make some changes around here and you don't fit in the new plan. I'll need your keys."

Whether we like it or not, our husbands, wives, brothers, sisters, sons, daughters, and many entrusted friends, customers, vendors, bosses, and strangers have invested part of their lives and maybe even cash into our little enterprise, Me, Inc. They trust Me, Inc. to perform well in every aspect and to maintain and increase share value for the investments they made in our persons; trusting in our ability to create ever increasing financial security through accumulated wealth.

These folks are our stakeholders whether they like it or not, whether we like it or not. And if we have any sense of responsibility and interest in fair play, we must consider the value of their investment in Me, Inc. when we make decisions that, ultimately, impact them. We must be thorough in researching opportunities and careful in our responses to market trends and forces and consider every angle and every angle of every angle... There's much expected of us and we know, deep inside, we can't to do this alone. Maybe it would be best to get another opinion, another set of eyes on the business plan of Me, Inc., other lifetimes of experience offering new perspectives on the matter at hand, before we make those "oh so critical" life defining important decisions.

No one man may possibly expect to have all the answers, so my Me, Inc. is run by a Board of Directors to keep my Me, Inc. on track, to guide it through the rough spots in life. We, each of us, have only one shot at Me, Inc. There is no Chapter 13, reorganization option available in the Christian model. Sometimes I wish God had engineered us with an "undo" or "reset" key that I could hit to reincarnate and start over; get it right the next time. Nonetheless, this entity, Me, Inc. must go on living despite incredible hardships and personal setbacks. So far, my Me, Inc. has survived and will continue to survive the cyclical downturns, competitive pressures, supply chain short-comings, increased demands that are difficult to meet with the staff on hand, cash flow issues, and the loss or death of key-men. All the things that happen in life, Me, Inc. faces and has faced and will continue to face and will survive regardless of a short sighted fearful death-watch of a dream. But, only through constant prayer might I focus on being an integral party to the work for the benefit of all and my mind clearly sees the possible positive outcomes that are guaranteed by God's Wisdom heard.

However, the question remains, what shall I report to my shareholders that keeps them from bailing-out and more so, entices them to continue to invest their valuable time, energy, and trust in Me, Inc? If Me, Inc. is to truly succeed and make a difference in the world and do so with confidence in the positive, safe, and sure outcome that I know is just around the corner or sustainable beyond this "best year ever", I must know, without a doubt, that my plan is correct and that my ego isn't the Captain of the ship.

~

So, let's take a step back and determine our purpose for being in business and develop a business plan that considers a "higher purpose"; a purpose higher than simply feeding our egos and filling our bank accounts. We can spend months writing it, we've already spent a lifetime developing and deploying it, but we each have a unique purpose and a plan to follow and it's best to get it on paper that it solidifies our commitment; that it becomes our reality.

To begin, let's ask ourselves, "Are we happy with whom it is we have become?" and "How interested are we in being that person times 10 due to the results of maintaining our current course?" We must ask ourselves if we are fulfilled; are we living a life of purpose, and are we fully exploring the talents God entrusted us to share with the world? Do we love our work so much that we would do it for free? "Rich Dad Poor Dad" is a great book. It asks that question loudly. But, how do we best put our core talents to use so that every day is an adventure, an exploration in how we might stretch ourselves and how best might we serve God and our brothers and sisters here on this planet?

We each, deep down inside, truly know what it is we are born to do and may envision ourselves successful at doing it and we've found it and are living that amazing life fulfilled or we're well on our way to reaching Nirvana or we don't know how to get there (wherever "there" might be) and we're too scared to make the first move. And which move might we make to find our part or maintain course? We each have many and varied degrees of assets and liabilities; talents, strengths, and weaknesses and it becomes a daunting task to sort through the infinite plausible and possible scenarios to determine our best course of action and best use of time and resources to deploy to be successful beyond short term – say, next 10 years or so – goals.

After many successes and failures in business and in life, the only fair way for me to honestly stand in front of my shareholders and sell my new line of ideas is to give up control of Me, Inc. and hand it over to my "Board of Directors" and follow their guidance, explicitly; stand back and take their lead. This Board I'm alluding to has proven itself time and time again to guide me out of the darkest business and personal storms and into my highest state of performance and unimagined success. With free and often unsolicited advice and direction from the Board, there's no room for doubt, only hope. They have the inside story, a huge database, and an Eternal perspective; far beyond mortal vision, far beyond human fears.

In 2005, long before I had full need for office space for my security camera distribution company, I was working from a comfortable home-office and for some reason was compelled to place an ad to hire a salesman to help me grow the business. I could see my business plan starting to take shape in two distinct areas and needed help. I had a few calls from the ad and one morning met with a very talented and astute businessman with loads of sales and sales management experience; Rene Zamora. I'd greeted him at the front door of my home; we sidestepped the cats in the entryway and sat across from each other at my dining room table for an interview; of sorts. As we discussed the business opportunity, questions flew back and forth, he interviewed me and I him when he finally asked me, flatly, "Bill, why are you doing this?"

It was a great question that I had no prepared positional and practical response. So, caught off guard, I listened and went with the "Bump" and grabbed my pen and notepad, stood, and moved over to his side of the table. I drew a circle and said to him, "I have a Board of Directors and there are three members of The Board." And on the top of the circle I wrote, my Father, below Him, His Son Jesus and then the Holy Spirit. He smiled and understood and from that moment we began to share common interests in God's works and guidance systems and instantly became brothers in a higher mind of doing business.

I didn't employ Rene; he formed and is now operating a successful consulting business in the Bay Area, www.salesmanagernow.com. However, for the next five years we worked together on several ventures, each very important and successful. But, more importantly, he and I have learned to call on each other in the midst of battle to hold an ad hoc "Board Meeting" to help each other through the current most difficult task or decisions of the day.

It's the obvious solution to manage fear of the great unknowns; give them to someone with more experience – more power to get things done. And how is it possible to have a more committed board of directors, a board more interested in your absolute success, which is in fact my absolute success? The Board has no hidden agendas. There is no guesswork required. It's a loving and fully vested Board that, by-the-way, created Me, Inc.

So, I approach The Board for help anytime anywhere without an appointment or need to set up the conference room or spiff-up the office... prepare reports... When we meet, whether impromptu or planned, I do so with no fear of reprisal for putting them in an awkward position – without notice – or being shamed for making selfish and "oh so foolish request" for advice. The fact is, I am and we are God's creation and He wants nothing less than for each of us to know His Love and for each of us to succeed and to find joy in the work we do for one another.

Try it!

Have a quick Board meeting as you open the restaurant door on the way into an important business lunch or as you lean in to listen to your customer in the middle of a sales call, while preparing a proposal, before sending an email or text, during a performance review, or staff briefing, while in a difficult customer support call with a client... before and during a conversation with your child. Take every chance you can to include The Board and give up the learned agenda that makes us each compete for favor or need to win, that another loses, and cooperate with God's agenda. There's peace, as well as power, to be found in letting go the reigns and leaving nothing to chance.

The great caveat:

If you're not completely certain you can give up the reigns, don't try it with only one foot in the stirrup, you'll likely be thrown by the power not grasped. Plus, as the old saying goes, "You can't ride two horses" and the parable about serving two masters applies well in this regard; serving to gain and protect market share or serving without thought of reward provides two distinctly different outcomes; the latter being the greater – more sustainable.

It takes courage and patience and a willingness to be second, to truly give up control and to allow God to design and implement His Holy strategies. But, once who is in control of Me, Inc. is agreed upon, there's less fearful energy exerted and more of His Goodness that may be put in motion to fulfill His "Great Plan". The Great Plan of which we've had little knowledge its grandeur or ability to be a trusted accomplice in completing.

Place your trust in "The Eternal Plan" and have dumb-patience (quit thinking so hard) as He lines up the contacts from His Eternal file of connections and relationships, as He queues us into action with precision, gives us the words and phrasing, and provides the opportunities He knows full well we are prepared and fully capable to meet the unique demands.

Just smile and say, "Thanks!" when you see it working.

But, of course, it's a tough thing to do, giving up our dreams in place of the Eternal Agenda. And let's say that we do and it works for a while, we'll find great success and joy, yet we'll most likely return to old habits and try to run things on our own, that's human nature. So, I've found it necessary to go to The Board every morning to prepare for the day. I get out of the driver's seat and give Jesus the wheel. Sometimes I have a more formal meeting where we sit at a table and I pray. On paper and in ink, I consciously open my life up to Jesus; everything feared, open for exploration and correction. I write them down; my plans, apprehensions, anxieties, successes and failures, both business and personal, which by-the-way there is little difference when you love the work you do.

During these Board meetings, I write down the names of those for whom I wish to pray and list the tough unanswerable decisions I currently face.

In these meetings, with everything out on the table and Me, Inc. empty of agenda, I give up my version of truth and am ready to let go of my dreams and material desires and relinquish to the Board everything I own or think I must control and I pray to accept the Board's greater

Will; in its place. With my reality and intentions open to every Board scrutiny and examination at mystically parallel dimensions of Universal Thought I may receive Absolute Direction. My action-plans are thereby spiritually determined and miraculously and quite expectedly I receive a clear course of action for at least this single day; which is, in truth, but all we have.

The Board keeps me sane, on track, on purpose, and it's on constant standby – ready to hear from the President of Me, Inc., me; in my prayers for the truth and from my impassioned and private screams for solace.

~

So, what about The Game of Money? Bottom line; let's look at The Game as one of many ways in which to measure our ability to listen to The Board and to serve well the world in which we live. When played well, the reward in cold cash might be one of many statistics that measure the growth of our souls, so don't be afraid to be rich in cash; that the wealthy cannot get to Heaven. As we succeed spiritually, we learn to serve without thought of material gain. So, played well, we are released from need to own or control neither hard-assets nor the talented and influential people that come and go in our lives. These people are sent to us; they are the keys to unlocking our fiscal, if not, Eternal net worth. To play well, include others and, as we experience each relatively minor success by doing so, we've learned to trust more fully in His Grand outcome than in our own selfish designs.

The "Big Lesson" being that material wealth is no indicator of our Eternal net worth. Yet money moves the world in which we live, so choose to play the game well and God rewards us with more responsibility that may require more cash to flow through our bank accounts although, not necessarily for us to keep.

The Game of Money helps us realize the spiritual way to success by understanding the universal forces that lead us to wealth and, in the same lesson, frees us of a wealth that must be horded or stored away in safe deposit boxes or that fills our climate controlled storage units. The Game of Money's wealth is not measured in the sums reaching vulgar vastness, but in the balanced person we become in playing The Game well. The Company assets and cash-on-hand we control is merely an IT, but how we get IT and what we do with IT defines who we are, who we have become; our legacy.

Spiritual Logic

Each of our life's decisions is important to God in fulfilling His Will for a loving Universe of His Creations and we get one lifetime on earth to make good our agreed chosen-path and it's in this one and only day that, and in this singular moment, we might affect the Greatness of His Plan. So, we must get it right today, and that places an immense burden on us. Yet, there is no good to be found in stressing or obsessing over this seemingly intense responsibility to perform God's Goodness.

We must learn to let go of the burden; an incremental daily learning.

In that, I'm learning a little more each day to step back and allow "The Board" to create, Now/Here, through my being, Me, Inc., and I'm learning to be fully satisfied and appreciative of the sometimes glorious and sometimes apparently benign outcomes of a day lived well; in communion with God.

Life is simplified, as I'm here to do only the best that I might to listen and follow my Father's Will. I may do this, as I remember to choose to live complete within this day, within this moment in time; not yesterday, not tomorrow. For it is in this moment in time, only, that I am me; completely.

In this moment, only, I am completely alive, loved, forgiven, forgiving, humble, energized, and absolutely curable. And I am cured of me; alive in Him.

In this instant, I realize that I'm sorry, I'm wrong, I am forgiven, I'm thankful, and I love and am loved. For in this moment, there is nothing to regret from the past nor may I fear for the future. This day lived to the full creates no room for regret or cause for anxiety and this moment is far too important to waste. Yesterday is gone and tomorrow will take care of itself as I reside completely in this moment in time; this Eternal Now, uninfluenced by fear, in this place God resides, life is perfect.

When I'm at my best, Me, Inc.'s gifts to the world come in the form of a transparent being who takes no credit for simply doing my job well or functioning as I'm asked. The good that Me, Inc. accomplishes is not a notch on my belt or a reason for a parade in my honor; it's merely the result of my ability to remain true to the moment, freed of my agenda, and quickly respondent to God's loving Nudges and Bumps. And I pray that this uniquely carved individual, with a lifetime of cuts and bruises, may travel to the world-beyond having added more to this world than it has been given.

The promise God makes to each of us is clear: The Board, unbiased, guides us, our Me, Inc.'s, with perfection. He entrusts us to work towards the successes that only the Mind of God knows we are capable to achieve. Yet, to keep our part of the bargain, each of us must consciously choose to abandon our selfish desires and surrender ourselves completely to the moment in which God resides; Now.

In each exasperatingly simplified/glorified moment, we may choose to ask to become Eternally purified and, in this request and with His immediate reply (Grace) we may experience greatness within the mind and heart of God.

And our Eternal legacy is salvaged; sanctified; survived and lived.

The Miracle at Forest Ridge

JUNE 2005

As with most every amazing experience in my life, my first meeting with "The Board" was completely impromptu. The idea of meeting with The Board came to me on a sunny summer afternoon, at the home the boys' mother and I rented in the mountains, 20 minutes southwest of Wenatchee, Washington. We lived in a little piece of heaven in the forest about 3,000 feet elevation above the valley floor and with another 4,000 to the peaks above. The Wenatchee valley is carved from an ancient lava flow of which over the past couple of million years the powerful

Columbia River chiseled its path to the Pacific Ocean on its long journey from Canada. Surrounded by forest, it was far enough from the city lights that the stars shone bright at night and in the daytime the sky is brilliant blue 300 plus days a year.

To top it off, I was minutes from a rustic and relatively underappreciated ski resort; Mission Ridge. Its steep slopes, narrow chutes, and surprisingly light, dry, and Utah-like Powder gave me absolutely no cause to yearn for my home-town ski resorts near Salt Lake. Having found this place in the mountains made me think of Wenatchee as my new home.

I worked from a bedroom converted into a comfortable and workable home office – no water cooler distractions. The quiet of the mountains allowed me to occasionally take my work outside to the deck, where my laptop and I could contemplate strategies undisturbed, at the patio table.

On that afternoon of my first meeting with "The Board," I remember the mountain air fresh in my nostrils, the blue sky clear except a few puffy clouds lost from the pack, drifting slowly; sitting still bathed in the warm summer breeze, calm, butterflies and squirrels mingled with Bambi and Thumper… Ok… you get the picture. But, the smell of the summertime flowers and the pine sap is a lot of what the soul can use to break up the hectic day and the lonesome solitude of a small home office; working long hours to solve issues for my clients scattered across four time zones.

My young Company had yet to prove its business model that would one day require a staff and office space; increased overhead, but a butt-load more of the offsetting revenue. Still, I was struggling with the idea of packaging a distinctly new offering that would require the startup of yet another company. The new company would provide marketing support for an association of dealers across the United States and the project was beginning to get legs under it. The big question was, can I or should I enter a race riding two young horses.

The prospect of starting a business division before the other ran smoothly was causing a deeply divided war in my soul. The inherent risks to a steady cash flow were driving my shorts ever more tightly over my head in a galactic self-inflicted wedgie. Uncomfortable and frustrated, I grabbed my computer and phone, notepad, and pen and headed outside to the deck. As I sat in the shade of the tall pines out on the patio and as I took a deep breath and laid out the scenario on paper, with an exhaustive breath, I pushed it "all" out into the middle of the table – laptop, notepad, and phone, as if to abandon the effort and say good bye; good riddance.

Within a few deep cleansing breaths, my soul began to calm. Even the animals in the forest circled quietly, some knelt, but all gazed upon the scene with loving support, as I prayed to God for solace, for direction... And in that quiet moment, when all was still, I opened my eyes and looked across the table at the three empty chairs and surmised: Wouldn't it be cool to give my company to God and go to work for Him. If it's His Company, I needn't be responsible for these life-defining decisions and I could just go to work!

I could simply give Him controlling interests, including my earthly dividends, but most important, He'd have the controlling vote to sanction or forbid which of my well vetted biz-ops to work on. I could count on Him, only, to guide me to the only door that would lead me out of my confusion and into His world of universal clarity.

Why not give Him control? If anyone knows, He knows the Way. He created the Way!

But, my mind was tainted from puny and mostly materially-limited thinking and I was sure He'd tell me to pass on this never-before-attempted marketing plan. New technologies needed to be rewritten and deployed in ways never before had they been.

So, I was certain He'd say "Forget it" and that'd be the end of it.

He'd tell me, "Stay focused on the business that's working. Don't screw this up by taking your eye off the ball!"

New plan abandoned, I could relax and get to work on the safe thing that was working; no time wasted on the huge unknown. So, in preparation for the "great relief" I stopped the wheels from clanking around in my mind, took a deep breath, and prayed.

"I'm confused God. What would You have me do?"

"This is Your Company, now. Here... take it!"

"It's Yours – here's the keys and final authority on all decisions."

I prayed that my thoughts were His and that I'd have the courage to follow His guidance and put His ambition to work, but only in His time and as He'd direct me.

The chair across from me was now filled. God, the Father Instantly took it and I began to feel somewhat relieved.

Then, quite naturally I prayed, "Jesus, I'll step aside completely for You to take the second seat at the table here to my left. Guide my words and hold my tongue and I'll stand back and say nothing from my private and fearful mind, otherwise I'll speak, as You would direct me, with Your words, with Your Love and nonresistance, and in Your confident and knowing tone."

The chair to the left of me was Instantly filled, and I was beginning to see a trend.

So, I prayed, "Holy Spirit, take the third seat. You've guided my actions and I trust You implicitly and I promise not to resist Your subtle Nudges. Yet, when I do resist I pray for a solid Bump that I cannot ignore. With You here next to me, I'll get out of the way and follow Your lead and do the work You guide me to do."

In that moment, I spiritually and metaphysically had transferred the ownership of the Company to God, the Holy Trinity, and then and only then could I take direction from these, my most trusted shareholders. I agreed to operate the Company as president directed by my faith and trust in the leadership of "The Board". I became a foot-soldier doing God's bidding and stepped aside to allow God to make the business decisions for His Company and, ignoring my habitual earthly interference, I would do what was asked of me; one day at a time.

~

So, the big question of whether to start up another Company wasn't for me to decide nor for me to initiate creation or guarantee an outcome. And if it flopped, I could simply tell the boys' mom that it was God's fault… His idea! Right?

OK, she had plenty of reasons to think I was too easily distractible and might be better off working within the confines of a corporate structure with a humanly educated hierarchy to which I'd report. She'd have been given ample supply of ammo to have me put away. With her skepticism in full bloom, I kept the meetings to myself.

And I know what I know and only share this with you because it's pretty cool how God works in the lives of His willing accomplices. And whether you believe this or not is not in my control, I'm here simply to tell the story and you're on your own to determine the level of lunacy or truth you're willing to ignore or accept. But, for me, at the time, I was absolutely "set free" by giving up control of the tough decision-making to God; the Creator of all that exists; I found freedom from the fret of deciding; putting it squarely on Him.

Why not take advantage of the Gift He promises; Grace; and put it to work in business?

"Ask and you shall receive."

So, I was determined to make full use of this promise and ask for relief and constant guidance to get me to the right place in business that He would have me, to work for whom He would have me work, and to serve whom He would have me serve. At that moment of acquiescence, I was emotionally, physically, and spiritually prepared to ask my first question of "The Board".

"OK guys, this is Your Company now. What do You want to do with it?"

Before the question was fully asked, I heard these words. Not in a voice that could be heard, but with that familiar whisper – without breath, a thought delivered without processing.

I'm guessing He's fluent in every language, but to me, He speaks in English. And when He speaks, I know His Voice; as does the sheep know the peculiar nuance in the tone of a protective and loving shepherd, calling. I recognized Him without doubt and He said, "Stay with it."

"Crap!"

That was me that said, "Crap." And when I did, the disturbance caused a ruckus and all the animals flinched and scattered and nature began to move again... And, said Eeyore, arriving late, "Who called this meeting? Nobody tells me anything." "Pathetic, just pathetic" as he clumsily wandered away.

Shaking off the surprise of God's desire for me to continue down the path I'd been researching, I agreed to go to work on it – fully vested, but not happily. I was a bit upset that a new responsibility had been handed me. Absolutely the last thing I wanted to hear, as I was certain I'd be freed from the notion; certain The Board would advise me to drop it. So, as a matter of course, I had to ask again to know it wasn't my ego-Bill-self that got in the mix to twist my thinking; my ego being in constant lookout to fulfill its dreams of fame and fortune.

So, I asked again, more specifically, as we're sure we must when we don't get the "right" answer.

"God, do You 'seriously' want us to start another Company and go after this unproven line of business?"

"Yes."

Well, "OK."

It wasn't easy, in fact it took most of the rest of that summer to put the plan together, tie up the loose ends on the technology and determine the finer points of the go-to-market strategy. But what was to come, was incredible. A few days before our scheduled meeting to pitch the plan to the Company in Chicago; Monday, August 29th, 2005 … all hell had broken loose in America…

Lou, who worked for the Company I was about to make the presentation and who was key to developing the plan, lived in New Orleans. And two days before the meeting, on Saturday August 27th, he was the receptor of a mandatory evacuation of all residents, as Hurricane Katrina hit him and his family. And Katrina was still hitting hard the day we were to meet.

Lou had worked hard to set up the meeting and lined up the key players for the meeting; the President and CEO, the Founder of the Company, and the VPs of Marketing, Operations, and Information Technologies. Yet, there was no way to contact him to find out if the meeting was still to be held; considering Katrina's blasting his home and cell service was sketchy.

Spiritual Logic

Come to find out, Lou had evacuated his family to Dallas that weekend and, with the overloaded cell services, his office couldn't reach him, so I'd no idea if the meeting was still on and was certain it was not.

So, more than slightly unsure of what to do, on Saturday, I met with The Board and was sure they'd advise me to cancel the trip.

"Should I fly out tomorrow, as planned?" I asked.

"Yes."

"What? Are you crazy? This is pushing a little too hard... Don't you think we can back-off a little and give Lou a chance to get his house in order?" I abruptly prayed, mostly respectfully, but a bit incredulous of the order... and I needed to be real sure of this.

"Go."

So, Sunday, I flew to Chicago, as planned.

When I arrived in my hotel room, I received the next bit of bad news. Joel, my technical support partner, who was to meet with us and make mad passionate Geek-love to the VP of IT, couldn't make the meeting. His new truck broke down in Sioux Falls, SD after having its first oil change – less the drain plug. Saturday, he and his family were stranded nearly 700 miles west and Joel had no economical way to get to Chicago. Cars rented in South Dakota may not be driven beyond state lines; so I learned. Needless to say, he couldn't be there for the meeting.

OK! Lou and Joel were out. Now the VP Operations, who was my first contact with the Company couldn't make the meeting, either. He and his family lived in Tennessee and Katrina had blown a tree over on his house... what next? Who's left?

"Keep at it." "You're in the right place."

"All right, I'll be fine." Or so, I had to believe.

With everything seemingly at work against me, I was never so sure about making the presentation to whoever was left standing. When I arrived at the 1:00 PM meeting, I was greeted by the CEO, the Founder, and the VP's of Marketing and Information Technologies.

Lou and Paul would web conference from their locations and, after much prayer and preparation meditation, The Board and I made the most succinctly intelligent and persuasive presentation of my life. Never could so much have gone so wrong, yet I had a well-developed proposal to present and with my psyche shored up after a brisk morning run and hours of prayer and meditation under my belt, God had instilled in me an inner sense of absolute confidence and I could not deny its source.

The unfettered poise I demonstrated throughout the presentation literally took me by surprise as I presented the case for doing business with us. I struggled not to smile too broadly for the inside secret I'd put to use so eloquently; fearing I'd appear insane.

I held control of the meeting through the technology and marketing presentation and the tough Q & A that followed. I might have been alone physically, but I could feel the presence of Angels in the conference room on all sides of the discussion; as I'd prayed there to be. As I wrapped up, I asked, "Are there are any more questions and what direction do we need to take to move forward?"

The CEO immediately stood up and reached his hand across the table to shake mine and said, "This is very well thought out." "Can we have a few days to think this over and determine how to move on this?"

After a full year of working out the details with department heads and attorneys, we signed the contracts and a Company was formed; which led me to open an office, hire a much-needed staff, and to generate the biggest revenues in nearly 10 years.

~

God's Will is generous and mysterious and sanitized of mortal judgment. It's embedded in our intuition, honed by trial and error; moving with and against His Bumps. And, over the years, I've developed a rock-solid belief in His ultimate Way, moreover, with faith in His determined desire for mine, yours, and our happiness; rescued by Heavenly-guided actions in our work. We needn't justify actions to those mortally-bound that might ridicule and exhale damaging and limiting judgments upon us to secure their selfish ambitions reached or worst fears avoided.

When we take a moment and ask The Board's direction, we find every answer quickly; more so, we walk a path to success that never before might we have found or forayed alone. From these private directions from this unassuming and all powerful Board of Directors, I owe any financial success, as well as the seemingly devastating failures that have led to many character building and immeasurable personal victories.

the Hope in Entrepreneurialism

CHAPTER 10

THE GAME of MONEY PLAYBOOK

"In a world of all we want
is only what we want until it's ours."

Train

The Game Objective

The Hope in Entrepreneurialism and "experiential objective" of The Game of Money is to "Not think!"

If you truly believe that God the Father, the Creator of all seen and unseen, is the all loving and knowing Being of this and every Universe, and He, through Jesus Christ, by Grace and Mercy tells us "ask and you shall receive." So, why not take Him up on the offer and put His Thought processing mechanisms to work to Think through our every issue, problem, and challenge brought by tragedy, poor planning, or accident.

Opening our Hearts and Minds to God to Think through each of our problems in life, trusting Him to do so in our behalf, and granting Him power of attorney over our conflictive mindal-estates; He levels every unscalable mountain and dulls the edge of every imbalance of justice. His Eternal Knowledge and Understanding bypasses every unnecessary solution-derivative that we concoct/explore and He Instantly provides answers previously unthinkable – unprocessable – by our relatively puny mortal minds.

With our relatively limited processing power to access stored intelligence from our studies, experience, and collaborative associations, we have little to zero chance to solve complex issues without help. And in these days of instant global access to multi-disciplined, multi-generational, multi-language relational-information solutions, available now, plus the unwritten answers, to issues, often used by the disconnected – analog information inaccessible by Google search engines, but conveyable by ancestral stories of methods successfully deployed in days-gone-by – in faraway places.

We have so much information available to us and the answers to every problem may be resolved in this Now, if we could simply do God's job; if we could efficiently process, associate, and communicate multi-dimensional procedures derived from the correct correlated data of multiple sources or from accurate memories of previous similar experience and apply today's pertinent nuance to the problem.

But, we're not asked to do God's job. His Eternal Mind Knows the answer before the question is asked and He wants us to Know, as well and step in for Him where He cannot go.

If we truly believe and have believed in His Brilliance and Ability to Create, why do we think we might do better in our attempts to "think" our way out of trouble or into pleasure or away from disease and suffering and into good health, wealth, and a perfected day – all around? If we really do trust that He has the answers to each of our problems and issues; that He knows the Path because He created it; what makes us think that our *"thinking"* about how to solve a problem is more effective and might be more expeditious to resolution than letting Him Think for us and instill "His Thought" into our minds and hearts?

> "If you abide in Me, and My words abide in you,
> ask whatever you wish, and it will be done for you."
>
> John 15:7
> NIV

10.1 The Art of "Not Thinking"

Overthought, maybe, but a happier more productive and fulfilling life might be led by practicing the art of "not thinking", specifically, when "thinking" is fraught by the landmines sprinkled throughout habitual notions of how to protect ourselves from the myriad of frightful conjured illusions – our calculated negative outcomes to every feared event or issue.

However, there is a seemingly unnatural alternative to thinking and planning and that is to "Not Think". To actively "Not Think" frees our minds to focus attention securely on the moment lived; on being. For only in this moment in time might we access our inner source of Truth; Mindful, Universal, Timeless Truth; that is the Thought of God.

Simply put, as we learn to place our trust and Faith, wholly, in the process to meet God's ends *begun and finished* in this particular moment in time, we discover and uncover God's Desires and Perfect Plans for our lives. Focused on this singular moment we've aligned our thoughts with His and become whole; without question. Trust that God is more than a memory or envision and that He exists Infinitely Dimensional everywhere, however, only in this singular moment in time, Now, and we access His Thought.

Why wouldn't we? He's given us this perfect Place to exist. So, do it!

And when we stop our minds from "thinking", take a breath, relax our eyes and shoulders, and listen closely we are privy to His Thoughts. His colorful clarity brightens our day. And this day's journey becomes His day; Perfected. A simple, yet extraordinary process: Stopping the wheels in our minds from spinning "alternative facts" and perception into its own shade of truth.

When we stop our wheels from spinning our emotions up and down and "let go" of the earthly attachments and allow His Love to take its rightful place, Love initiates an answer. His Thought instantaneously ignites the truly natural thought processes – void of our thinking – and our fears are Instantly displaced, if not vaporized. And when once our precious time had been wasted on hatching schemes to gain approval or defend ownership, without thinking, when choosing to live wholly within this moment in time – Here/Now, we might enjoy the returns of our investments connected to thoughts of the Universal Mind and we more naturally strive to serve others selflessly.

In selfless service directed by the readily accessible Thought of God, we reap unexpected rewards that our mortal thinking cannot originate.

In this selfless and scary act, to consign the search to answers by our energy and mortal intellect to the Eternal resources of God, we take the bold step to trust His Mind over ours, on purpose, and we've, by de facto, chosen to believe in Him and His Eternal Love and Universal Want for our good health, welfare, and safety. And we slowly and more frequently begin to place our trust in His Eternal Knowledge, Understanding, and Compassion that answers the question of our significance and plight.

If this is accurate, that He wants exactly what's best for us, then His Thought, first and foremost, must be His unalterable desire for our happiness. And by "not thinking", when we place complete Trust in Him and grant Him access to the world He created, He can work through us to Create a better and more loving world. In this arrangement, He might have satisfaction in His benevolence, with immediate results, fairly distributed to all whom we might affect by the ignorance of our self-proclaimed brilliance; accepting of His Genius; relinquishing ours. And we may survive ourselves and the outcomes of selfishness, as we choose to "dumbly" focus our complete attention on the Truth, Beauty, and Goodness of this particular and precise moment in time and we thrive in the exact vicinity of this place, only. With our Father, we are complete.

~

"Not thinking" doesn't mean we don't study our problems or investigate the world's many challenges or that we're required to play dumb or remain ignorant to the Truth we're led or to allow the lies broadcast to us by negatively charged individuals attempting to defy truth's gravity to destroy our good intentions. No! "Not Thinking" doesn't give us an "out" from living right, but by being thoughtful of our conscious connections to the Mind and Heart of God and All His creation we're inspired to Create with Him all that we might; Instantly. In this Instant, we instantly ignore the lies that distract us from truth's goodness.

But, wait...

Even Jesus sought refuge from the madness of our natural human thought processes that drives our fear of the unknown to escape, defend, or convince. Remember that, exhausted, Jesus extracted Himself from the fray and prayed for resolutions not discoverable by our pesky *mortal* thinking. He, Himself, sought our Father's Thought in relief from His own.

By not tapping, solely, into our experience and learning and intellect to think through the myriad of process-options, we are open to humbly ask and to earnestly "listen" to our heart, which allows for a clear transfer of God's Knowledge to our consciously open heart/mind. *Transferring* responsibility to God for the answers we seek, in every situation, we choose to be open to His Thought and a spark ignites dialogue with Him and with those He leads us to convey His questions – become ours – that leads us to Instant resolutions and plans for Heavenly derived and supported actions – Genius.

Yes, it is difficult to give up our most learned ways. We might think that thinking about a problem is the right thing to do, as "thinking" is what we've been reprimanded we must do "before we speak!" and "before we leap!" And when confronted with challenging problems and issues and "thinking" has worked so well in the past, why wouldn't we "use our heads" Now?

Yet, how might we trust *our* thinking in the face of so many personal, family, and career issues piled-on by the horrors displayed, sometimes live on TV? Horrific life-ending-acts brought by poor decisions of so many of our brothers and sisters. We have instant access to the most troubling information; some information better never shared. With our bright and conscious minds, we're given every opportunity to worry and obsess to the point of over-thinking every issue, issues not in our wheelhouse of expertise to affect change, but we scavenge for answers and worry ceaselessly, still.

In our primal survival thinking roles, confronted by challenge, we think it our duty to react intelligently, so we think hard and our eyebrows raise, our foreheads become furrowed, our look becomes intense with worry, sincere smartness, or with gratuitous anger and our voice changes in tone and decibel, veins protrude recklessly from our necks, our jaws clinch, teeth grind, and, for the most part, we frown seriously as we press forward. We experience serious spiritual-awkwardness triggered by these manufactured and magnifying fears being unnaturally addressed by constant "thinking" and "re-thinking" of the illusions' plausible resolutions.

"Thinking is the self-damning curse of the intellectual."

Delores Dogood

And if shame is possible, it's well-polished when we relinquish intuitive exploration of Truth, Beauty, and Goodness only discoverable in moments shared with God, close family, and true friends and we forfeit living peacefully within this moment. We've chosen to find answers in the usual manner; by the drudgery of habitual and learned inspection and protection of our justifiably smart judgments of the world around us, especially the actions and words of others and of the lot they've chosen to defend or of the exhortation of their well-intentioned proclamations made with, from Heaven's perspective, an obvious lack of Hope and Genius.

Thinking (lower case) is especially troublesome and trouble making, as we think about how to judge another's problem solving tactics against our self-made esteem, yet we do and we judge ourselves, as well. We spite ourselves over our multi-flavored memories that might've been seasoned differently "if we had only _____" or as we drift in thought to prepare steps that most efficiently complete our sacred to-do lists or as we scheme to maneuver Game Pieces to outflank competitive forces that are sure to steal our happiness or as we learnedly derive the quickest pathways to well-earned recreation and relaxation or in our derived conspiracies meant to streamline fulfillment strategies of our self-imposed mightily ambitious obligations promised or in our plans for the slaughter of loss or the accumulation of wealth; all of which fantasize a happier place and time than the Here and Now could possibly hope to provide.

God's Promise tells us to unburden our souls, but to "not think" leaves us vulnerable except that we may choose to abide by what we secretly proclaim to know – "I trust the Creator of the Universe to pre-instantaneously Think for me; in my behalf; in our behalf." By entrusting our lives to God, we are more able to remain in a peaceful state of mind not requiring us to answer every problem and fix every issue confronted. And we become the unburdened souls, living our lives fully alive.

~

When the Art of Not Thinking is practiced well you'll be confronted by the Constant Question: "When a problem is resolved, did I think it through to resolution or did I hear right and act on God's Thought?"

To which mechanism do we attribute the initial thought that ignites the incredible mindal sequences of ideas strung together from tangent or adjacent memories or from our ever-evolving thought patterns in problem solving that urges us to study similar cases or the trains of thought that gives us the nerve to ask the timely and poignant questions to derive or calculate a proclaimed workable solution?

To whom might we attribute our genius? Think about it; or not!

Well, today, as you begin to realize that you're not required to answer the question – fix the issues – solve your life or fix the lives of others – or that your thinking must be right or necessarily worth exploring, you may find yourself physically, emotionally, and spiritually Bumped to connect with the Mind of God for the answer/s. And you'll begin the natural habit of asking and receiving, from the Creator of everything that which He's prodded each of us to rely; His Smarts and His Grace.

~

What if, in the face of great or simple challenges, we were to cooperate with God and use our minds to think only about existing in this moment in time? Instantly, we choose to follow His Thought process and our knowledge base syncs with His.

When we allow God to lead us to the Truth, beyond mortal thinking, we automatically ignore the insane and illusory thoughts initiated by fear and we access His Mind filled with solutions triggered by Love. In our stillness of mind, in a distraction-vacuum, in this quiet moment with God, a brief moment grasped between anxious human intervening fear-initiated thoughts, we may trust in His Mind over ours and over the fears others project.

Once proofed through a year or a lifetime of replicated experiments, we might choose to determine to move when He tells us to "Move!", "Speak up!" when He asks us to speak, and act decisively when He says, "Do your job." And we might understand the power to trust "numbness of mind" when otherwise we might have asked a manipulating question or make a proclamation in defense of our learned stance or we dive too deeply into an issue that distills a solution from our low minded "fixing-thinking". And by stopping and not acting on our intelligence, we might avoid embarrassment or worse.

If we simply stop when we hear "Stop!" and abide and show our esteem and trust in an ever-loving God, this quickness to follow Him exhibits our true Genius.

Thoughtless of issues and problems and schemes for success or survival, we naturally realize an eagerness and courage to explore the Truth embedded in the Eternal fabric of each precise moment in time. In this Here and Now we've been given a unique moment to experience life and living and we're Instantly blessed to enjoy the smells sights and sounds of the place in which we exist, as well as appreciate the once ignored life-form standing next to us in line, and we Instantly appreciate the Truth-lesson Heavenly-ordained in the struggle to survive maddening thoughts and self-creations and frightations.

~

In this particular moment, Here, only, might you expect and accept the Bumps, Heavenly-initiated, that drive you to serve well others and do so with an eloquence only God might choreograph into your performance – become effortless – "In the Zone" – without thinking or planning – especially, without thoughts of self or need of approval or appreciation. Alive in this moment, only, and with joyful gratitude of the opportunity given to breathe and to love and to serve; serve the world spontaneously Spiritually-conscious, today; more able than yesterday or just moments ago, and as you live alive right Here and right Now, you define Genius and have become you.

And, "Oh, the places you'll go..."

"Oh, the places you'll go! There is fun to be done!
There are points to be scored. There are games to be won.
And the magical things you can do...
will make you the winning-est winner of all."

"Fame! You'll be famous, as famous as can be, with everyone watching you win on TV, except when they don't because sometimes they won't..."

"Out there things can happen, and frequently do
To people as brainy and footsy as you.
And when things start to happen, don't worry, don't stew.
Just go right along, you'll start happening too!"

So...
be your name Buxbaum or Bixby or Bray
or Mordecai Ali Van Allen O'Shea,
you're off to Great Places!
Today is your day!
Your mountain is waiting.
So... get on your way!"

Dr. Seuss, Oh, The Places You'll Go!

And in this Eternal adventure in Time and Space you'll encounter everything unknown and, as with His Understanding, Forgiveness, and Grace (Holiness), the blessings found in "not thinking", you'll realize that, once the Holy experience is known, fear is resolved by the experience and learning and, ultimately, your survival, and spiritual growth Just Happens and does so with the increased trust in God's Loyalty, Love, and by an ever increasing knowledge of your abilities to believe in His unfiltered expressions through your words and works. And you'll succeed at living miraculously, at every opportunity, not by your will, but His.

> "And will you succeed?
> Yes!
> You will, indeed! (98 and ¾ percent guaranteed)"
>
> Dr. Seuss, Oh, The Places You'll Go!

In doing so (succeeding at living wholly within this moment in time, otherwise known as conquering the illusions brought by thinking) you'll more naturally and effortlessly "not think" and you'll have an ever-increased humbled ability to navigate the lies spewed by your inner enemy, as well as the fearful associate and you'll more easily step over the poo-poo left behind by the adoring spectators of the liars. Thoughtless, your focus remains on the Good in people, as you more easily ignore the scent of failure and accept the Truth in each moment. And you'll do so without a whimper for the struggle of holding your nose; which, in reality, is no big deal.

And your Heavenly-initiated dreams are realized as you've Instantly beaten the three-headed dragon of Fear, Pride, and Vanity and won the Instantly waged war between following Truth and believing in the illusions maintained by a lesser self and by those unwilling to seek and heal the wounds inflicted by their thinking-demons.

And by loving yourself and others, first, without judgment, you'll naturally be more patient and compassionate and more comfortable in receiving and giving blessings for the earthly assets acquired and required to do God's Work. You'll defeat the ambushing dragons by making each moment on this journey count, while realizing each moment is a blessing not a random occurrence awaiting your reaction spit from fear-lined behaviors that oppose God's fearless Truth-expression.

In Summary: The Game objective is to recognize the difference between your thoughts brought by calculative thinking and those Eternal Truths brought by the Mind of God. By surrendering temporary dreams of earthly riches and comforts – for the audacious dream of serving the whole of humanity selflessly, one good deed at a time derived by consciously outsourcing your every decision to God; your fearful thinking exchanged for the power of God's, you are Now known to be naturally intuitive, savvy, having taken the high road... be one living a life lived free from chance – being Unthinkingly Naturally Brilliant.

And a single most important battle is won, as you appreciate God's reward without comparison to that of another's station in life. For, when The Game is played for the audience of one – God – His rewards are simple, they're beyond your wildest dreams, yet as big as is God's Mind; unimaginable!

It's an endless battle, though, and when pride loosens your hold on His Plan you'll feel helplessness, as does a lost child, and the reward of peace, joy, love, and gratifying work is slipped away.

Remember, He is constantly forgiving and when you make that Instant choice to be thoughtless and get out of "your head" and your heart enters the Game with Him and in behalf of your brothers and sisters, His rewards are instantaneous. And, as per usual, you'll be more comfortably unsurprised as He ushers you past the trolls of selfishness and grants you unfettered access to every place, every talented person, every coveted relationship and every great and valuable material thing required to serve the world well, as you are His willing surrogate; His Eternal accomplice in this conspiracy to be and do Good and serve selflessly; on an Eternal scale; limitless.

10.2 Zero Zero Vision

Why does God instill within us a Vision; a play, a method, an idea – if not to have His Will be done?

If we see everything around us as something or someone God Created and we appreciate His Vision for us in the form of a Good Thought, that Life is His Gift free and clear, then let's take it to the best possible conclusion:

> God instills within us His Thoughts as a Gift to Himself – for Him to accomplish everything Good necessary to share His Love with His Creation using our ever-increasing confidence in that Love that we are Gifted and shall overcome the struggles and appreciate the joys of living on earth, by His Glory fulfilled.
>
> So, we need only listen and see; see and listen; and appreciate all that we sense as would He. As He sees with our eyes and hears with our ears – taste, smells, feels, and enjoys every sensory and extrasensory interaction with all things living He truly is alive within our body minds, and spirit. The

Goodness and Joys we experience are sparked by His Knowledge of everything and our happiness complete improves His Joy to Sadness ratio. It's the ultimate Win Win!

10.3 Rules of Engagement

There are two kinds of money. The money you own and control; that you've learned to call "my money" or "mine". It is earned or stolen, saved, or inherited, but it's cash, hard and cold and it's "all yours".

The other is the results of service to spiritually aligned shareholders and the Board of Directors of your personal, yet Universally held, Me, Inc.

The Board's money is not ours, yours, or mine to control. It is of Holy origin. But when played well, money received by acts of God, money directed to you, unmistakenly, by The Board, is merely money only yours to steward, not to own; solely. Yes, this sucks; I agree. Sorry, not my rule.

But, you might ease the pain of lost ownership by Vulcanizing your view of money, as would Mr. Spock and purifyingly objectify your view of money; ignore human emotions as you begin to play the Game knowing that service is rewarded by unknown deposits made into your "character account" that attracts wealth. It's not that simple, though, as basic human fear of loss or desire for security and safety underlie nearly every money decision you've ever made.

And when you've given up control, be prepared for the waves of confusion that disturb the soul, at times, when making even the simplest of money decisions. To find relief from the loss of control, before splitting your soul in half, you must objectify ownership of money by separating yours from that money derived from God's work and call His money IT. The relief might be; IT is not yours, so not "mine" to control.

If you've really become detached from ownership you'll know the power of freedom from the responsibility of ownership, as any amounts of IT is subject to Universal Laws not under your smart and savvy scrutiny to control. You'll find relief in the knowledge that ITs natural growth may not be hindered by your emotionally charged interference that once might have moved you to hide it away as did the coward with his talents. Or it might move you to overproduce to prove your value and create "derivatives" (lies) upon which to speculate or manipulate returns in a plasticized financial marketplace.

The creation of any amounts of IT is filtered through Goodness and grows exponentially, as it is truly of God's origin and no lie can work Universally to help you earn more of IT. So, be aware that your lips will stick together and mind becomes limp in dumbness, as you attempt to overpromise a return on investment or dramatically convince another of your grandness; once you've enjoined yourself in The Game of Money and committed to managing IT for its Heavenly Owner.

To recap and to begin playing The Game and to appreciate the privileges associated with any and all amounts of IT, you must observe and follow The Game Rules that might multiply and self-perpetuate under knuckle-Nudged and inevitably surrendered-stewardship:

1. The means to earn or acquire Universally balanced sums of IT is through "Board Certified" services to others.
2. Whatever the quantity of IT, large or small, is of no matter; it's not yours, so if IT is to be invested, saved, tithed, and gifted it is done so ONLY as directed by the Owner of IT.
3. IT is honorably taxed and likewise honorably paid, ("...give unto Caesar what is Caesar's..." with a smile rather than a grimace or smirk) IT not being yours and with the knowledge that "there's more IT from where it came."

"Keep your lives free from the love of money
and be content with what you have, because God has said,

'Never will I leave you;
Never will I forsake you.'"

Hebrews 13:5

10.4 When to Use the "No-Look" Pass

Choose anytime anywhere to give up your agenda for God's and you're connected to the Power of the Moment – You're in the Zone of living the Truth of who you are. You're just being who you are – perfectly who you are.

At any time anywhere choose Him and in stillness you'll hear His Word. When I asked Jesus for clarification about this subject "How should I know what to think about to be most productive; in the grand scheme?" in prayer, this is what I heard from His breathless clear voice. It came to me, while hovered over my notepad, seated in the aisle seat on a flight from Seattle to Tucson, and Jesus said:

- Think about doing and being Good, not what's instore for you for doing and being Good.

- Think of others' plight for no one is immune to significant dangers in life and living.

- Think of my mind's purity. Be this purity. It is (the) only truth unencumbered by weakness and fear.

- Be pleasant and positive in the face of the unknown – fearful thoughts do not drive your actions – I will to do My Will through and for you.

- Be pleased by My Creation it is only part of the whole and it's incomplete without your appreciation.

- Seek Me in your judgements of others. It is important not to seek imperfections but rather to find purity in the thoughts you have towards your brothers and sisters.

- Find Me in the far reaches of the mind, although on top (of mind and) in front, easily seen and known.

- Find Me in the things seen and felt. Be at peace, not of others' thoughts and judgments.

- Know nothing is certain, but My Love expressed through your heart.

- In times of struggle and despair, my mind is blocked from expressing itself to you by your choice to exclude Me and My Holiness.

- Take time to spell yourself from the situation to find Me regardless of imposition it might exert on others. In the end, all resolves by the lesser of the inputs not of Mine Thought.

- Be still; envision Me with you; really with you, by your side.

- Talk to Me, with Me, (and) have your deepest discussions with Me.

- Let go of your fears or apprehensions, shyness, or wisdom and be involved in a conversation with Me.

- At each moment give (Me) thanks.

10.5 Trial Game

Today, without ignoring the spiritual and material values of IT begin the adventure to discover the Truth about your long term monetary value by redefining the impact you might expect IT to play in your life as if you were to humbly give up control. Give it a try, but beware as it's much easier to be humble when you've been humbled than while "riding high", before you've made too much or become owned by the lure of controlling more and more and more of the uncontrollable IT.

Run a Trial Game and you'll face risks to character that come with wealth and might, while fully knowing it's only a Trial, avert human-nature's lure to control more and more of what really isn't yours. Detach yourself from the results of winning before becoming accustomed to the anonymous gaze upon your grand and glorious being; other souls wanting what you so mysteriously have won; worldly praise; that you are special. You might take fond notice, as "they" shyly peer at you in amazement, brought by rumors of your incredible wealth. Yet, you're tempted and might fall from Grace's embrace in prideful claims of victory and you begin to expect a place of honor at the table for your grand idea and your self-wrought childhood suspicions of specialness; now perfected, as you find yourself drunk from the "Specialness" your admirers confirm you are due and you are, in fact, "Noteworthy".

But, the emotional bling weighs heavy when things begin to click beyond your makings and you've forgotten the Trial Game being run and you deem yourself Special. That's precisely when you're spiritually penalized for "excessive celebration", for doing the "idiot dance", in the acceptance of large or even small portions of IT you were meant only to steward. So, before you become bloated with pride and self-absorbed in your grandness, reconsider the lure of money and remember it's an inanimate object that, once survival needs are met; your belly filled with prayed for "daily bread", to be fair, you must accept the weaning of ITs ownership in an ongoing Trial Game.

It's a constant Trial; relinquishing ownership, as He gives you potentially teetering power and higher-pay-grade responsibility from which you might fall when enamored by the relatively enormous sums of IT you're to manage. Don't look down, you'll realize how high you are and think you've found the top, of which you've forever known you deserve placement.

On the other hand, it's as easily difficult to "think on your feet" when you're scrounging for money; fearing lack; really sucking for air, financially. But, in your monk-like reconciliation of the ownership of IT to the Creator of IT and belief that He doesn't play games when your happiness is on the line; you're saved from hell and the Trial is proven worthwhile. And you're instinctively transformed and emotionless in your considerations of temporary lacks of or handling of extreme amounts of IT that happens to flow through your accounts.

Before beginning your Trial Game, wipe clean your money-memory and ITs influence will have less hold on you; no hook. IT is merely numbers on a piece of paper if it's not yours. Objectively detached, you'll find safety from your selfish thoughts and from today's lack or massive amounts attained; less interested in what you can buy or control with IT or to which accounts you must pay or that which must be received when due, to save your home or feed the kids or make you and everyone around you happy, comfortable, and appreciative to you for your hard-smart work.

Forget about it... except that the Universe hates a vacuum. So, before you run a Trial, be sure to empty yourself of the earthly lies and prepare your soul with affirmations backed by solid principles based on spiritually logical perspectives to form new beliefs that fill the vacuum, beginning with:

#1   Surrender Lack and Accept Abundance

Simple? Just try remembering the simple prayer to let go of thoughts of loss or gain and remain true to the Brand, who you are and your slogan, "Here to Serve!"

#2   "The Top" Where You Are not Where You're Going

Pray for the strength to apply #1 and it's much easier to see yourself succeeding in finding "The Top". Accept that the Universe (God) is on your side and you'll discover that "The Top" is attainable beyond yours or a family member's vision for your success. Also, notice "The Top" isn't an earthly place as much as it's a better Way of being; you being more confident in your abilities; Here-Now. Be careful, however, not to expect "The Top" to be the estate finally fulfilled with every material glittery thing and the trappings of ownership's natural fears of losing the wants of your life; losing any part of what's finally yours; deserved.

Knowing that "The Top" is simply your new Way, a spiritually instilled way of being, of coping with tragedy or fame, it's a way of attracting others to do good, to lead well, and the way by which you might work with others and trust in the good you might accomplish together.

"The Top" happens!

And it happens Here-Now, as you connect with your true self, unafraid, in this moment in time, you plug into God's being; His Will; and all that is good connects you with others of like mind; in service to the world. That's His Plan for those at the "The Top", in this time in space, Now, when you are who you are absolutely and you allow others to be who they are absolutely; completely. And together we succeed.

Yes, the view is great from "The Top;" disturbingly great. You'll clearly see a world with disturbingly limiting patterns, confrontation avoidance that ignores the perplexing problems of greed acceptance; but you'll also see the lie for that which it is and you're driven to play your single role today in "the great repair".

You are Now, Here, looking beyond the jungles of the world's darkest fears and might wonder why it was so difficult to get here and why more people aren't here with you; to see the show for what it is. At the same time, look around and notice that you're not alone. You're not so special or different after all. You're here with lots of really good people who see the world through spiritually logical lenses, as do you; talented, interesting, committed people who, while vastly different and ironically dissimilar, are very similar to you in values and ethics.

When you've chosen to work for God, knowingly, willingly, or unexpectedly, you'll notice He loves each of us the same and that you're in good company to meet the demands of His Will for your individual happiness and the world.

There are billions of us; His beloved. Yet, we are unique individuals.

We're each a beloved and singular characterization of His glorification; in human form. And our lives are a blend and balance of the world's entire history of personalities; women and men with varying degrees of freedom and talents who've cleared the path ahead of us to get us here; who've struggled and sacrificed to create a better world for their children; while discovering whom it is they might become. We live in a world, the results of their good work, so remember them and thank them, publicly; privately, Now.

~

Today, together, you and I are tasked to perform the work we've been blessed by God to perform; work learned from our ancestors that challenges us each, entirely uniquely, as we are entirely interconnected beings, past – present – and future. Each of us performs his part in a spiritually orchestrated dance to do good and care for one another and the earth and its every critter for every "next generation" to come, benefits, as well it should.

By appreciating your role in your family history, your life's projects miraculously turn from a longing and lonely whisper of a dream in the dimness of your mind's eye, into blinding reality; beginning with the vision that "The Top" is Here-Now.

And in this moment; there is no bottom, there is no middle class, and the need to reach for the once cherished "Top" vanishes, as the top lies within the mind and heart of God shared within your vision, of which we are each guaranteed a sacred place. And a large sum of money has nothing to do with extended moments of happiness of which the liar has had us fooled that it would.

#3   **Don't Allow *Your* Goals to Interfere with God's**

> "Planning is incompatible with an entrepreneurial society and economy.
> Planning is the kiss of death to entrepreneurship."
>
> Dr. Peter Drucker

Man's goals aspire, generally, and from an earthly perspective to comply with fully imagined unbroken strings of success or recoverable failures resulting in wealth delivered, status preserved, or estates protected. Unrealistically and unsustainably and most usually our goals for annual incremental increases in earthly wealth are derived by agendas fueled by greed.

The obvious problem:

- Greed lacks love and is fueled by fear.
- Greed's ambition exploits worldly resources at the expense of "the forgotten".
- And since greed's material gains are the results of well-timed, selfishly directed, and overly cherished ego's interpretation of its abilities to constantly outperform others; at peak levels; relentlessly and regardless of cyclical burps and unpredictable markets' exhaustive wheezing; we suck even harder to breathe and everyone we love suffers in the stale fumes of our self-made stress-sweat.
- Anger at our losses and pride in our successes out-smells a warm summer afternoon stroll at the dairy; a well-known fact.

And no matter what we've learned through experience or extensive calculations, there's no "earthly-formula" for success that may transfer, in whole, from generation to generation. But, in our earthbound and humanly supported confidence, based on our past personal or ancestral success, our shareholders' expectations are fixed on forever repeatable success. And when Wall Street's or headquarters or spousal expectations are missed someone must pay the ultimate price.

Intense fear flashes through our beings, as we're sometimes uncontrollably shaken in the struggle to meet goals; the goals set by an ego's dreams of finding heaven on earth or just saving our job; which is Goldman Sachs associate's written #1 goal, "Keep your job." Not "Serve the Client!", but "Keep your job and you'll be wealthy."

And the screeching sound of the three-headed dragon of fear, pride, and vanity is exacerbated by our visceral understanding of the acute limitations of our plans derived from a mind trapped in a physically limited three-dimensional experience; trained by a lifetime of peer-reviewed self-perceptions of our class-limitations or masking weaknesses. Our perceptions are clothed in the armor of our singular greatest past experience and we succumb to patterns filtered through waves of sometimes lonesome and relatively harsh failures of which we hold ourselves unilaterally responsible for unrealized dreams or seemingly avoidable financial catastrophes endured.

Otherwise known as, "Am I able?" "...worthy?"

And the success of our mission is complicated by the notion that we are capable of success, but only by employing our gifted talents relentlessly; individual smarts put to work hard; working hard and enduring the yawn of boredom and stress-overload of extreme challenges by the pure strength of superhuman willpower. Our work and dreams hampered by the memories of pains of loss and failure – great plans for success derailed, despite an "eternal optimism". "Great ideas that must be pursued" and "working overtime in overdrive" are and have been our only surety of success.

But, of course, everybody knows it's a 60/40 chance that "chance" will betray us, so those of us "born to succeed," as are you, we are convinced that working "extra hard" will guarantee we reach our strategically derived goals (goals based on assumptions and numbers pulled out of our you-know-whats) and that chances' torturous failures may be mitigated by cleverly working smart and "giving 110%".

As anomalies of fate destroy the plans we so carefully set into motion, there's no foreseeably positive outcome for "extra-hard" work. Forgetful of Grace, we fear chance; the chance that we may lose again or we'll be given no other chance than this to succeed. And we certainly cannot fathom surviving a repeat of our last worst-failure.

But, what if?

What if we were to remember Grace when everything around us sucks and we ignore time's influence on our daily schedule; abandon cultural, ancient, family, and Company assigned roles and routines forever held sacred by the well-respected brilliant men and women of our day. They know precisely how to succeed in our chosen career, but do they know of Grace or do they care about what's right for us? ... or for "the forgotten"?

Consider this: Strategic planning and the over-performance of mortal tasking required to meet our ass-derived greed-induced goals strategically interferes with our ability to remain present; for the fear of losing, and ironically, we lose. Setting forth in our work to meet goals, solely, takes us out of The Game, as we've forgotten to be human, which is our greatest asset and means to achieve success.

In our ill-fated quests to perform tasks for the satisfaction of performing tasks proven to deliver results, we've forgotten to smile, relax in the moment, and enjoy the journey of serving, of doing what it is we were born to love to do – be human – be who we are.

~

Our eyes relaxed, soul fortified by calm breathing; we're Now engaged in the business of serving rather than survival and we'll ask the compassionately-valuable questions of our clients or the market and we more easily comment in a discussion rather than delivering a well-rehearsed pitch. And we've sought God's ultimate direction, as to which tasks He would have us perform that best serves His agenda in the question:

"How may I help"?

God's Will cuts through selfishness, escorts us through rush-hour traffic, makes esteemed introductions with movers and shakers, and knowing this is our new agenda become real, we become less hurried, more present and confident in the direction we're traveling. And we exude a James Dean coolness in our being that attracts goodness and instills in others a calmness that smart decisions might be made and everybody wins; not just you.

So, smile!

By avoiding the need to hurry; hurry to perform well and experience glory quickly or quicken the relief of pain, we realize that it's okay to shut-up and listen. As we listen quietly for His Word delivered it comes in a small still voice, a shocking whisper, or out loud in a client's appeal for relief to his most current problem. Confident in God's certain positive outcome, we muster the courage to ask the selfless questions and to probe the client's ambitious, as if a trusted friend, and we experience "living the dream" rather than scurrying to earn it.

Grace, unearned, is experienced simply by remaining Here present in this Holy moment, Now. And in this Now, our spirit is fully activated in service to a brother or sister, which results instantaneously in "the dream" come to life.

> "Convince yourself to quit trying so damn hard to 'make it'
> (whatever it is)
> and, instead, appreciate the fact that you have
> 'You're alive.'"
>
> Delores Dogood

Yes! You've "made it" simply by being Here-Now; by living today only; by loving who you are enough to love others; by appreciating yourself enough to forgive your latest failure and compliment another's brilliance without comparison to yours; by caring for yourself enough to care for those God put in your path, Today. And, Today, you'll be freed to perform life's God-instilled dream of 20 years ago, un-obscured by ego's limitations brought by fear.

~

God's miracles run wild when we collapse our ego's storefront mannequin, forgive ourselves, get out of the way and into His, and agree to allow His Love to express itself through us. And only our disbelief may stop His train of thought that leads to peace and enduring happiness, Now.

> "God, forgive my disbelief."
> and
> "Thank you."

(my two favorite prayers)

Detached from earthly goals, you may choose to serve generously and let God's plan be fulfilled through you and, at such time, you'll appear the hero for making sense of the insane and diplomatically negotiating a path through personal, Corporate, or Legal bullshit, and you might boldly act, while others stand by: idly; their mouths ajar; blank stares; a slight drool.

But no, not you...

Here/Now your "True Grit" forms a dangerous jawline; a slight breeze blows back every hair; the giant and glowing "S" on your chest pulses magnificent, fully revealed for whom it is that you are; hands on hips, chin up, shoulders back; you are "The One" who boldly acts!
Yes, once you realize the heroes of wealth are simply people who, like most of us, are just doing their job, in this Holy Now; you may perform limitlessly heroic, as well. Without trying, limitless, become a truthful unit with our brothers, us, together, standing in line (enjoying common interaction) processing collaborative solutions to our common quests for security, health, safety, and happiness.
And we succeed in this moment as we reprioritize "wants" for monetary riches with God's; as we replace well thought, over worn, self-serving, committee approved strategies to meet quotas and, instead, we gain wealth with that "great unknown" plan God has for our combined and cooperative success. And we've allowed Him to create – evenly balanced life-work that straddles the material and spiritual worlds; by His miracles; through His Grace and a willingness to give up dreams of empty wealth and accept His limitlessness.

"Remain thirsty my friend."

The Most Interesting Man in the World

Thirsty for Truth, reprogram what you've learned about finding success and being successful and abandon the man-made goals that out-perform our last goals met. In this Moment, you've exceeded earthly goals a relatively tiny mind might contrive. And as you learn to appreciate and accept the perfectly formulated and limitless Goodness that comes with an unclothed desire to serve without thought of reward, the unexplainable, incalculable miracles of living a spiritually logical life flow freely through your emptied being; unplanned; unscheduled; unlimited; but fully imaginable and real.

> "Strategic planning is not strategic thinking.
> Indeed, strategic planning often spoils strategic thinking
> causing managers to confuse real vision
> with the manipulation of numbers."
>
> "The most successful strategies are visions, not plans…"
>
> "Strategic thinking in contrast (to planning), is about synthesis. It involves intuition and creativity."
>
> Henry Minzberg
> (From his book, "The Rise and Fall of Strategic Planning")

#4   Our Inherited Purpose Usually Conflicts with God's

Be careful how you speak about IT, most won't understand that the money God's directed you to earn isn't really yours to spend. He's led you to IT and IT to you and there's no cheating on this. When you were close to giving up, when you could see no hope – He showed up and shown you the Way. He's always been here for you, me, and them and continues to work with us, as we work for each other; despite our simplemindedness and selfishly muddled vision.

Proof of His Love, lays in the fact you're still breathing, living, and here to enjoy another day; beyond your most horrific fears of defeat or death. You're not forgotten and hopefully you have a dry roof over your head and food in the refrigerator and if you've made it through yesterday and here to live yet another, beyond the acts of "the crazies" within and without, the logical conclusion for this daily occurrence is:

You're here for a reason and you've been awarded Purpose.

So, given another Now to live, you're required to fill today with "Purposeful Action". And within this Now, and only Now, you may trust in Him to guide you to the work you're meant to do, to be the person you're meant to be, retrieved from hell, and forgiven of past mistakes you're alive today fully knowing that the money will be here today; money of which you are blessed to steward for Him. The money (IT) finds you when you quit looking and begin serving. And today, in gratitude for this tender morsel of Eternal Knowledge, you'll earn and spend specifically, as He Wills and you'll gift and tithe with "the faith of Abraham" and nothing will stop the gifts from coming your way; except your decision to evoke greed for the fear of losing.

Remember that IT is not yours and greed and fear of losing is merely the cowboys of your past-life shooting blanks at the Wild West's targets of success and those thoughts are not God's and they have nothing to do with reality.

Jesus gives you the ability to earn and enjoy your life's work as if it were recreation. And He's sent IT your way and knows where it's needed. IT has Purpose beyond your reach or limited vision, so listen to Him as you're moved to share, spend, or invest "Board" money. Don't think too hard, you'll receive specific instructions for whom to hire or to which vertical market to attack or where to deposit His Cash. He guides you with favor to the right and true places; perfectly timed with perfected intent, as you give Him the final word in distributions; His Purpose fulfilled.

Knowing that His earning and spending budgets are preordained and require a super majority vote by The Board to exceed limits; you're Instantly freed to spend or not to spend, as it's no longer your decision and you'll be surprised at how relieving it is to know He's got your back. He's put His trust in you, as you've given His Will veto power; financial authority over yours. His Will has become your safety net and in this pray for the strength and ability to hear absolutely, to know clearly His direction, and to accept His Will over yours and His Will, in time, becomes yours by following Him gladly; possibly toothless; a mouthful of gnashed teeth; but thankful and gratified by the struggle now proven worthwhile.

10.6 Determining a Winner

Imagine that immediately upon your death, death accepted, that "better place" found; you were handed the following form. In death, do not worry there's no waiting, be prepared, however, to go over a few details before moving forward. As a word of caution when filling out the form; the auditors have known you since before you were born. They know if you fail to accurately report all assets and liabilities listed. Do not attempt to hide or exaggerate details… the discrepancies will only cause annoying delays in the process and, invariable and quite unnecessary, embarrassment when Instantaneously brought to light.

So, to begin, add the amount of cash on hand at your earthly demise to that amount of your estimated net proceeds of asset liquidation; including your share in your home/s, stocks and bonds, insurance policies, toys, and vehicles; land, sea, and air, etc., etc., etc.

Enter that number here. _____

Also, add the amounts of monies you've given to worthy causes or gifted to the poor, tithed, or to develop entrepreneurial ventures, scholarships, etc. during your lifetime.

Enter that number here. _____

Add to this number any and all amounts spent on family or friends to recreate, vacation, and paid to maintain physical or mental health-care not covered by insurance.

Enter that number here. _____

There is no allowance for corporate junkets to lure favor of public officials, drinks after the second, the costs to purchase or maintain an Urban Humvee, and any and all other expenditures that might be considered extreme self-indulgences or bribery. Deduct these amounts.

Enter that number here. (_____)

Time spent doing laundry while others watch TV or time given in service to community, school, or church may be multiplied seven-fold the hourly wage based on your family's average annual earnings garnered over a lifetime.

Enter that number here. _____

Deduct seven-fold average hourly earnings for those excessive hours, not so selflessly given, in care for others or for the time donated to charitable organizations, school, or community that took you away from your family or friends in an attempt to escape home or to fulfill *excessive* call-to-duty-urges or in search of ego-boosting, pride-fulfilling, parades of thank-you's, or any other attempts to receive public accolade and award beyond a simple "thank you."

Enter that number here. (_____)

And, of course, deduct earnings received from ill-gotten gain; stolen ideas, property, or cash; misrepresented sales, monies gained from shorting accounts or intentional broken promises or larceny in business practice or non-allowable tax deductions or insurance fraud or outright thievery by act or omission.

Enter that number here. (_____)

The sum of all the above is your gross asset number at death.

Enter the net total from the above activities here. _____

Living a life filled with the Eternally begotten answers to life's many challenges, wonders, and tragedies; blessed with a myriad of mystically derived careers (dull and amazing) that affected the twisting paths to fiscal responsibilities leading to our safety, security, and happiness; earthly rewards; you gotta know there is no absolute winner and there are no losers in the Game of Money. And now that you're dead, do you honestly want to take time away from your explorations of Eternal Knowledge to look back over the books to see how you fared against the "rest"?

10.7 Game Day

By giving up control over the gifts of the world and your need to exploit your full talents and those of others who cross your path, you'll have the tools necessary to complete God's work today and may do so without being owned by your belongings or by the privileges of success or fulfilling the world's view of wealth or promoting your inflated view of yourself or maintaining your right to the inherited powers of celebrity or coveting that which you might think you must own; you are Now freed of the world's ethereally shocking hold on you; Here-Now.

Once you've discovered your Position in The Game and correctly selected a Game Piece (career, profession, or enterprise) and joined a Team; be prepared for change. A lifelong position at a Company is not guaranteed, as The Game changes ever so slightly year after year and as your abilities become more attractive than of those who oppose God's gifts; they who suffer from self-fulfilling destiny-acquisitional-disorder-syndrome tendencies and who are forced to live by chance or luck. If you choose to be spiritually-charged, change is good, but not without stressful disruption and resistance to growth.

But, you are and have grown. So, don't be surprised as you see the truth of the matter more easily and might smile watching the melee, as others duck for cover from the truth being spewed so effortlessly from your newly released life-filled being; as your preemptively disarming smile tells the world to relax. And you know that it's OK. You can handle the truth in well-deserved self-deprecation or honest appreciation, as you defuse defensive stands and ease the terseness, of which is the result of "tough love".

An honest tongue often has nothing to say, but when Nudged, your loving words are spoken with unplanned charm and with a glimmering eye you'll assure another that there is no agenda more valuable than seeking the Truth.

And Today, you're fully alive, as you evaluate the meaning of our totality of existence filtered through "how may I help?" As The Game teaches you that we are born to succeed, to enjoy our work, and to live safely and productively within our means in service to others, together *with* our brothers and sisters; not separately, not comparatively, not competitively apart; you've won, as you've outlived the need to control the money you were blessed to receive. You're Now-Here freed from the gravitational pull to succeed by enforcing the rules of greed and instead attract Goodness in its place by just being you; selflessly magnificently you, as God created you to be.

So, that's it! Those are The Game's objectives, rules, and score sheet. Good luck and remember to play fairly and have fun; The Game is moving at full speed and is over in a blink of an eye; relative to Eternity.

Being Present

NOVEMBER 2003

You meet interesting people when you pull back a little, ignore the device vibrating in your hip pocket, and take a look around at who's standing right there... right next to you. Just smile and say, "Hello."

    The evening I met Mr. Arthur Richman, I'd also met Molly Holly who, at the time, was the reigning WWF World Champion women wrestler. I offered to carry the suitcase of this young woman up the stairs when she immediately became buff, smiled, and with no effort hoisted her luggage up the stairs on her own. As we walked through the Cincinnati airport to separate connecting flights, she introduced herself and within a few minutes we were in an interview so deeply personal that she comfortably spoke about what her parents thought of her chosen career, her thoughts on motherhood, intimidating boyfriends with a sleeper-hold, and so on and so on...

On the next leg of my return visit from New York City to Spokane, I met a man who worked with James Cameron to film the movie "Titanic". His company rented the mini-submarines from the Russians used to get the footage of the sunken ship for the movie and documentaries. He showed me photos of the Titanic that he had taken and told me a great story about how they got the shots for the movie and what it was like to see the ship with his own eyes. He went on to tell me how his company had recently discovered 180 million dollars in gold coins off the Carolina coast in a sunken frigate lost in a hurricane, while on its mission to fund the south during the Civil War; kind of an interesting guy, to say the least. I read the story in the New York Times, about the discovery, a couple of weeks later, just as he said I would.

Then, I met Mr. Arthur Richman. Waiting for my bags to come off the carrousel, I noticed a stout, well-poised, elderly gentleman wearing a black suit and tie and what appeared to be a military cap from the ship or squadron he served back in World War II. He stood out from the crowd of late night travelers and I got a "Bump" to step up and say hello. So, I carefully approached him, smiled, and made eye contact, and quickly glanced at the insignia on his cap and back to his eyes – seeking permission to read it. Without saying a word, he smiled and nodded approval and with my head tilted back to read through my bifocals, I noticed the details of the Presidential Seal of the United States of America.

"Wow! How do you get one of those?" I asked.

"You save the President's brothers' life.", he said.

I thought he must have been a heart surgeon back in the day. But, he proceeds to tell me the story of how President G.W. Bush's younger brother Marvin was fighting colon cancer and at the same time struggled with a severe bout of depression. His emotional health had deteriorated to the point where the doctors couldn't put him under with anesthesia to operate, for fear of losing him; a healthy mind being the necessary engine for healing.

"G.W. knew how much Marvin loved baseball, so they called me."

This guy's got the goods over Molly Holly and the Titanic guy, I thought to myself.

"OK! Why'd they call you?"

"You ever hear of Arthur Richman?" he says and smiles with a gleam in his eyes. "Well that's me."
I didn't know the name, so he proceeds to tell me the story about how he works for George Steinbrenner in the Yankees front office and knows everybody who's anybody in baseball. And the story goes; when the President calls him to describe the problem, Arthur went to work to line up the players; Hank Aaron, Mickey Mantle, and the like. They agreed to fly in and meet the President's brother and they cheered him up, simply by being there, sharing challenging experiences, giving him encouragement, and got him to a healthy state of mind where the doctors could operate.

Did he save the President of United States brother's life? Yes, I guess you could say that!

Well, that was just the beginning of my evening with Mr. Richman. I'd met this amazingly strong willed, witty, and funny octogenarian who's standing in front of me and incredibly willing to share great stories with a total stranger. But, as we said goodbye and he walked with his luggage down a darkened corridor that led to nowhere, I did a double-take and offered him a ride into town. He was so grateful for the offer his eyes lit up, he smiled and accepted immediately. I was honored that he would accept my offer, yet *he* was profusely thanking me; he being a little miffed that no one had sent "a car" for him.
Mr. Richman was in town for the funeral of Ken Brett the brother of a famous third baseman for the Yankees. It was nearly midnight on that very cold Saturday night at the Spokane airport. The parking lot was a sheet of ice, so arm in arm we slipped and slid together across the lot to my car. As I put his luggage in the trunk, I smiled remembering there

were two Yankee hats in my bag, bringing them home from my first trip to New York City. And when he offered me money for the parking, or whatever he could to repay me for the lift into town... I thought of those hats and here's the guy who hired Joe Torrey and who intimately knew "what a jerk" (his words) Joe DiMaggio was. He knew Yogi Berra, Thurman Munson, and anybody who's anybody and he was sitting right next to me in my Toyota Camry, in the middle of nowhere, USA.

Of course, I turned down the money, as well as a Papal Blessing he said he could arrange; explaining that he was such a large donor to the Catholic Church that the Pope owed him one. He chuckled to himself at the prospect proudly divulging that he, himself, was a Jew. Needless to say, I'd rather hear more about him and his life, so I asked him to tell me some stories in lieu of a tip. Well that opened the flood gates and I selfishly made it an incredibly slow drive into town. As I pulled up to the hotel, one I'd never heard of, but found on the first pass without directions, he invited me to come to the funeral the next morning and meet everybody. "I'll introduce you to all the players." he said. "I'll put you up in a room." What a kind man and a generous offer, but how do you crash a funeral? I respectfully declined and he insisted on getting my address and asked how to spell my wife's name. And that was it; an end to an amazing miracle-filled evening on three flights from New York to Spokane, Washington.

Well, three weeks later a package arrived with a note from Mr. Richman thanking me, once again, and giving me an open invitation to tour Yankee stadium, next time I'm in the city; which I did a year later. But better yet, there it was... a framed, signed picture of a horizontal Derek Jeter, flying towards second base, diving for a ground ball that was about to hit his mitt.

"To Tere, Best Wishes... Derek Jeter"

As I was admiring it with my four-year-old son Michael, at my side, he wanted to know who that was in the picture and what it said.

I read it to him and he asked if he could show it to his mom... "Of course." I agreed and as he skipped off out of the room, he began singing... "Mommy and Derek sitting in a tree... K I Z K M O G ...

Ya!"

?

Obviously, he knew the words, just hadn't picked up on the spelling.

Big and small, there are miracles standing by ready to happen without notice, in all shapes and forms, and in every direction God Wills for us to choose. Miracles are being prepared for us, as I write and you read, with God in the front office directing, His countless Angels are busy connecting us with others who may impact our day or whom we might prove well to impact theirs. There are no coincidences in life and God has a grander purpose for us in this moment in time in preparation for the next; even in the smallest of life choices that lead us to stop the wheels from churning that might crystalize into fear and instead we let go of our fears and realize this exact moment in time with Him, Here, is safe. He's on our side, and everyone has a story worthy of our honest respect in the currency of our time. And we smile and greet a stranger in passing and something memorable simply just happens; maybe a story worth telling and retelling...

CHAPTER 11

Survival vs Spiritual Logic

"Success is not final, failure is not fatal:
It is the courage to continue that counts."

Sir Winston Churchill

Once the Game Objectives and Universal Principals have been agreed to be learned, recognized, and followed (as outlined in The Game of Money Play-Book); it's time to accept the Spiritually-elevated value of your place in this world. By doing so, you also must accept the consequences of accountability that comes with position plus growing pains; the inevitable addendums to this agreement. But, you've agreed to a "fair fight" against pride and vanity that feeds your ego (the barnacles of our spirit – the enemy within) and decided to meet God on His playing field on His terms relinquishing yours. And the battle begins.

Now, in humility and gratitude, you may safely activate the genius of your well-crafted "Game Piece". Yes, Here-Now it's time to activate your fully-loaded, previously well-hidden genius that God created within you, uniquely and unmistakenly, that you may ignite its passion to play your part in this Universally-approved, high-stakes, Game of Money; Today.

And now, you may activate God's Genius. Simply press the "Go" button. It's not easily found, at times, hidden so well within your fluid consciousness, previously cloaked by shameful patterns meant to protect you from fear and doubt. Acknowledged and engaged, you may Now accept the belief that you, specifically, have been well prepared and spiritually and emotionally readied to fulfill the roles God mapped for you; Today; today, only and every day you agree to engage the "Go" button; from here to wherever forever finds spiritual-stability in Time.

Remember, though, that God cannot lead you astray. That's the trouble with accepting the consequences of agreed upon accountability. When you've made a mistake and decided to take command of your destiny and you fear destinations unknown, take pride in your genius, succumb to temptation, or simply procrastinate the performance of that most difficult task, you might fear you're being misled and that you're alone and that even prayer won't help.

But it ALWAYS helps to take your eye off doubt, stop thinking negatively, and gamble on hope; in prayer. And don't forget: It's OK to screw-up and that by doing so it doesn't make you one, and by doing so doesn't mean you haven't learned valuable lessons from the process. It's what we humans do. We screw things up. And when we do, we think that because we make a mistake, that that's what and who we are or fear we might become, so we attempt to cover up our messes or polish our behaviors or work overtime to make up for something we do naturally; disobey!

Don't be so hard on yourself, though, for disobeying the Source of all that is good, as He leads you to that perfect place and you've ignored the Bump; when you've acted too slowly to make the connection; Heaven Sent. Don't worry, you haven't lost; you'll get lots of chances to make good and Jesus takes our messes from us, anyway. So, just pray that you might ignore one fewer of His Eternal-streams-of-rolling-Bumps-and-Nudges, Today by living more true to the moment in which you exist, present in this Here/Now moment in time.

> God's miracles are perfected in Eternity
> Drawn of every minuteness and magnitude
> Delivered to you at no charge.
>
> Delores Dogood

And today is a perfect day and right Now is a perfect time in which to free your genius. Not tomorrow or in an hour, but "Right Now". Right Now, you may simply choose your genius' investigations and interactions over your ego's fear-based distractions, and the day is perfected. Today is perfect regardless of your past mistakes or hereditary judgments that have led you to distrust yourself or the world and God's rewards for your loyal obedience are His Promises fulfilled; possibly just in time to make the mortgage or payroll or save a brother or sister in need.

~

To play The Game well and live entirely in the Now/Here is the Objective, but highly impractical given the multitude of earthly distractions and challenges. However, the realization of the Truth of "who you are" is the relief required when you find yourself missing "The Point" (Eternal Ambition for the Day). When you drift, just pray to be fearless in your quest for the Truth and for the courage to leave conformity and comfort behind and remember to check in with God before making that all-important career decision.

Ask for His guidance and in silence question Him, "Is this Your Thought?" "Is this Your Will?"

With these questions begrudgingly asked and simply answered with an instantaneous "Yes" or "No", you'll Instantly know who instigated that very important directive that seems absolutely critical for survival, to end struggle, to care for another, or to appease the bank's request for payment.

Is your salvation brought upon by clever thinking or conniving from a protective place within your mind or is it God's Thought; freeing you from antiquated ways; freeing your genius?

With an answer received, get to work and don't think about the past or try to forecast the future; these thoughts paralyze genius. Here/Now, you might imagine yourself sitting next to God in that safe-haven (Heaven) above the fray where no earthly agenda can supersede that which is of God's ultimate good; a place where nothing could possibly muddle His Absolute and Grand Design; a design culminating through "time and eternity" in a Universe filled with His limitless aspirations met for each of His beloved children; you and me, included.

Now, take a slow deep breath and look at your life from this purely spiritual perspective, watch The Game being played here on earth viewed from the comfort of a seat in the grandest of all "Sky Boxes". And from this purely Holy Place, you might appreciate the wisdom of the unfolding of your life rather than the appearance of life haphazardly being built then falling apart then somehow pulled back together again; an accordion of trial and error; financial and relationship success and failure; failure, failure, then success; work then play; sadness then happiness; health, sickness, then health, and sickness; suffering, struggle, and peace... then death...

God, help me; I hate accordions...

But, from this Heavenly perch, the Angels and Saints see us as children; easy to love. And if we were to view our lives from this perspective always, we'd more easily see God's plan unfolding and recognize the wisdom of His directives, as His many Angels take Heavenly queues to protect us from ourselves and the evil that lurks within those who seek to destroy us or pinch the results of our work. Yet, from this perch, your attitude isn't tarnished by the microscopic view of the struggles of the daily mission; a mission distracted by fear, dull toil, hurtful envy, and misfortune that otherwise might cause you to scrounge through your educated memories for a worthwhile answer that proves your worthiness; your Genius.

From this perch, we can see the happenings of our lives as neither good or bad nor right or wrong. We see the happenings as would God's Angels and we may respond to stupidity without resistance, without reacting, but fully alive, in the moment, prepared to display an objectively loving act of courage in defense of the Truth; even when stupidity crosses the line into evil and your genius must be activated; trust that it is, as well as has other's in this seemingly endless battle.

Now/Here accept your dynamic role in daily living and the reality for that which you've been prepared, as did His Son, and you're Ultimately compassionate, forgiving, and a passionate defender of Truth. You'll do your part today only and isn't that all that's asked of us anyway? So, choose to be a skilled warrior with the full strength of Eternity's Power that carries you firmly into battle with the force of undying love and you are a loyal soldier whom He may call upon, at any moment, to defend and be the Truth; to create with His Goodness.

When once you might have played poorly with another to make things right, prove the grandness of your well thought theories, and defend yourself from that enemy you fear the most – and The Game had become laborious, Now, viewed from the Sky Box, with The Board at your side, surrounded by Guardian Angels and a myriad of Heavenly Hosts, you may more easily see that playing The Game well and with integrity is The Game. And the "final score" (your net worth) does not mark the end nor is it the tally worth risking your character to achieve high rank. Loving your work, being who you love, loving who you're with and serving them well, by doing so, is your net worth revealed.

~

Today is the day to realize and accept the fact that your ability to live comfortably, to live life freely, to excel at anything worthwhile, and to earn immeasurably is in direct proportion to your ability to choose to accept your role in service to another, in your ability to remain in the moment, "in the zone" and to trust in God's plan; if not tomorrow… for just this single moment in eternity, for just this single day. And the truth is obvious, appreciated, humbly accepted; and together we win.

By making this conscious choice to seek and accept the Truth for today, you've gladly given ownership of your will to The Board and God swiftly exercises this pre-negotiated right to enforce an agreed upon imminent domain over your will and He leads your mind and guides your words and activates your skills; previously unknown. Extremely and seemingly unresolvable complex issues are simplified and solutions and amazing concepts formulated from out-of-nowhere and many new and unexpected relationships; progressive and positive images; and abstract associations meld to lead you to resolutions beyond your fears and beyond the ceilings built over a lifetime of relatively limited materially-logically derived survival-goals met.

In prayer, Board instilled Instincts are highly tuned and guide you to avoid disasters or to achieve greatness. Be aware that to verbalize thought instilled by the Universe's frequencies of Truth, you'll appear unbalanced and crazy, to the well-educated and worldly experientially-sophisticated associates. As you more easily speak Universal Truths, you may more confidently present opposing opinions and seemingly half-cocked and fiscally risky proposals and receive loud criticism; ostracized.

Historically, Board initiated proposals of progressive thought have been met with strenuous objection by society. So, expect business partners, who might filter decision making processes, solely, through an educated survival-logic, to object furiously or they might be deemed insane, as well, for following your absurd trains of thought.

But, in a Universal Connection, we are privy to a Higher Knowledge of which we may not deny nor fully disclose its source, as instinctive and trusted directions originating in private prayer might be unbelievable to most. Universal Truths realized through prayer and meditation, in this one and only moment in time, runs counter to the myriad of our egos' earthly-proofed guidance systems. God's Guidance, when secularly-presented, is naturally targeted to be quashed by the "unbelievers" and in your attempts to defend its "highest" intentions you appear radical, if not unworthy of a chair at the conference table.

Those who strictly enforce the methods proven to work in another time and place and who are fearful of exploring new lands, lands beyond the horizon, must reject "New Thought" as unproven. And many are blind, as are we, when we join those whose efforts support the bottom line, solely, and ignore their conscience in doing so; those who love people on surface, but are blind to the depth of character aligned with the Highest Power; the Creator of All; the power to discern honestly and to create Universally; Power that lay within all men and women; of every birth age, physical and mental ability, and human culture.

With an absolute Faith in God's directives, you'll learn to trust beyond your fears of traveling down an unknown path that might appear to lead to failure and you'll find yourself presenting a wildly-unproven business case with innate courage and instilled Faith and you may save the business from caving into the popular view; mediocrity; "business as usual". The initiative you present is based on a spiritually-logical perspective that defies the survival-logic's agenda and your plan that seemingly stimulates gigantic losses to your company's bottom line is presented with Jesus' Thought for selfless service. And new associations are made to solve complex problems before deemed too troublesome for all to employ

And from within your soul and with His Hosts of silent, yet powerful Angels at your side, your message delivered is received; maybe rebuked, but delivered well, nonetheless.

As you take this spiritually-defined stand and present well, with supporting data supplied by serendipitous alliances and spiritually invigorated research... the chemical plant in India is courageously closed well before twenty thousand innocent people are killed... toxic waste is treated rather than carelessly dumped into our rivers and seas and the irreversible toll on nature is avoided... budgets are approved for additional testing before introducing, modifying, or shelving the release of a new prescription drug with questionable results; lives are spared unknown agony... fishing nets cut loose at sea are retrieved before left to float aimlessly in our oceans; silently killing with no human benefit or interference... etc. etc.

But, how might we quantify the significance of an avoided massacre of life or lessening of avoidable suffering; avoided by courageous actions? The tragedy never occurred. Pain was not experienced. This non-happening was due in part to a Faithful decision to abandon a materially educated guidance system and you've convinced your associates to follow the Spiritual-Nudgings received in meditation to fight a battle of Highest import. But, when all is said and done, no one may know the wisdom nor the scale and scope of God's directive that avoided catastrophe. The catastrophe did not occur.

We may go about our daily business, making seemingly insane and expensive decisions that *did not* amount to anything of financial or self-promotional merit, yet lives and livelihoods are spared unknown anguish; anguish and pain that clearly would have been the result of our selfish quests to succeed in business; at any and all costs. And you've risked being hanged by the Company's board of directors, escorted to the door by security, and business-as-usual would go on without you.

You will have done what you must and God is your proven protector and you've been spiritually, emotionally, and experientially prepared for His next great Spiritually Logical battle being prepared just for you to fight.

Spiritual Logic

> "When we do anything from a sense of duty, we can back it up by argument; when we do anything in obedience to the Lord, there is no argument possible; this is why a saint can be easily ridiculed."
>
> Oswald Chambers
> The Utmost for the Highest (a daily devotional)

An ironic example of Listening might be found in the following. These excerpts are from various documents that tell the tale of the seemingly serendipitous series of actions that served to end World War II.

"It was the dawn of the nuclear age and the B Reactor, at the Hanford Engineer Works in the sagebrush prairie of south-central Washington, was the cornerstone of the top-secret Manhattan Project to build a bomb and end World II before the Nazis and Japanese could.

Mr. Farmer was the cover name for Enrico Fermi, the Italian physicist who helped design the reactor from scratch – a pile of 75,000 graphite blocks, 36 feet high, 36 feet wide and 28 feet deep, drilled through with 2,004 tubes holding enriched uranium fuel for a nuclear chain reaction that would produce plutonium. It was built in 11 months, a sort of seat-of-the-pants engineering feat." But, when the reactor went online, there were problems.

"The Hanford scientists were at a loss to explain the pile's mysterious failure to maintain a chain reaction. Only the foresight of DuPont's engineers made it possible to resolve the crisis."

The cause of the strange phenomenon proved to be xenon poisoning. Xenon, a fission product isotope with a mass of 135, was produced as the pile operated. It captured neutrons faster than the pile could produce them, causing a gradual shutdown. With shutdown, the xenon decayed, neutron flow began again, and the pile started up. It was Xenon reactor poisoning that played a major role in the Chernobyl disaster.

Fortuitously, despite the objections of some scientists who complained of DuPont's excessive caution, (which led to seemingly unnecessary delays in a race with Nazi Germany to construct a nuclear reactor) the company had installed a large number of extra tubes (which turned out to be the exact number required). This design feature meant that the pile 100-B could easily be expanded to reach a power level sufficient to overwhelm the xenon poisoning.

Success was achieved when the first irradiated slugs were discharged from pile 100-B on December 25, 1944. The irradiated slugs, after several weeks of storage, went to the chemical separation and concentration facilities. By the end of January 1945, the highly-purified plutonium underwent further concentration in the completed chemical isolation building, where remaining impurities were removed successfully.

The Los Alamos Laboratory received its first plutonium on February 2, 1945."

How ironic it might seem, that the horrors of World War II may have come to an abrupt end by this and many other interventions and acts of courage, of which we know not the magnitude nor understand the spiritual reasoning. And how do we not judge those who made decisions to use these bombs that inflicted such pain, suffering, and death in Hiroshima and Nagasaki? Hundreds of thousands of Japanese were instantaneously and quite horrifically vaporized; the results of this ambitious experiment to create a weapon of mass destruction, like none other in the history of man.

> "I am sick and tired of war. Its glory is all moonshine.
> It is only those who have neither fired a shot nor heard
> the shrieks and groans of the wounded
> who cry aloud for blood, for vengeance, for desolation.
> 'War is hell'."
>
> Lt. Col. Dave Grossman

Is it possible? Is it possible that, from the Sky Box, we might be privy to the immense pain, agony, and wisdom employed to make the decisions that averted further death, destruction, and human suffering inflicted by the warring madmen of World War II? The war ended by this ungodly event of mass destruction, but was a balance struck, of which we are not humanly capable of understanding that made these decisions "right" or were there other options "men in charge" simply chose to ignore? A warning shot into the sea, maybe?

How men choose to draw technologies' development roadmaps illustrates the constant human battle between good and evil and God forgive us if we were wrong to drop those bombs.

~

The gifts of the Holy Spirit run through all men and man chooses daily to make the most of these unrequitable favors of God, to whatever extent they may reach; for the good of mankind or, twisted, to its horror. Productively speaking, however, privately in our executive board rooms and behind closed-doors in public buildings, exemplary (from a spiritually-logical perspective) decisions are made; the results of which never make it to press... not exciting enough... nothing of visual consequence happened... but thank God these Spiritually Logical decisions are being made and acted upon by the saner of our leaders.

When we seek God's Will over ours, our world is safer and more productive and foreign are the notions that justify our intentions to take advantage of the unsuspecting. And unnatural is our desire to steal or coerce favor in what might seem to be the natural course of doing business or other seemingly justifiable methods of competing for our share of the money pie.

When decisions are spiritually led, the thought cannot cross our minds to bill 340 hours per month per associate nor do we consider creating a $900 invoice for a $40 hammer or push legislation to fund construction projects guised as Foreign Aid to seemingly backward countries. 'Confessions of an Economic Hit Man' reads like a spy novel, but it reveals, well, how American foreign aid, in reality, pays our leaders' friends in high corporate places to design and build the dams, power grids, roads, harbors... etc. etc. only to exploit the natural resources of the least powerful. The book tells the story of how, for decades, the West installs puppet leaders to rule with an iron fist the populace of these "lesser" nations to maintain an undisturbed supply of goods to fill the needs of consumer nations and stoke the fires of "big business".

And we have bigger problems to resolve in a seemingly sophisticated world teeming with intelligent and seemingly well-educated life-forms. For one, why does any child go to bed hungry? If we will only choose to recognize that human starvation is a worthy battle to be fought, we might activate the potential for resolving the issue, as did we to reach the moon within a decade. And with the proper sights set in our scopes, we may choose to view our business, public servant, and personal lives from a Heavenly perspective and make decisions filtered through our highest sense of Spiritual Logic – and the world brightens by our good deeds and thoughts.

The horrific problem of hunger may be solved, if we activate our ambition, as have we done with every unsolvable problem solved.

And to solve any problem, honestly, begin by surrendering your deepest anxieties and darkest fears of failure, as well as your most esteemed visions of grandness-ness and self-made right to sickening wealth. Become empty, weak, and let God be who He is through you. He is your Genius revealed and you may, in this moment Now, walk alongside your brothers and sisters not as competitors, but as allies, comrades, counterparts... You are brothers in arms, in this great adventure that God has led each of us to play a small but critical role; His army battling the money driven forces that would have us ignore starvation and economic inequality. Daily, we are given the Divine directions and authority to boldly proclaim the end of ignorance, the end of self-exceptionalism that provides for our comforts in living that makes us each too lazy to change, the end of our acceptance of greed as a worthy method to happiness through wealth and abundance of possessions earned and stored, and leads us to proclaim the unacceptance of the arguments that convince us that change is unnecessary; status quo is plenty fine – the stillbirth of a dream unsought.

But, as you find yourself cooperating with God more and more each day, increasingly one successful day leads to another and you'll succeed in life far beyond your self-determined earth-bound financial and survival-driven targets. Through the vehicle of Jesus' Wisdom, when viewed from His perspective; alongside Him in His Sky Box; you're enlightened by the view from His vantage point and receive your destiny (Heavenly established goals); as your fears are wiped away and Hope is instilled in its place. With Hope, Charity, and Love in your mind and your heart filled by the Spirit of Truth He exudes life through you; and you and I succeed together beyond ourselves; all encompassing; within Him, through Him, and beyond our individual selves.

God's Travel Agency

AUGUST 2003

Dave's "The man!"

    He singlehandedly had sold more product than anyone I'd ever met. But, I couldn't have known the weight of that when I was handed his card, hidden in a stack of 40 or so I received from Casey. Casey was leaving the company and had been instructed to give me any work-in-progress and contacts. With a bit of reluctance and little fanfare, he said "This guy might be a good one to keep in touch with." I had a full plate and set the cards aside for a better time; like never...
    You may know how it goes... a few months went by, it's now May of 2003 and I was Bumped to go through the cards and make a few calls. I caved in to the notion, begrudgingly, and reached over the box of paper clips and note pads to the very back of the top drawer of my desk. Of course, I may have as well picked up the yellow pages or searched Yelp, if it had existed, in any major city and started from scratch, but

some contact had been made and these calls turned out to be warmer than expected. Dave was in Atlanta and me in Salt Lake and he must have thought we had previously met, from the greeting he gave me. He treated me as though we were picking up where we had left off discussing a representative agreement for his firm to carry our line. He had a calm reassuring voice and always made me feel at home. After many conversations over the summer we had developed common ground and a friendship. In August, we each happened to be in California at the same time and decided to meet in San Diego. We set the meeting for that coming Sunday.

Carl Raubenheimer, a burly South African rugby player in his recent youth, our Company's sales manager and I decided to meet with Dave, together. Carl and I'd had a full week of meetings in Los Angeles that wrapped up in the late afternoon on Friday. From the office, we sped out of town; by sped I mean 30 or 40 miles per hour down the bumper-to-bumper, Friday afternoon, southbound I-5 Freeway. Arriving Friday evening, would give us a full day on Saturday to unwind on the beach. I knew the area fairly well, so we stopped in Carlsbad, just a few miles north of San Diego to find a room, but there were no vacancies, which was not a good sign. This was the middle of the busy season and we had no reservations, but I didn't feel overly concerned. I knew we were being directed to meet Dave and there would be no serious road blocks unless we were taking our roles too seriously; becoming prideful or otherwise self-directed. So, there we were, eight o'clock on a Friday night on Pacific Beach driving by one motel after another, each with a "no vacancy" sign in the window.

Carl was uneasy about our options, but I didn't notice a lot of urgency or apprehension in my being. I'd an unearned confidence in the plan and when we pulled up to the first motel in the middle of the row of motels on Pacific Beach, Carl went in to check if they had a room while I waited in the car. He came back and excitedly said, "They have a room, it's $170 a night, but only has one bed. She'd get us a roll-away, though." That was easy. But, we can do better, I thought. So, I asked Carl to let her know we'd be right back. He did and we went on the search to see if we could find a better deal or at least two beds. It didn't take long; maybe 15 minutes before we raced back to grab the room. There were no rooms, anywhere!

While checking in, the young lady at the desk told us she never under-books on the weekend and that they never have vacancies that late in the evening especially on a Friday night that time of year. Then she said something else, "You know, when you first came in I was wondering if it was you that I was saving this room for."

We had a great place to stay; right on the beach and had an amazing Saturday, as per usual, and the trip went well. Met Dave on Sunday as planned... and by the next month, in New Orleans, Dave had connected us with the group that built the sales and support channel we used to launch the product nationally and internationally. And it happened just like it was supposed to happen; by staying in the moment, uncrumpling an old business card, picking up the phone, and acting on God's quiet, but life thumping Bumps, I did my part in a grand purpose of which I had no idea or could suppose such a brilliant outcome.

the Hope in Entrepreneurialism

CHAPTER 12

A Spiritual Neural-Pathway Rewire

"The biggest human temptation
is to settle for too little."

Spiritual Logic

Fr. Thomas Merton

As you'll discover and are discovering by the surrender of your will to that of God's, in this exact moment in time, every single thing is correct, correctable, or being corrected. And, if you've committed to conducting your life under the direction of The Board, you'll find that you'll be in no hurry to win. Winning is not the objective of life; it's a fact. And, by accepting and receiving Salvation, you have, in fact, won — know this and get to work, as His surrogate for Him and with Him.

Know in your heart that you've won the Game simply by acting on that which you've discerned and truly believe is our Father's guidance. Act in His behalf and your faith opens a conduit for His Will to unravel sin; mistaken as good intention.

Committed to your Salvation, imagine the Creator of all that exists creating all that He might through you, and your reward is simply, shared-happiness. He answers your prayers when you're ready to receive and to appreciate the answer. So, be constant and consistent in your requests for help, but more importantly, in your thanks in advance of prayers fulfilled. Advanced thanksgiving helps you appreciate your ever-growing Faith's ability to ignore the pains of spiritual clumsiness.

Your relative belief in His Spiritually Logical pathway relatively fuels your ambition and inevitably leads you to great places you never imagined you're justified to inhabit, based on your sketchy financial historicals or ill-fated business plans; mediocre earnings complicated by debt-sanctioned spending; perceived greatest personal achievements and expectant glorification; or self-made ceilings of your highest possible corporate advancement.

Simply and horrifyingly horrifying is the act, but if you place your Trust in God and quit trying so hard to win and just take His Holy advice; you win at life.

In small bites, you win the prize; delivered peace. Just learn to appreciate the taste of His Truth; hard to swallow at times, but He wants for His children's success at every seat around the table. And, in spite of rapid-fire cliché and overuse of metaphor that eases my burden of explaining what I'm thinking and having to explain in more depth, of which I fail to find the words in which to do, you'll get the point and, in time, find peace in non-resistance to His Love, nonetheless.

From this new perspective, you'll more easily recognize the insanity that is perpetrated by the illusions of fixed business strategies designed to win, by defending and controlling rather than freeing God to create through you and your associates.

And if you choose to manage your business defensively, you can't hide your agenda from the quietly "Knowing" people surrounding you. You might've, as well, pasted notes to your forehead saying, "I'm only here to make deals." And "I'm not so sure I have time for you and your problems; go away!"

People are not stupid. Even the "Knowing", at times, are just too lazy to stand up for themselves, as you dismiss their fears and needs. So, your day might be condemned to putting out fires as you've selfishly abandoned critical moments when you might've behaved well; selflessly. And tapped out the fires, but your management team is left unmanaged to focus on their fears of what hell will certainly manifest, brought by the illusions of a world that works against them; as they've been led to believe that it does. Nice work! Another fire!

> "... my favorite lies:
> 'Competitors are the enemy.'
> 'The customer's always right.'
> and 'They won't pay the price we're asking.'"
>
> Delores Dogood
> (from the companion book to "The Cookbook for Bookkeeping"
> entitled
> "Workbook for Cookbooking")

However, a sublimely strict adherence to The Board's recommendations, assures success, as well as the success of your competitors. Why not? God picks no favorites, so ask yourself these questions when you lose whatever it is you're sure you should've won:

- Do I or do I not believe in abundance?
- Did the customer win by purchasing from the other guy?
- Do I truly believe in the infallibility of love?
- Am I willing to serve without thought of reward?

From a solidified foundational thought of "How may I help my sister get what she needs, so she can get what she wants!" you'll unconsciously demonstrate an unusual confidence in performing the day's tasks selflessly; directed by service. As you succinctly deliver the reasons for your recommendations; the Eternally Thought remedies to "Why does it hurt?", a higher purpose is accepted and followed based on a client's earned confidence in the fact you haven't condescendingly placed honor upon her, only to win favor.

Remaining "Present" she subjectively and emotionally understands that you care mostly that her pains are relieved, first; with or without purchasing your Brand™.

Honestly prepared to walk away from any negotiation without your remedy purchased soothes the buyer's fears of losing. You've become an invaluable counsel fully vested in doing what's best for your sister-client / friend.

~

Fair-play and fighting to increase profits cannot coexist emotionally and materially in the same space. But spiritually there is no separation in regards to profits brought by Eternally driven solutions sold. Throughout our lives, tragedy presses us into action and we rescue those in peril; however, in business the unexpected disastrous earnings report sends the market into an auto-pilot fix-it spree of varying strategies based on greed or protectionism, but rarely fair-play, as when human life is in jeopardy.

Yet, lives are put into jeopardy when increased profit is the primary answer. As the world's response to threats of physical harm contrasts with threats to our financial security, our Board-approved Directives often run contrary to worldly directives. These Board Directives instill in us the surety that we must continue to tactfully and confidently move forward. In Faith, we walk strangely comfortable amidst the ruins brought by chaos and the world looks upon us cross-eyed in bewilderment, as the value of God's Eternally lifted Directions are impossible to qualify or quantify; spatially or temporally. Yet, you progress courageous, defiant to fear of failure.

And of course, there is skepticism to your mystically-driven seemingly fiscally irresponsible marketing plan, as the process driven by God has no earthly track record by which to forecast an outcome. So, your money-blinded associates are simply doing the job for which they are paid; respect that, turn down the volume of their arguments, pray for the Truth and for your ability to convey reason, and move forward until you win them over; or you're fired.

Regardless of temporary setbacks, we ultimately win when we comply with God, as we cannot fail with His inside-knowledge and elite Contact database. And, over the years, you'll begin to know, from that deep place within your being, that success, while a difficult road, is immanent. And in your humility, with dogged resilience to fear's clutches, with Faith in His Direction growing firm in your soul, you'll begin to envision more clearly, day by day, His Thoughts of success and your direction for each day becomes of more certainty and a true compass by which to travel.

The Holy Truths by which you may choose to conduct business are Eternally dynamic, so today's mission must begin from an absolute Truth graced to you from our Most High Source; for this single moment in time. And your Mission Statement is immediately transformed when you choose to follow your highest sense of selflessness and trust in His best intentions for doing business. With each minutely incremental step towards God, your path to success requires that your abilities be magnified and you become ever more, and involuntarily, in-tuned to His use for your talents, Today.

~

Dragged away from comfortable habits, screaming and clawing, you might be terrified that you'll under-perform in these many and elevated God-directed tasks. Yet, as you're escorted from the comfort of the known, you'll be assured by the occasional Bumps and Nudges throughout the process telling you, "Yes!" you're in the right place and, "Now!" you're fully capable of this Center-ring performance.

As difficult as it is to place blind faith in His rolling Bumps, the realization that you can do far greater things than you thought possible provides pain-amnesia in the euphoria of the win. And much like childbirth to a new mother, your privately-experienced publicly-shared ordeal becomes a favored memory to cherish. So, cherish the fact that you listened and swiftly acted upon what, in hindsight, was an obviously brilliantly instinctive act of selfless courage. And as the challenges faced become of increasingly higher importance and more spiritually-critical, far beyond your mortal imaginings, your mettle has been strengthened and you've proven to yourself and others that you're able to handle more and more responsibility; you are "One to be trusted".

Yes, of course, we fear the great unknown and the possible negative outcomes may loom ominous in our minds. But, as we round the corner of the path never before walked, the new day opens itself to a welcomed vista. So, be prepared for anything to happen, for in this new day, you'll be recruited by our Lord to perform a great task, the task that must be completed as His surrogate.

Thinking Spiritually Logically; if you've never performed as He's asking of you, doesn't mean you can't. As well, if He's recruited you, He must know you're ready to perform, so just face your fears, and do it? Why not? Confidence is built and sustained with due diligence (inspection, introspection, forgiveness, and prayer) and by taking the first step, as if it's the only step, then the next; and so on. And each right-experience increases your confidence. In answer to prayer, all is in order, as you're guided to take just one single step at a time, experiencing life in this one single moment; right Now; then the next.

~

In January of 2012, I was asked by a friend to co-host an auction for the Catholic Family Services fund raiser dinner to be held on St. Patrick's Day. This is *the* big fund raising event held each year with hopes to raise around $10,000 to fund programs in the Diocese of Central Washington. I was honored to be asked. Kim said I was the logical choice, but, I didn't understand why she'd think so. I'd never hosted an auction or any event, for that matter and event lasting three hours; before 300 guests. With Carol my cohost, it would be our job to keep their interest through dinner and to run the auction. But, I truly was puzzled. "Why choose me?"

Honestly, when I got the Bump to commit and accept, I said, "Yes, I'd love to do it."

"Yes?" Crap! What had I done? The word came out of my mouth so quickly... It's such a small word... and it took, maybe a nanosecond before my fears of failure and the magnitude of embarrassment-caused stage-fright began to churn in my gut, as I'd committed to run this very important auction. I'd attended a few, but what makes me think I could Host one???

Huh?

Well, Carol and I had eight weeks to prepare for the show. We met a few times and determined not to over-plan it. It couldn't be too scripted, as we each are much more comfortable speaking impromptu; in the moment, rather than trying to remember and deliver a prepared message; awkwardly delivered. Rather, we chose to invest time in meeting the staff of the CFS to better understand the needs of the agency and figured the development and delivery of the message would take care of itself.

Emotionally haunted for having committed to running the auction, I was talking with my brother Sean, who lives three time zones away, about our preparations for the event and about my recent public speaking fumbles that I'd brutally self-suffered and he reminded me about Toastmasters. It's a great organization and they could help me prepare; build my confidence. So, we hung up and I went online to find a Wenatchee group and discovered they met once a week and, as per usual and not coincidentally, they were meeting in 20 minutes and, as per usual, being adequately Bumped to take advantage of the so-called coincidence, I shed the cloak of my most negative fears of disgrace and made it to the meeting, just in time.

It was great! I was welcomed to the meeting by sympathetic members and given an immediate opportunity to practice speaking before a safe group. And, for the next year or so, I'd take every opportunity to practice speaking and working out the bugs in my head that blocked nature's performance. Right up until the moment of going on stage with my heart pounding audibly in my chest, I feared the worst and made myself crazy with an imagined worst performance fueling my anxieties.

On the afternoon of the show, I prayed like I've never prayed before, to prepare to go on stage to begin the evening festivities. I'd emceed a few programs in smaller venues, but this was a Five Star event with a fully catered dinner and Carol and I'd be the focus of attention in front of a packed house of the community's high-profile donors, friends, and special guests from around the state; including the Diocese' Bishop and the CEO of the national Catholic Family Services from New Orleans. I tried not to freak myself out, but I get a little freaked out just writing this. It could've been a roomful of kindergartners and I'd have been equally messed up.

So, I called in the big guns, The Board of course and minutes before going on-stage, I called Sue, the love of my life and, at the time, my new girlfriend soon to become my wife. We had only known each other for six weeks, but I knew she was "the one" and I could literally trust her with my life. Sue was at home in Portland waiting for my call, as planned,

Spiritual Logic

before going on we'd pray together. Praying over the phone was weird the first few times we had done it and it's quite awkward unless you stop, become still, and imagine you're physically with the one on the other end of the line. Nonetheless, that loving prayer gave me the encouragement I needed to breathe... stand tall, relax my eyes, smile and perform fearlessly and comfortably in this venue; a performing venue I would never have taken, on a dare.

Bottom line: the night went great! Carol and I worked well together and raised $33,000. We received great feedback from the audience after the show and shared ideas for next year's event, as if we'd be expected to return.

God guides us to that safe place He knows, full well, we are fully able to function perfectly and perform perfectly above our previously held self-restricted abilities. He gives us the spiritually corrected thoughts and words to use and if we accept the mission and stay true to His path, the notions of grand performances are more than plausible. This new expectation *is* our new reality. And we've immediately become more able and, having endured hell we have a new Heavenly "Endorsed Skill" simply by being more faithful to His guidance. He loves us and reminds us of His closeness by His miracles that save us from going mad by self-applied pressures to out-perform our self-surmised barriers to delivering His message well.

The moment God knew I was prepared to "stretch", He set plays into motion by Bumping all involved to convince me I was more capable than I'd been willing to believe. And through much prayer and in my painful emptiness, where pride and dread of failure cannot coexist with humility and love, I was instilled with the strength and humility to perform well for Him.

~

Now, take a step back and imagine how much greater were the pains Jesus suffered during His short visit to earth. He had thrown Himself into the fray of human spiritual blindness when religious pride had meticulously gouged a path through the truth to a favored, but fictitious, righteousness of which only a chosen few were invited. Ignoring that love is the answer to fear, the self-made holy men of the day controlled God's forgiveness by payment to the hierarchy, and for Jesus' good nature to survive the human-blindness He often would sequester Himself to the loneliness of the desert, in prayer.

To escape debilitating thoughts that scratched and bit at Him with every empty question and culturally-corrupted prideful pronouncement of inherited spiritual wealth and favored rituals to our Father's honor, presented; He'd disappear. And it might have been humorous to Him, if not for His compassion with pre-knowledge of the consequential suffering, the results of ignored Grace; His children's pride displayed and fanned by religious specialness demanded.

So, Jesus prayed for strength, rather than be drained emotionally and physically in the battle for Truth against the Pharisees' passionately ignorant teachings; teachings that ran contrary to His first-hand knowledge of an ever-loving Father; a Heavenly Father who loves each of us evenly and beyond our comprehension; without fee.

Bombarded with spiritually abhorrent questions from the multitudes believing in "payment for favor", Jesus might've doubted His messages could be received. Could the spiritually-ignorant be forever changed by His short stay on earth? Could His beloved really understand the importance of the simplest of messages...? "Love one another."

Imagine that Jesus would have allowed a painful thought of mission-failure to be trapped within His human mind and that these thoughts might become internally thunderous, to bring Him to His knees, exhausted in prayer. But, by allowing Himself to experience fear and despair; to be truly human; that He must resort to prayer, Jesus could know from our human perspective the pain of losing the Grace-connection. By prayer and meditation, He'd once again find peace by connecting to our Father's Will; through the emptiness brought by human physical and emotional suffering; Now erased by Grace.

In His weakness, He'd be strengthened to reenter the fray, invigorated that His efforts might just make a difference in the minds and souls of the Grace-ignorant masses.

So, if Jesus prayed, why would we think we're immune and should not be required to pray to escape the crazy thoughts that instill fear and hopeless visions into our minds? Yet, we forget that the link to certainty and peace is here for us, always.

Never forget to pray.

Prayer is our lifeline to safety, to His sanity away from an insane inner and outer world of endless pressures and terrifying occasions to perform beyond ourselves. In this single moment, He places us directly where He's sure we are poised perfectly to succeed.

But, fearful of losing, we often forget the option to abandon our worldly demands and replace earthly agendas with our highest missions to serve; that we may live more fluidly, coherently, and confidently in a fashion Jesus would choose.

We simply forget.

Yes, it's easy to forget Grace especially when we're so proud of our accomplishments and self-deprecating in defeat. With the many distractions of the world, distractions we might choose to endorse, it's easy to be lured off course and forget that the simple act of selfless service performed spiritually perfectly results in our rescue from fear of failure and fills us with peace and soulful happiness to achieve beyond our best self. And our Holy Spirit within us protects our Bumped travels and guides us; with a sharp elbow to the ribs, if needed, or a decapitating numbness disconnecting selfish conductivity; and our mind is dumbed. Stupefied, we cannot ignore the ache that gnaws deep within our back and shoulders that makes us want to shudder; and our emotions run eerily and mystically painful by our bad choices, procrastination of duty, or prideful oratory conveyed; regretfully.

~

With this newfound gift of your increased spiritually sound decisiveness, by quietly following the blocks your God-guided Angels set for you, your seemingly well trained actions are simply the result of an unearned knowingness and trust. You'll surprise yourself as you exude clear confidence that by your agile footwork and infectious confident smile; a smile fills the room, for no special reason. And your aura colored by goodness attracts the look and attention of passerby's and they surround you with good thoughts. This "goodness cycle" instills in you increased and potentially favored status among those who wish to be as are you; "at peace on the unmapped path". And your trust in this new awareness of all that is good in others, your strange, incredibly talented, and oddly behaving brothers, enlightens the path and you intuitively understand precisely what you must do to play your part to affect necessary change to thwart evil and pursue goodness.

You'll be surprised, as this "knowing" attracts good people from every direction, as they stand at your side and want for the same for all. Try not to be surprised, rather accept your ability to mystically command respect and attract collaborators from varied paths to bring about much needed improvements to the landscape of trial and error that's been, forever, the main impetus for people's survival and learning.

Today, you are a leader in the revolt against stagnant social longing "for better" at no risk to one's comfort. You are one with the Universal Thought that deems all participants in this new journey towards inclusion of thought of God with that of all men and women demanding change to the unruly world fashioned by earthbound men and women; until this very Now/Here.

And the byproduct of this Holy Rewire, instigated from your brand new; daily renewable; Eternally rewired brain – your thoughts purified – is your new ability to Instantly provide resolutions to your family's and the world's ever increasing challenges to safety, security, peace, and happiness.

Give up control of your earthly learned mind to God's Eternal knowledge-base and try each day to become more comfortable with blindly following Heaven-sent Bumps and Nudges, fully expectant of amazing results promised. With an ease of access to the Truth derived, the payoff is so real the benefits from the effort to let go and the need to cling to God's Thought conjured cannot be argued. In an appreciation of your thoughtless-mind's brain's ability to function amazingly on its own without controlling it to your satisfaction, but by letting God take the Game controller for His Purpose, you'll have no intention of taking credit for the outcome. Pride disconnected, you're naturally in a space of constant thanksgiving for the position you're given to play in this incredibly fascinating, globally effecting Game Jesus has set into motion, years ago, Now-Here today being played-out.

Morning Reprogram

In thoughtful prayer and the thoughtlessness of meditation; in your emptiness; detached from the needs and wants of the world; easily attached to the mind of God – without judgment – without judgment, yes, but with compassion, understanding, and courage – let go of your schemes for success and fears of the unknowable outcomes to scheduled plans and ask God to Rewire your brain's neural pathways – to physically heal your living data processing circuitry.

Each morning, take a moment before meditation and prayer and select three character aspects from the list below or add others that might mean more to you – more pertinent for today. When you're ready to be readied for your personal time with God – imagine your body, mind, and spirit being fully enwrapped and filled with the Light, Love, and Goodness of the Father, Son, and Holy Spirit and ponder these three traits aligned with Jesus'; in this stillness, know you're being healed.

Be still....

Now – Here in this moment breathe-in the Holy Spirit and with this breath you are empty of agenda and God fills your body with Holy Light. Imagine Now that this room is filled with Light, this home, this State, this Country, Planet, and Universe. God fills your heart and each of the hearts of our brothers and sisters, your family, friends and allies, business associates and clients, our community leaders, our country's leaders and political and corporate leaders from around the world each filled with Light. You might actually feel a tug pulling and detaching old-thinking pathways; you might have a real sense that you're being worked on. Go with It!

Empty and Filled, you know God's Truth and Act Fearlessly as He works to un-wire and re-wire each of these trait-connections to the thinking processes of our brains' neural pathways to re-connect them directly to His Holy Circuitry. Rewired, we are the whole persons He intended us to be – Connected in His Holy Thought. Now/Here, His Holy Thoughts Sanctify and Invigorate our intentions and actions and Clarifies, Economizes, and Powerfully Delivers the Words – Jesus' Truth – through us. And we Listen carefully to the completion of another's Thought sent by God and we ignore the rest. To Jesus' Words we Respond, as He directs, as each of these many aspects of our beings are Purified and we're Gladly Perfunctory to His Will and are mindfully:

>Compassionate
>Introspective
>Imaginative
>Industrious
>Thoughtful
>Supportive
>Honorable
>Optimistic
>Respectful
>Inquisitive
>Interested
>Confident
>Generous

Spiritual Logic

Pragmatic
Forgiving
Engaging
Prepared
Friendly
Trusting
Humble
Positive
Devout
Honest
Artistic
Loving
Joyful
Caring
Frugal
Polite
Loyal
Kind
Sure
True
Fun
Still
Pure
Cool
Quiet
Loved
Happy
Candid
Valiant
Sincere
Sharing
Selfless
Present
Curious
Fruitful
Faithful
Fearless
Mindful
Truthful
Pleasant
Grateful
Intuitive
Resolute

the Hope in Entrepreneurialism

>Powerful
>Believing
>Inventive
>Reflective
>Ambitious
>Energized
>Apologetic
>Humorous
>Expressive
>Supportive
>Courageous
>Sympathetic
>Unassuming
>Appreciative
>Adventurous
>Complimentary

In this Holy Rewire, feel your mind's brain being reworked and untangled. Know that this is the new you being re-created by your open invitation to God to enter, at His Will and Time, your mind's brain to mend your thinking processes. Your brain realigned by the power of the Holy Spirit; Sanctified by the Spirit of Truth; results, enjoyed by you and God and you're remade True and Complete in this Here and Now by your trust and volition.

And all throughout this and each day, when you're befuddled by evil, weakness, or accident, act decisively – take a break from the craziness – and allow the Holy Spirit swift entry into your mind's brain to complete the reconstruction of these new spiritually architected neural-pathways. And today, more so than even yesterday, your mind's new brain is processing information more directly with more clarity – simply, objectively, naturally, and more spiritually logically. Your Holy-Rewire Eternally tunes your brain to ignite reflexive and naturally intuitive, courageous, and compassionate behaviors with Heaven-sent instilled Knowingness and confidence in the Way.

Your Way, today, is the Way instilled by God, as He adjusts your thoughts to deliver His Goodness to the world in His Ultimate and Eternally Creative Way. And you may in each moment live your life fully alive as would Jesus; unhampered by fear; fully vested in Love.

CHAPTER 13

Remembering to Remember

"... if it feels this good being used ... just keep on using me ...
'till I'm all used up."

Bill Withers

It's humanly impossible to relentlessly refuse our materially wanton desires, ignore comfortable bad-habits and debilitating patterns; generations in the making that assures our family's needs are met, our livelihoods are secured, and our multidimensional values proven. As we set off for work in the morning, to slay the dragon, survive our bills, or to earn an enviable living we take personal the responsibility of being the "Knight in shining armor" to those who rely upon us for safety and financial security.

Yet, we may choose to deflect this enormous responsibility; this act of required heroism; by prayerful abidance to "do the Will of our Father in Heaven"; forwarding responsibility to the "highest source" our Creator. We have a choice to give Him the reigns to make straight our way to productive earnings. Although, in doing so, one might argue, by giving up our will for His, we are simply being God's good little puppet sent to rescue another without supplying thoughtful input or to evoke courage mustered. If this role of the nonchalant do-gooding-puppet is accepted, what is our real purpose for being? Why doesn't God just do it Himself, if His work is so critically important?

To act gallantly, does His gift of "Free-Will" offer us another option where we might reign victorious without conscious prayerful adherence to His every Thought, as it occurs? And of that bad and tragic thing that just happened, is it really "God's Will"? The heavy weight of tragedy lightened by accepting that it's "God's Will" rings of lazy theology, as I suffer in profound agony the emotional costs of a blunt smack to the side of the head; physically or emotionally. And as I anxiously await the next unforgiving blow, I uncontrollably flounder in pursuit of an answer to "Why me?" How could this horrible thing be God's Will?

Be careful how you consider the happenings in life as "God's Will". In its worst definition, the enemy might be guiding you to stand on your heels and take a punch directed to inflict pain not teach a lesson. Do you honestly believe God would have us suffer misuse or abuse at the hands of evil or to use "It's God's Will" as an excuse to avoid a good fight?

Well.... I, for one, will fight relentlessly against injustice and lies, but as His Will directs I've learned not to hurry into battle without a thoughtful plan.

Yes, I've lost, painfully, too often by thoughtlessly or egocentrically entering a fight in a spastic uncontrolled, ADHD induced punching fest, with no sensible battle plan, and been thrown into too many brick walls along the way to want to chance repetition of insanity. So, today, I will wait for God to Bump me into the ring knowing that in "His time" I've been fully prepared to win smartly; focused; undistracted; I'm certain to be "on mission".

Spiritual Logic

I've learned, through painfully loathsome trial-by-error and seemingly endless waiting, that to enter battle ready to win, I'm better served when I appreciate my place as His indentured servant on earth and let Him choose the weapons, the battlefields, and most important – the time.

And if it is, in fact, His Will that I suffer the pains of loss, to be lowered from my self-made pedestal of great grandnessness, in those times I've won BIG and overspent earnings, well... so be it. If suffering helps me to understand the value of the emotional pains of harsh defeat, the results of selfishness and pride, that I less often repeat the Game's infraction, I must be grateful for conscience?

Many times, I've suffered alone and survived and it wasn't pretty, in fact it sucked badly. But, Now, with the realization that I am never alone in my suffering, that Jesus resides within me, filling my passions with forgiveness and fortitude, I suffer with less of a grimace and better manage the emotional pains of the tough lessons that lead to God's better outcome; a far better place than my ego had advertised inevitable.

~

God has given us the freedom to choose to be within Him or not to be; to serve intelligently in every instance or abandon Truth in our pride and lowest energies of Superior Specialness. And, while I'm not one to be identified as a tool, when I immure my ego, I may selflessly serve others and be fully oddly me rather than admirably Special. To be just me, the me God created, His incredibly powerful me, I'm comfortable being a tool, a good soldier, God's human puppet; with purpose. And oddly me, I'm less special to myself and more special to those I am here to serve and to God; I'm confidently empty filled to the full; alive in His Truth.

As His puppet, I choose to be His surrogate. And, as His surrogate, I merely allow Him to work His miracles through me and with my relatively benign "great ideas" discarded, His Power, His Grace is sensed by all involved and the miracles in living flow unhampered; miraculously.

Another option: Agree to be the puppet of this world and dance to the tugs of our ego's fantasies of success and happiness or skittishly scurry to protect "your" estate from endless fears of failure; of which we're certain the world controls the multitudes of strings. A puppet of the world has no chance for lasting happiness only contrived defenses, endless battles for superiority, and fleeting moments of ecstasy. A worldly puppet cannot be her true self and enjoy true moments of bliss, as she is not free to dance as she desires; her gifted talents muffled by fear of being judged poorly. A worldly puppet has given the world control of the strings and reluctantly performs to each tug, fearful of reprisal or loss, or she'd severe the attachment long ago.

But, a time may come and in that single courageous act of selflessness she chooses to cut the strings and she's suddenly freed to seek and know the truth and be her true self, fully. She's unstrung from the world and immediately included in the whole and heart of God; living a life inspired; whole.

We "believers" are not puppets, for a puppet cannot make a tough decision to do that most difficult and integral task that goes against conventional thought or, in his passion for work, persist tirelessly and, as a result, feel a sense of purpose and reward in the accomplishment; at the end of a long tiring day – smile. When is a puppet able to create, if not inspired? And when is a puppet given time to enjoy moments of amazing beauty and un-earnable grandeur because of the many hardships and pains survived in daily living?

Being true to ourselves, Now/Here, we are freed to laugh at ourselves or openly share compassion with a friend over a great or tragic experience. Freed from our fears of being found out to be "different", Now, we can be our true-selves and to act within each moment as a part of the whole of God; not a puppet, but as a partner in the act of living.

> "We are in a strange partnership with God.
> We cannot do what God must do.
> And, on earth, God cannot do what we must do."
>
> Author Unknown

God encourages us to cut the worldly strings and escape the illusionary comfort of status quo and promises to protect us as we enter the "Great Mystical Unknown Uncontrollable Life" led by selfless goodness. In agreement, we find His Way offers the highest rate of return for the pains endured in life. Yes, God is a loving Father, but He's selfish for our love, as well, and He wants to experience a happy life with us and through us, as we wholly explore the Eternal depth and breadth of our abilities.

He's here with us guiding us to recognize the beauty in the day and to help stop the wheels in our brains from churning just long enough to appreciate the talents of our brothers and sisters, beyond want to control. He does not demand our allegiance nor does He force His agenda upon us. However, from the simplest task to the most life-challenging altercations faced, in this single moment, God has a perfect design for each of us and we have no idea or recollection of the perfect import or where this perfect connection is intended to lead us; perfectly. But, we need only remember to cut our earthly strings, let go and shadow Him to find what new "Great Adventure" He's got in mind for us.

Scary!

...except for the fact that He's painstakingly designed a huge safety-net for each of us... woven with Forgiveness and Grace.

~

He has a Will for each instance in our lives and His Will is dynamic as it changes from moment to moment, as we desecrate or otherwise screw up the previous moment's Will. He tweaks the original Will to accommodate our mortal frailties and failings. From the Sky Box, we may imagine how subtly His Will changes for us from one moment to the next as we stubbornly or foolishly abandon His Plan for that of another. As we race blindly in this haze of our over-committed selfish ambitions to conquer the world or to simply control outcomes, we drift off course. And, as we drift away, He re-redesigns the next best path for us that maneuvers us beyond our selfish, prideful, and fearful selves to that place He knows we belong; a place at peace within ourselves, at home within our being, lovingly compassionate and accepting of others, as well as, of ourselves – forgiven. In this new moment, we discover that God's forgiveness and Grace uncovers our destiny, which is, in fact, Here/Now to experience.

Today, the Eternal conduits established by of our newly wired neural pathways, of which we meditate God's cure, have become our New-Thought pathways. And selfless battles survived and successes enjoyed strengthen the foundation of the pathways, through our brains, to the Truth. And we are more easily at home, alive in this single moment in time, like no other time were we able to construct. Each experiential thought traveled along this pathway is a new adventure with Jesus and as vital as it may seem, it's not so scary, after all.

God's revised Will has our name on it and, if we so choose, this new Will may become our redemption from the misgivings of the past. We are forgiven and the peace we discover in our hearts is proof of His Eternal Compassion and Love.

And as we recognize an update to His Will, that we are guided Instantly to His Holy Purpose for this particular moment, we experience life with no thought of self, fully alive "In the Zone", completely Here, committed to Now. And we're intuitively convinced of the safe and simple yet glorious outcome that He knows we are readied to appreciate.

Today, remember to pray for the strength to freely hand the reigns of your life to God and pray every day for the courage to accept His Way over that of the worlds. I know without doubt, I'm at my best, when I've stopped everything in the midst of battle and cut the worldly strings with a short prayer for guidance. It might be a simple, yet powerful three-word prayer "God help me!" or I've repeated the perfect Lord's Prayer on the way into an important presentation.

We may find great relief and immediate direction in a quick release and reconnect in a simple prayerful request for Heavenly Strength and Truth.

So, try it; say a quick prayer under your breath on the way into an important meeting or before making that terrifying call to "close a deal" or "follow-up" on an important presentation. And, at least for this single moment in time, you'll have remembered and instantly connected with Him. In this quick-connect, regardless of fears or absolute hopelessness in the current situation, expect nothing and you'll receive nothing less than a myriad of miracles to be worked through you and your friends; in the quest to fulfill the Eternally Willed redirected Will God, so long ago, set into motion.

~

The battle is relentless, so we must be patient with ourselves in the winning and losing, for our memories are short and distractions catch our eyes and we lose sight of our missions and begin to take credit for our wins and the blame for our losses. We vacillate between selflessness and pride and we begin to walk our paths alone without realizing our prideful/fearful mistake and we miss-step and second guess ourselves and begin to judge our every move and mostly have forgotten to consider that Jesus is *always* here. Jesus is standing here; right here next to us whether we're ready or not.

Being Eternally un-handicapped and omnipresent, He is completely Here-Now, regardless of wherever else He is. Incomprehensible, His presence is Eternal and all-encompassing and He cannot pick and choose where to be or with whom to love? He is boundless and loves each of us, beyond our ability to understand. He inhabits every nook and cranny of our minds and He loves us – even when we so desperately try to hide our sins or fearfully procrastinate fulfilling our duties or when we can't or won't have patience with the Spiritually Logical process. A process that is sure and steady; true; timeless.

> "… Ask and it will be given to you;
> seek and you will find;
> knock and the door will be opened to you.

> Luke 11:9

We've been preached this sermon time and time again, since before we could possibly understand its import, but we mostly forget its power. And any Preacher worth his salt teaches passionately that Jesus wants nothing more than to be included in our lives, our decisions, our words, as well as our actions. He patiently waits for us to seek Him in *every* simple and worldly-magnified hardship and challenge and in those horribly lonely moments of boredom and despair; He cannot leave our side, for us to "go it alone".

So, we must consciously decide, Now and in each and every Now, to include Him or not. In this conscious recognition that we have a choice and we remember to ask – He responds. Jealous for our safety, like an attentive and loving father, He knows what we're up to, He knows our mischievous ways and convenient shortcuts to comforts; He hears our cries for attention and need for Love.

Our loving Father sees where we're headed on our journey, far in advance of our short-sighted material focus, and He knows the outcome before we take our first step. And when we drift away, He patiently awaits our emptiness; our prayers for relief from the growing-pains caused by His Nudges and Bumps ignored.

~

Yes, it's a simply natural process of living a human life; following gallantly or drifting away in pride or vanity; failing and momentarily succeeding; and asking for forgiveness and directions for the way out of our most currently feared hell. Yet, we either forget the simplicity of the "Top Two" Universal Laws or we simply ignore worshiping our Father in Heaven and loving our brothers and sisters, as do we love ourselves.

Selfishly, we struggle anxiously to provide our brain's contrived-solution to a client's needs or we exacerbate efforts to win business we are certain will benefit all concerned or we ignore the need to clear our desk at the end of the day and we race to the store or to get our kids to soccer and we fail to have time in our lives for our marriages. We get so caught up in the business of living that we forget God exists in a constant ready-state to be included in our plight for survival. At no physical cost, we may synchronize our mind with His, in a split-second of prayer.

In a single troubled thought encountered and released well in prayer – peace restored – we may breathe easier, our eyes relax, and we discover the Truth. Once again enlightened to our mission and the mission of those whom we are guided to serve we Glow again, but soon we forget to ask for Guidance and we struggle to receive the Promised Grace.

Admittedly, some days are better than others as we shine and perform well or, even better, we remember we're in The Game with Him and He's in The Game with each of us. In those times of amazing performances, we play on-queue absolutely and completely "In the Zone." And these days begin to connect with one another and our Faith grows and day after day and time and time, again and again, we begin to experience unexplained compassion and hope and dreams fulfilled. We've found success beyond measure and we discover treasures beyond ourselves, beyond our fears, and we've included God in The Game and at every chance we discover there is no such thing as chance.

~

However, when once we've "Won Big", the thrill and excitement may send our imaginations into the realm of, "Finally, it's my turn to 'Live Big!'" And the party begins and over-spending and excessive celebration places self-control and common sense at risk. We've witnessed, too many times, the price paid for self-elevation, by the despair in the face of a brother as he realizes the gift had been squandered and the hole that was dug is deepened by excuses and pride; by people who should have known better; people like us; me.

> "Our emotional highs are as high as the lows are low.
> There's no middle ground when we travel alone."
>
> Delores Dogood
> (from her book, "Bribing God for Goods")

But, it's not easy and, in reality, we shouldn't expect to master total communion with God for a few hundred billion years or so. Lucifer's fall's a prime example of how the battle continues well beyond our short-lived lives on this planet. Not only did he forget to include God, he determined that *his* great works were by his will not our Father's (sound familiar?). And the story goes, He felt whole heartedly that he had earned dominion over what he insisted were his own creations and that he, in fact, had earned mastery of Creation. By his many and wonderful God-given gifts, his amazing beauty, and creative talents he had earned the right to rule dominion and He had no need for God's "input/interference" to create through him.

He was a pretty clever guy, but talk about Most-zheimers. He mostly forgot the true source of all that is good and powerful, and his unbridled pride got him in a hell of a lot of trouble and he's caused us all a hell of a lot of pain and suffering along the way. And his chosen, deeply-embedded arrogance and conceit couldn't allow him to admit his wrongs and accept God's forgiveness even when given a chance for redemption.

And once he cut himself off from Goodness, he got angry, vengeful, and then evil; and things began to get and have, ever since, got ugly.

But, try to imagine for a moment how he could possibly forget the source of all that is good and great. We do it almost always, every day. But the guy had the ocular gift of God's Presence. He had a readymade instant connection, proximity, and access to everything Universal going for him. He had knowledge of Time and Space and the functioning of God and felt immensely loved by Him. He knows of God's goodness and witnessed the effects of His all-encompassing Love, yet he blew it.

And it, more than just a little, annoys me that he's so selfish and hurtful that to be justified, he must convince the rest of us to join him. At the same time, it scares the crap out of me; because sometimes I do. I fall into the same trap protecting that which I think I must own. My fears of loss make me angry and I passively or overtly lash out or I fearfully protect a pattern that worked in the past, yet ignores God's path to fulfill a promise made to a colleague, vendor, client, employee, or loved one.

While Lucifer's fall cannot be ignored, let's not give him the energy and attention he would like.

Agreed?

OK… Now, take a deep breath, relax your eyes, and let it go… nothing to fear… calm down… breathe... come back to "Now" … OK, here we are… we're back in God's arms, nothing to fear.

You OK? Good... we had to tackle the subject, sooner or later.

We really mustn't be so awfully hard on ourselves when we forget to include God in our ambitious creations or quick fixes to problems, which in fact, are beyond the scope of our job description or Me, Inc.'s core competencies. Caught-up in the battle for survival or recognition or due reward, our misaligned self-focus takes our good attention from God's subtle messages deliverable to guide us through the day. Or we fail to take the time to notice His presence in the eyes or face of a stranger or to see His brilliance in the simple gesture of kindness, which seems to be of no immediate consequence but reveals itself, immensely important, to whomever it was we endeared ourselves; in that precious moment in which we shared.

~

It's very easy to forget He's here for us, that we may go directly to Him for the answers – no middleman – no cost, but honest intention. While He's quite invisible and materially-unprovable, He's alive in our hearts and minds and He's also outside and within all that exists, omnipresent, omniscience, omni-omni... And while we can't physically touch Him we can personally know of His want to know and believe in us. So, how do we fix it in our minds to believe that He's really, really, really… really here, always?

Well, let's try a little imagery aerobics.

First Step: **Open your eyes wide... and breathe, two, three, four...**

We each require experiential knowledge for Faith to be sensibly explored, but short of that and not to be obtuse, when we open our eyes just a little and look at what's in front of us; we may see God's influence in the living world; in life. We needn't look too hard to see His signature in a sunrise or set, in the excited surprise in the eyes of a learning child, and in the simple acts of kindness that occur for no apparent reason. His love is as penetrating as is the defused sunlight on the cloudiest stormy day; greyness that serves to illuminate our paths through the density of Mother Nature's unforgiving storms. Take a deep breath and let me have this one; that there's a force in nature that triggers Creation and while the existence of light Creates life by triggering the chemical reactions that make us possible; let's let light be a symbol, if not the reality, of His existence and we're ready for the next step.

Next Step: **Look up... and breathe, two, three, four...**

Have you ever thought about how privileged you are to see light from the dimmest and most distant star in the evening sky? This stream of light has averted untold objects on its seemingly endless journey to hit your very own personal eye ball where it then travels onward to your brain for processing as part of the evening scene. On the next clear night, quickly pick a single very distant star in the night's sky. Don't dawdle, select one. OK? Study it and ask yourself, how did that single stream of photons happen to hit your retina and not your forehead or the ground next to you; traveling from such a faraway place; on a journey begun so long ago; now arrived at its final destination?

Now, if you take a step to your right or left and look up again and breathe... two, three, four... There it is again, same star, different stream? Surprised? OK, but this exercise demonstrates that a steady stream of light that has traveled so far to hit us in the eyeball must simultaneously travel in every direction and permeate all space spherically, completely, and is everywhere in-between; 24/7/365 since the day it was spit from that very distant star. Allow this to be a symbol of God's capacity to be everywhere, all the time, day or night, from beginning to end and beyond; a simple, yet unexplainable phenomenon. And you saw it with your own eye.

Third Step: Run and Try to Hide… and breathe two, three, four…

Find yourself in trouble and run as fast as you can, as far as you can and try to hide or dodge the suns light or the light that escaped that oh-so-distant star. Try to manage on our own and dig a hole if you must… and breathe, two, three, four… Jump in with your comfortable and surly habits and insane beliefs and willing accomplices; try to hide. Unless you learn to enjoy the smell of your ill behavior and the view of your sometimes cruel and arrogant pride – thinking that you've outwitted God – someday you'll find you've had enough and scramble for fresh air. And, once the light of day is seen, you may again breathe easy.

His light finds us when we're looking and bathes us in forgiveness and is always here, as long as we're alive; before, during, and afterwards, as well. However, if we can't recognize His expression of love from the comfort of our self-dug holes, we've lost the chance to be near Him and we go it alone; in darkness. He's reachable, nonetheless and we can't shake Him; we only lose our ability to remember Him, as we attempt to hide from love; caked in fear.

Fourth Step: Stand Naked in His Light … and breathe two, three, four…

Envision yourself covered in muck, as you've exited the confines of days or months or years in hiding in the hole so well dug. With nothing to hide stand tall, upright, stomach in, chest out, and chin up, but butt-naked. Instantly, by this act of courage, you're stripped of layers of habits and exhaustive patterns that benefit self, ahead of your duty to serve the world; first and foremost. Humbled by losing the war after years of battling demons that mask your weaknesses and improve earthly stature, you're given the gift of Light – within and without – to bathe the muck from your being and purify whom it is you are; forever. Once you're cleaned you're more easily cleanable and it's only up to you to remember to forgive and be forgiven.

~

Spiritual Logic

Bathed in the Light of God and Knowing of Him personally, you might ask, "Where is He when I need Him – if He's always here, that is?"

In those dark moments of ceaseless toil, in the tedium of mindless work or during personal strife or tragedy and when you're caught up in the struggles of living on earth how do you find a place of peace when you have it in your mind that none exists – right here – right now? How is it possible to experience peace in the Hell of a deeply troubled time? In those terrible places where even prayer can't possibly help; where's God now?

Darkening the dark, in this distorted view of life, we become comfortable in our own hell; comfortable in our misery. So how do we break free of its pull long enough to apply Faith and remember His face and promises? We're fully engulfed in this, our most current panic, our most current drama compounded by confusion, despair, and possibly depression. How do we reach for light when we're not fully self-assured that it's truly His Logic and not something we've concocted, of which we're trying to base these important life choices or financial gambits?

The answer is no secret.

We must be diligent in building our Faith and we may do this, only, by seeking Him daily to show us the way. Slowly, but daily, become well-entrenched in thoughts of goodness and selflessness. Starting today make time to develop a well-formed habit of including Him in your daily plans; well before the day begins and "the crazies" have a chance to attack your soulful intents. Each day, inch by inch, reach for Him and ask to be reminded to include Him in your today's time and space.

Faithfully remember that He guides you effortlessly through each and every task to be completed well. And your Faith grows by making a commitment to a curious and conscious search for Him, by setting small parcels of time aside in a place of peace, to clear the slate and begin anew emotionally, mentally, physically, and spiritually. In whatever means you might, make it a habit to start the day with a commitment to clear your lines of communication with God. Regardless of your failures over the past few decades, years, or moments and with no thought of the imagined and oh-so scary future, begin each day with His clear direction penetrating your mind over the thunder of your negative thoughts and that of your brothers' fear-based battle cries or slyly silent manipulations.

Seek God through exercise, good nutrition, meditation, and prayer and you've prepared your psyche and spirit for success. You've prepared yourself to humbly receive; receive the plan, the means, the way, and the God-guided direction that exiles fear to its place of non-resistance; non-existence. And the rewards run the gamut from success in the mundane; smooth sailing; or exhilarating joy in the magnificent outcomes of His promise fulfilled. By clearing the slate each day, without judgment, forgiving of yourself and others; miracles come in rapid succession or as a much prayed for reprieve rescues you from hell; in the nick of time.

~

Trust this process and you're free to show compassion in your personal and business lives. You're freed from being owned by the need to control others or defend lies; your cherished ideas. Beginning each day, with Him in your heart and mind, readies you to trust the process He's created and by which He prepares you to focus your Time-Spotter energies on being the best at that which you love and reminds you that "to serve others *is* your sacred mission." You'll be guided to serve without thought of reward, yet receive reward beyond that which is harbored by this three-dimensional fear-driven plane. In this one single day, you'll instinctively know that which you were so skillfully, uniquely, and perfectly created to be; loving and lovable.

I write this at an early hour (5:35 AM) in the pains and throes of doing business with thoughts of that which might go so terribly wrong today, that which might ruin a vital relationship and kill my most incredible business plan. How will I fulfill my many promises to clients, investors, vendors, banks, and the IRS? Yet, at the end of this day, the unknown will have had light shed upon it and I will have endured and persevered and I will have exhibited great courage and strength; an indiscernible notch above my previously unexplored abilities. For it is my will that I include God in all that I do and all that I speak. And it is my will that I abandon all judgment, need, and want and instead I reserve my will for that of His, for this one single moment in time, Here-Now; in this Eternally blessed breath. And today I pray to remember God, for His Will to become mine; a daily and constant prayer; an affirmation; if not for this well-formed habit, I'd surely pay pride's price in forgetting His Love rules.

Morning Meditation

Do not be anxious about anything, but in every situation
by prayer and petition, with thanksgiving
present your requests to God.

Philippians 4:6

Ask and it will be given to you; seek and you will find; knock and the
door will be opened to you. For everyone who asks receives; the one
who seeks finds; and to the one who knocks,
the door will be opened.

Matthew 7:7

the Hope in Entrepreneurialism

In This Instance

In Stillness

I Breathe
I Relax
I Stop

I Pray

Jesus

Father

Brother

Thank you

Abandoned of self, I am Humbled
Empty, Your Love and Light Fills my Soul
Instantly Forgiven, Eternity Awaits my Presence
In this Unique Place and Slice in Time, I am Whole
Unhurried, I Trust You to Fill the Gaps at Truths' Edge
Trusting that by Your Selfless Sacrifice my Path is Cleared
As I Trust Your Grace to Save me from my lowest thoughts
Present, in Your Presence, I Accept Salvation and Run to You

Cleansed of my sins, I've been Freed to Be Whom I am to Be
Today, I Walk Tall with You and the Holy Spirit within me
Today, We Fulfill the Father's Will, Now Here Ours
That Together We may Serve Your Children
Identifying with Your Nature, I Know
My Abilities are Fortified by You

Letting go of whom it is I think that I must be
Whom it is I must Portray or Value Proofed
Cleansed of self I Cling to Your Thoughts

Spiritual Logic

You Tell me Where to Be What to Say
Unhurried in this Moment – I Act
I Know What to Do and Why

My Thoughts Up-Righted
In Your Service, I Am

In this Place and Time, I'm at Peace in Your Arms
In Stillness, I Listen for Your Heart's Thought
As Your Love Fills me and I become Us
I View the world by Your Kind Eyes
I Hear Your Guiding Thought
Speak Your Truth, Only
Filled by You, I Act

Present with You this morning, I Prepare to Serve the World,
as would You, in this Particular Moment in Time and Place.

I Know Who I Am.

Your Loving Thought Created me

So, thank you for me, who I am!

Now, be still

Listen for the Word, the Thought

And you'll know what to do, today, and when.

CHAPTER 14

Do Unto Others

"Do not seek wealth, it will find you.
Do not seek honor, it will find you.
Seek only to serve and you've done your part."

Anonymous

Spiritual Logic

A few minutes of reflection in meditation, in the morning, connects me with God and my highest Thoughts and reinforces the power of Love over my worst "fear of the day". Stopping my mind from running wild, with its survival driven schemes, saves time and wasted energy spent in going to war to protect what I have or earn beyond my God-given abilities or defending my work designed to fulfill my fanciful dreams that self-glorify or make up for past failures.

Beginning each day reinforcing my belief in Jesus' Sacrifice that Saves us, each and All, from our every sin and that by following the Path God has meticulously laid for me, you, us, each and All, delivers me everything necessary to survive the suffering and I experience abundance, if not materially, in goodness given and received. And by living by my Trust in His Unconditional-Love for me, you, each, and All and that His Love is free of charge and in endless supply – makes the rest easy. The "rest" meaning there is no "big idea" "relationship" "material thing" "territory" or "intellectual property" that I've been blessed to steward that I'm also required to protect or compete to own; each being of God's Creation and each being replaceable or vastly improved upon, in time and space, by His Ultimate Power.

By my, your, and our "good actions" instigated by a firm Trust in the Power of God's Abundance creates a mindset that yearns collaboration and cooperation and makes the long-awaited "Love Shift" possible that in an Instant obliterates generations of institutional greed and protectionism that's killing this planet, if not the peace in our homes. Letting go of fear and trusting love makes all things possible.

In the fall of 2007, I met Jeff Tucker at his shop in Walla Walla where he engineered the remote climate monitoring equipment I wanted to take to market; sell to farmers, vintners, and orchardists. Jeff and I'd spoken over the phone for months, but had never met and when we did, I found myself looking into his soul as a friend – eye to eye; with nothing to hide. I sought to find that place in which we might be comfortable, that we each might get to the truth of the matter; beyond who controls intellectual property, territory, and customer base; as we so often volley for control in business.

Without planning how I would engage him in our first meeting, when we finally met, we'd both been "Alpha-Dogged".

If you hadn't heard of it, there's a method used by dog trainers to take control of a situation with strong-willed misbehaving dogs (such as we might become) where the trainer establishes himself as the "Alpha-Dog" – the one in charge. When a dog attempts to take control, the trainer states a one word command and proceeds, firmly, to lay the dog on its side. Once the struggle is over and the dog knows it's not going anywhere, the trainer asserts authority by laying his chest over the dog's shoulders and, depending on the size of the dog, his arms and legs might cover the dog completely. He firmly holds its head in place with a solid grasp around the back of its neck, as the mom's paw to its pup's head. The dog must be held absolutely still with full control of its movement until it no longer squirms; for sixty seconds or so. He then releases the dog slowly, but won't let it rise from the floor until a command "Up" is given.

Now, the dog has met "the boss" and been properly programmed to submit to the Alpha Dog, of which the trainer has established himself.

Have you noticed in families and in business how we line up with those whom we want to control, maybe not quite that dramatic; men and women sprawled across conference room floors or at dinner meetings, arms and legs flailing in a fight to control one another. But we've witnessed the sometimes subtle, sometimes passive aggressive, sometimes blatantly combative process, nonetheless. We've had it done to us and most likely attempted it on others, but what I experienced that afternoon with Jeff, in that moment we first met, was absolutely unlike any flagrantly controlling method of defusing human ego that I'd ever experienced.

As I walked in the door to his workshop and approached Jeff as I normally would, I peered into his eyes as if looking into the eyes of a brother, but for some reason held contact for a fraction of a moment longer than is normally socially acceptable by business associates who have no romantic interests in one another. I gave him time to know me and me to likewise know him. In that shared moment in time, as I reached to shake his hand to assure him, customarily, that I was carrying no weapons, I noticed he was unarmed as well and we allowed each other into one another's soul, through our eyes; beyond the smiles.

The experience wasn't a conscious attempt to control the situation. On the contrary, it allowed the situation to be as Jesus would direct it without either party taking charge or requiring control. Without effort, Jeff's and mine strong egos were peaceably disarmed we immediately went to work. That was the "game change" moment in my career in ag technologies.

By giving up control and getting out of the way; selfless and trusting; a friendly relationship took form between his engineering and programming and my marketing and sales business. This collaboration, begun that summer in 2007, four long – very long years later, led me to align with the similar interests of Cecil Rock, the President of a Saudi Arabia company with US engineering based in Eugene, Oregon with proximity to Canby, Oregon where I would meet and, soon thereafter, marry the love of my life; Sue... and so on and so forth and so forth... A domino had fallen in 2003 when I moved from Utah to Washington that led to an amazing chain of dominoes that God had set up and continues to strategically place and, each, I trust to fall perfectly as they have since that day.

And as one day leads to the next, it wasn't necessary that I must be in charge of Jeff to start another business and to eventually marry Sue and that I'd continue to form Water Point in 2016; Jesus had been given the charge and we'd been Alpha Dogged, by His highest power for a higher purpose. Jesus had Alpha Dogged the two of us without a formal prayer, patriarchal blessing, or endorsement of any church... and see what happened?

You can't make this up; it just works – outside of church; mid-week; don't try to figure it out or control it and you'll see the miracles unfold, by just getting out of the way and letting your ego die on the floor of the meeting room.

CAUTION

Jeff and I forgave control of the outcome, unbeknownst to one another, and, together, collaborated on a metaphysical level, well beyond our individual creations. But there are times in life when you'll be asked to follow another or be driven to take the lead. Follow faithfully or, when you've been handed the reins and expected to take charge, as the Alpha-dog; as the human representative of Jesus; a Heavenly authorized 'man among men'; "go for it!" This is your time to shine and you'll be successful, as all parties come to an agreement and accept the Higher Good of your humble and mutually respectful leadership. And there's much more to be gained by your leadership than an ego's filled belly; pride being whisked away in collaborative work.

But do this ONLY if you're committed to allow the situation to be Spiritually right and be willing to give up control and work without whining as another submits brilliance that must be followed. Be strong and accept the role knowing that Jesus won't leave you hanging. He knows you're fully prepared to meet the challenges of leadership and He will not leave your side or the sides of all who follow His mission in service to His beloved children.

However, amid a spiritually-centered Alpha-dogging, if you waver in the face of the Great Feared Unknown, you're imminently at risk of losing to a stronger willed, earthly-experienced, and fully materially-centered Alpha-dogger. You might begin with good intentions to Spiritually Alpha-dog another then frivolously decide to do so on your own behalf by manipulating a seemingly weaker "other" and in an instant your mind exits the moment and the relationship suffers in your backhanded attempt to control another's will; another's will that is of no other humans to govern, but himself and his God's.

We physiologically grow in stature and feature when we become important by fueling our earthly grunt-machines with selfishly manipulative actions and words. And our thought-processes initiated from a more savage past begin to take charge, we become the great actor, and our propped-up ego is given charge. Yet our selfish agendas appear ugly; revealed through the shape of our eyes, as well as hundreds of uncontrollable facial expressions that alert an observant receiver of our selfish fear-based machinations that we're not being as good as our smile is so boldly working to say that we are. And the "moment of truth" is lost and we run a valid risk of being mortally Alpha-dogged, in return; and the tone of our voice is heard in a troubling minor key; less respected; doubted; uninteresting; boring – worse; resented.

> "I have never been able to conceive
> how any rational being could propose happiness to himself
> from the exercise of power over others."
>
> Thomas Jefferson

Great words; just ignore the fact that Jefferson owned slaves; but, know that he must have had a good heart. He just bought and sold human beings to do quite grueling and mindless, uncreative, and spiritually-sabotaged work at the hands of his hired "Boss-man"; a product of his time and economies. Still, his words live immortal.

If we actually think we're the Alpha-Dog in any situation and attempt to take charge by enforcing our will over others, someday we must face the choice to fight for control, succumb to neuter, or flee in fear; tail between our legs; running off into obscurity. However, if we've allowed Jesus to Alpha-Dog us and Him through us to others, it's not our creative energy, it's not our agenda or imagining, not our pushy designs; and we've nothing to control and nothing to fear in the losing; for there is no "losing" only "being".

Simply "being" conscious of God and that Jesus wants nothing more than to work through us; we become a part of God's process. Is it possible to be better at being ourselves? When vying for Him in His spirit, we've competed fairly and may be recognized for having accomplished an amazing feat or lived an incredibly charmed life. But in humble gratitude, we don't care what others find amazing or incredible; we've just done the job asked of us and might enjoy the ride along the way.

~

Our days can be propped-up by prayer, but prayer ignored, they may be filled with disaster and calamity. An entrepreneur's life is far from boring. Living outside God's meditatively delivered intuition and instilled courage to act upon the heard-messages, we quite often find ourselves living reactionary lives. Creativity dumbed by habit, we lethargically enjoy the comforts of our well-formed abilities to put out the fires lit while transacting daily business. And as these fires are cyclically set by ourselves and others, we steal time from being productive and serving a brother; distracted by the noise. Rather than boldly leading the herd to safety ahead of the first spark that might ignite into a confusing and devastating flame, we may get caught up in "crap-thought" and can't seem to climb out of the greyness. That's when we must reach into our quiver filled with guiding answers and quietly pray.

And, though you and I are certain a prayer can't possibly bring color to the greyness; for grey is grey; prayer can and does change things for the better. Remember, light is light and God's light neither may be changed to anything less than brilliant brightness nor may it be destroyed.

So, as I begin the day in prayer and meditation, especially when Sue and I pray together united in marriage, as challenges arise with our children, our work, or within our marriage and the world and in those times we're humanly convinced there's no answer; in prayer, there is. Sue and I've become wholly complete in incredibly challenging moments and, in our belief in the "power of prayer", we've been made aware of the perfect place that the Here-Now is. And the problems seem to fix themselves, as the humanly unavoidable and unfixable is Now mystically and spiritually fixed through our prayers.

But, how does prayer work?

We've been taught to pray since childhood and, out of duty or belief, we make efforts to pray our way out of messes or for another's healing. And if Jesus prayed and taught us to pray, there must be a reason to expend energy to ask for God's intercession in our lives, by these sincere requests.

A word prayerfully spoken or uttered under our breath; if it's willfully spoken, might it help somehow?

Our good thoughts and prayerful words must affect change or why the requirement and natural inclination to push ourselves thoughtfully – spiritually in prayer.

And if our prayers are answered, is the action of praying the reason for the answer? If we had not prayed would the suffering continue unabated for its absence? Would God allow the world to work its evil to its bitter ends or weave its complex webs of greed and fear-driven ways around and through us to our destruction if not for our prayers and acknowledgment of His Love and forgiveness?

If our prayers are answered and we witness something we asked to change be changed, shouldn't logic tell us that the action of praying makes us the instigators, if not the co-creators, of that mysterious change? That would make our thoughts a Thing.

> "... I tell you, whoever believes in me will do the works I have been doing, and they will do even greater things than these..."
>
> Jesus

And if we choose to use these "Thought-Things" well and for good, selflessly, we've given God's Goodness a means to work and His rewards are our prayers answered; miracles.

Remember to pray and remember that our thoughts become things, as Creation is God's direct response to prayers. The deep answer to the question of prayer might lie in the results of prayer and by our willingness and natural motivation to pray; in our request to be rescued from sorrow, suffering, struggle, illness, and danger and we may learn to do so, by thanksgiving, first.

In our quiet meditations and prayer, we're taken to a place far from hysteria into the sampling of nirvana – strategically alive deep within this particular slice in time – we may exist fully within the most relevant Universal Thoughts; the Greatest of "Thought-Things"; the Thoughts of God. In solidarity in thinking, we may ask and receive and, in the asking, the streams of goodness are directed towards our Beings and towards the Beings of one another.

The "law of attraction" winds freely between good thoughts for our lives and for those for whom we pray. Forced by our good intentions, Now, activated by the truth that another might benefit from our prayers, if we believe our thoughts are powerful, not by our will, but of our Father's goodness then goodness is directed by our God-conscious' will, as we trust the workings of this Universal flow and our prayers benefit another.

When we ask passionately compassionately – pre-instantly – our thought is known by the Universe through the mysterious channels of communication sparked by the Eternal Spirit of Truth, actuated by God, and heard by a myriad of Angels and Saints. And action begets goodness and, in reality, affects the whole. In this Holy Thought sequence, we have done our part in the achievements of mankind, in the universal growth patterns needed to make us wholly alive and He reigns dominant over our fears of loss and lack and failure – we are made whole, instead.

"What the mind can conceive and believe, it can achieve."

Napoleon Hill
(from his book, "Think and Grow Rich")

Our thoughts are powerful by every sage's instruction and admonition. But, training the mind to function well doesn't require retraining; once trained it only might fail by laziness or lessoning degrees of willpower. Train it once to improve its depth of peaceful awareness and meditation – preferably twice daily for 10 to 20 minutes per session – only adds to its ability; by incremental measurements.

~

If your thoughts are powerful and they materialize in time, propelled by will and faith, your thoughts appear to be cogs, albeit necessary cogs, in the process of Creation. And if you "get what you prayer for," isn't it a good idea to know what you want? The one way to find out what you really want, in the most personal of effects, is to begin the day in a conscious connection with God, by meditation, and you'll know.

In "stillness" ask the burning questions without fear of knowing what's right and wrong but in readiness for the answers to flow towards you and to be gladly received. In honest reception, there is no question of priorities or of how to expend and extend thoughtful energies when you're tapped to support another who is suffering or when confused about your most imminent tough decision or when you've been hit with a teaching-brick to the side of the head and feel numbness to move in any direction.

Thoughtful, without complaint or a grimacing look on your face, by material preparation in spiritual meditation, you're recharged, you're prepared to live with authority and gratitude, and more able to stop the dogs from barking in your face and fight to stop them from attacking the face of others. As you've learned to take time to give thanks and invite Christ into the conversation bringing Universal Truth with you to your work battles, with you for your clients, vendors, employees; you'll mystically hear and speak His words of hope and peace; openly, simply, and painless to all – you offer sage counsel.

But being recharged daily doesn't guarantee days full of blissful business; happy interactions and transactions the whole day long; closing deals right and left; left and right. You earn your keep by solving problems and some days you'll earn a babysitter's wage; no amount of remuneration could possibly mean enough. And we make it harder on ourselves as we weigh the value of what seems to be unproductive time invested in service and support to that time which may be invested to generate new revenue streams.

Selflessly, negotiate the swift currents of the unknown and move with the gentle Nudges that the Holy Spirit ensues you to fulfill the promise that might appear to have no immediate financial return or productivity-reward. And yet the promise kept is emotionally rewarding nonetheless; rewarding beyond payment in cash. And you'll comfortably enjoy the "Art of Serving", following selflessly, and your true character is revealed to others, but more importantly you've defeated your selfish ego-self and proven to you your Goodness.

However, there are Bumps in business that will and do cause serious pain. These are the Bumps you ignore, as you drive business ahead at full speed, refusing to listen to the marketplace or the requests from authentic clients and you react slowly to their needs and invaluable input and once again your best efforts become little more than a grey story told in fictitious colors. These manufactured stories have no honest basis and you'll have worked overtime to make up for a lazy attempt to appease the market with a rightfully abandoned solution that is merely a bandage for this day's particular case. And you might bump your head against another's to force the solution in which you've grown too comfortable, a story of a warrior fighting a war of yester years; the charm surpassed by obsolescence. And...

"You're dead to me."

Kevin O'Leary
Shark Tank

Follow your comfortable ways and expect the phone to ring and for your stomach to churn in apprehension of the inevitable screech of a pissed-off client for whom you have no credible answer for shameful laziness or misrepresentations of abilities hampered by an old road traveled poorly and to nowhere.

~

The Truth is quite often too difficult to face and ignorance too comfortable to confront, as when you've held a firm grip to life's controls and know you're right and insist on providing proof that it's so. Yet, as you may become more practiced at staying in tuned to the Will of your inner Christ, by daily meditation and prayer to accept His, sometimes uncomfortable, Bumps and Nudges you'll move more easily and Instantly with the flow of these Universal desires. And you'll do so more and more easily by the remedy of perfection in repetition in making His spiritual connection a singular focus of your drive throughout the day.

In repetition, you're far more at ease and more successful at letting go of your self-righteousness and more able to accept the unexpected; more able to accept the Truth for at least this day. You'll discover peace in living within the mind of Jesus and notice you're Graced with an inordinate ability to work with the Truth that, Now/Here, powers your ambition. With repetition of consciously seeking time with Him, you'll more intently serve another with a better version of yourself and you'll more easily ask better and more pertinent questions and speak words of truth not conjured by selfish dreams and you'll do so without self-serving editorial or monologue.

Set your desire for the best outcome for your clients and you move freely without an agenda, rather a real desire to serve. Light shines through your being as you ask probing questions ignoring the natural, yet spiritually-opposed thought, "What's in it for me?"

The miracle of meditation repetition is in its incremental growth; growth in awareness that happens when – one upon another – each meditation practice encountered feeds the next with increased ease in connection and benefit in depth of peace. And you'll find that, quite often, you more easily espouse great edicts and prophetic utterances filled with simple and amazing wisdom and Universally governed directions fall from your mouth and you experience great courage and strength from a place in your being, well beyond your mortal/ego ability and design; but only by acceptance of God's Will; without resistance.

And you'll find yourself needing time to absorb the beauty of the words uttered or the calamity eloquently endured and in that moment, you'll have a chance to share success in fulfilling a Will of which you had no previous knowledge existed or envisioned possible. Time and time again, as you learn to accept your singular rolls in Jesus' Game plan, you experience an unearned sense of peace in your being during times of intense conflict when, otherwise, surely you might've crumbled and fallen and now you're amazed that you were not, just now, left for dead.

~

"Selfless" agendas manifest openly your interest in another's life to the point you'll honor another's abilities, acknowledge another's input, and set a place at the head of the table for another without competing or proving your equality or most-worthy place in the lead. In this particular or is it "peculiar" moment, if you take a back seat, you may find it easier to allow another to have a say and contribute substantially when, in reality, you'd much rather make the rules for yourself, be heard appreciated and admired, and control the entire process on your own terms.

When you're true to the moment and share the stage with another and realize the world isn't so bad after all, you're on your way to finding real peace in the journey to succeed in life, cooperatively rather than competitively. The truth is, God made all of us capable and fully able to be happy and most people most of the time are friendly and find joy in helping others overcome struggle; even tragedy. So, in this and in each particular moment in time, "Now Here Place", selflessly driven, you're freed of self-thought and have the clarity to determine what the "truth is". Freed, exponentially by time in meditation, you're Spiritually prepared to be acutely accurate in discernment of another's agenda and issues.

As you become more accepting of others brilliance, place, and pains, you'll find yourself in broad associations and drawn to people of very like minds, interests, and capabilities that may emerge from vastly different backgrounds and, at times, from many and faraway places and times. In this great miracle-expectation, great things begin to happen in these sometimes odd and, often, all-too-brief associations.

> "Most people happily help.
> A few deliberately hurt.
> Unfortunately, the latter are shocking...
> ...they make the News and drain our ambition."
>
> Delores Dogood

On the other hand, there are those times when we come face to face with people whose job it is to cause pain; those who might seem to savor friction of which they are the cause. I'm not speaking of full-blown evil, but pressing its borders; these are our so called tough-customers, insensitive strangers, and self-acknowledged jerks. However, when we view the moment shared with these folks, from the "Sky Box", from that higher perch, we see them as human and cannot hate them or become angered by their insensitivity, their broadcasted stupidity, or blatant disregard for peaceful resolutions. On the contrary, from this Higher perspective we instinctively fight fairly and are forced to grow in character much faster than would we have otherwise, had we not been confronted with, what appears to be, destructive behavior.

Sometimes we're forced to grow at light-speed, as when friction is faced squarely it's of greatest value to our growth. It forces us to immediately seek and accept the truth about ourselves and the situation we together inhabit. Our friends and allies wish us their best and they prefer to cooperate in our success rather than compete. Yet our toughest customers, employees, partners, and bosses; especially the brutally honest ones may teach us much more about ourselves than might we have possibly liked to learn. And from a Higher perspective we understand that they are our brothers and sisters nonetheless and whether we like them or not, at this moment in time, they play a key role in helping us become that better person we know we are meant to be.

~

What if we looked at each instance, good or bad, as just another place from which we may learn to serve another and to thoughtfully grow our character, by the lesson faced squarely? In the spirit of selflessness, whether we deem an interaction as good or bad is of no concern, if we make time to help another; free of judgment; free of charge, we each may win.

I found most of the following in the Urantia Book and paraphrased some to offer a simplified take.

> *If a man is drowning and we know he is within reach, wouldn't we swim out to save him? And isn't a man's soul of value, as well? In those moments he has chosen to treat you poorly, when you're taken for granted and overworked, unjustly accused, lazily misunderstood, or publicly betrayed; for your sanity, you must step back and take in a broader, more spiritually objective view of the situation. Since you truly know kindness and are entrusted with truth, look at the situation as it may be attributed to God's doing that we are each put together for a reason? You may be in a place to be the catalyst for change in the heart of an otherwise brittle or hard minded man. And the good in you is given a chance to overcome the evil that lies within his intentions; that you each might learn valuable lessons from the interactions that are led by the Spirit of Truth to endure.*

Maybe just as difficult to digest or enact...

> "The beginning of love
> is to let those we love be perfectly themselves
> and not to twist them to fit our own image.
> Otherwise we love only the reflection
> of ourselves we find in them."
>
> Fr. Thomas Merton

Mindfully-perceived views from the Sky Box, having been experientially-inoculated from laziness and pride, filled with life-tested anti-ego spiritually fortified character traits and attraction to selflessness, you'll smile more broadly and more easily see a brother for whom it is that he is. And nothing, except blatantly smug iniquity, is so serious that it might stand in the way between you and your ability to wrap your soulful arms around him to bring comfort and honesty to an otherwise unbearably tense situation.

Without condemning or criticizing another for their fearful words or laziness displayed, these drawdowns from charm and good character are defused and you're prepared to admit your own mistakes, as well as forgive or otherwise come to an interim, if not long lasting, consensus that allows for discovery of truth and lasting acceptance of another's core goodness. And each of us may grow experientially and find a peaceful path to travel. From that point of discovery, whether you choose to travel separately or share a berth together is of no concern, if it's peaceful and for the betterment of the whole; which, from an Eternal perspective, is for the betterment of you, for us, each, individually, completely.

As we each learn to accept others for whom it is that they are, investigate the story behind their eyes, accept their role in even the briefest of encounters, and allow them into our lives; our life-accomplishments become a "We did it!" rather than "Look at what I did!"

Exploring who that person is seated across the conference table becomes more valuable to the process than selling your ideas or pressing for fulfillment of a personal agenda. When you seek to understand another, you'll realize you're OK with or without your ideas being paraded or championed or their cooperation being earned or bought and living in the moment is your one and only true agenda. In this moment, all is forgiven, accepted, and life can be lived fully and the group's agenda may instantaneously evolve to that of God's, as together you agree to drop your guards and explore the truth in this particular moment.

~

And we all win, whether in business or in personal associations; for each move made forward towards peace, goodness, and fulfillment of God's agenda benefits the whole of society and of life on this planet; for our families and for each of our brothers and sisters, as it is and will forever enriched by mindful goodness. While Jesus wants *us each* to win, He's taken no sides in the battle to survive and succeed financially beyond our fears.

In the battles, we fight, realize that, while each of us holds a very special place in His Heart, individually we're not exceptional or special in comparison with ANY other person in the entirety of humanity. We each are the most beloved in His creation; none may be more beloved than is the next. Eternal Love doesn't work that way.

Understanding the depth of "being equal in God's eyes" helps us downplay and disregard our fellows' unrealistic over-expectations and cultural needs to out-perform our past best efforts; as they'd expect of us. Whatever it is another person expects of us or expects us to be or what we should have accomplished by this stage of our life; under, over, and above our promises to God; is not important nor is it 100% in line with Jesus' version for us.

You're at our best when you ignore another's expectations and stop the wheels from churning in your mind that would have led to a shallow defense of personally and Holy inscribed activities. By appeasing another for fear of mishandling their needed approval, you might accept a quick compromise to a Bumped task to do and be Good and with an elaborate and clumsy scheme backed by selfishness and pride or fear of failure you might choose to work overtime and over-promise your ability to perform. In this extra work, the attempt to gain approval of the spiritually-blind, you exit the moment and betray a promise to serve in hopes you're appreciated for your work, when no amount of effort might be appreciated in whole; in a spiritually dearth reality.

By staying in Jesus' Way, you need defend nothing; procrastination is put off for another day as you act decisively; Now. Now/Here, you move with ease and confidence within the Spiritually Logical flows of life. Your thinking clings to Godliness as it's adjusted by your private thoughts fortified by well-forming habits of letting go in thoughtfulness. Selfless, you are non-judgmental, non-resistant, and non-cooperative with another's destructive fears. In this quest for truth and happiness, your soul is perfectly in line with that person God created you to be and, in this perfection, except for distractions strewn by the jealous is there anyone so pure that they might judge you less loved?

For all is well when you are true, even in sadness and despair you may find forgiveness, grace, reverence, and peace within the Truth found within yourself; the Gift recognized in this Here and Now.

~

So, we each play an important role in each other's success. Only by including and supporting one another, as would a good teammate, may The Game be played well. Untold friendships are here to be made from the simple acts of kindness and understanding that we experience in cooperation and by playing well in the world of business. For in the world of business, God's created a natural venue by which He might express Himself to All, as we forge sometimes lifelong alliances and friendships through acts of charity, kindness, understanding, and support in the course of doing business. From this Most High mindset, the rewards are great, many, and far reaching.

As a bonus, just for you, and Today only... as we come to understand that God is our one legitimate and ultimate source and single reliance in all that we succeed in business and in our personal lives, the two lives we lead become indistinguishable in the ways of our beings. From the "pews" to the so called "real world", there is no intentional difference in our agendas and we find ourselves more easily able to support another during the trying times, moments of exhaustion, and in those exhilarating exchanges and happenings experienced while playing The Game at our peak levels. And the truth is more easily accepted, more quickly accepted, and more often appreciated.

> Universal Laws are naturally enforced universally
> by the Nature of God.

God's Loving Compassionate Nature naturally enforces the Universal Laws; "That which we do for a brother we, in fact, do for Him, thusly, ourselves"; a quickened circular benefit to self. And the converse is true regarding that which we might choose to omit or discolor. The truth is; words matter and we're all on the same team. The responsible word spoken well often prevents calamity that may have required a lifetime to repair. And the word of praise and support that initiates another's thought to greatness is a common result.

But, in envy or primordial fear-driven competition, we each pay for the other's mistakes. In contrast, we're rewarded as we might glow in another's success, as we each benefit by the cooperative unified structures and selflessly supported business processes developed and followed collaboratively.

We've been thrown together into a giant pool of water called "living on earth". And we're fighting an unending war between man's ego and God's Truth and when we extend that inner war outside, to fight amongst one another, the stir creates waves that affects the whole lot of us and destroys the ease of living; beauty and comforts of successful interactions lost. When we fight amongst ourselves, the waves might become rough as whitecaps and when the cyclical, yet unpredictable storms hit, it's exponentially more difficult to keep our collective heads above water.

What is it that brings us to the point of declaring war? At war, we struggle to tread water in this selfishly created storm with our hands around one another's throats; neither may survive; wholly, again.

Trusting God's goodness and appreciating the breath we're given, in gratitude for these simple moments in Eternity, our minds slow from the rush to succeed, create, and to protect that which we've created and we notice the blessings in the material world surrounding us and we may live more peacefully; be more productive and Creative, listen with more compassion, and share our true selves with more understanding towards one another's well-treasured seemingly "special stories".

Being of the same species and on the same team – genderless – without discernably Special spiritual-status, creed, or race – we must be supportive of one another's growth. Hold one another accountable to make the best of our talents and we together may thoughtfully enjoy one another's hardships and pain; lessening the terrible impacts on happiness. Together selflessly, we are instantly forced to be nothing less than spectacular, in this particular moment in time. And with an acknowledged love and respect for the other guy, the oddball, the great one, or the awkward dork (of which we share his pain, secretly known by personal experience) together we win.

If we'll remember we're in this battle together, we may more easily remain calm and thoughtful and less dramatic in our attempts to defend our versions of truth. We neither attack failure nor protect success nor do we selectively love only those who are like us; then exclude, corral, or kill the rest. We recognize and appreciate our brothers and sisters for their talents and struggles recognizing that we're here on earth doing the best we might with our inborn weakness and limitations and seemingly justifiable fears. Compassion embodies us and we refuse to kill the so-called evildoers or fight today's enemies "to the death".

A mind molded by meditation and prayer to forward the agenda of peace may calm the waters and peace has a chance to survive and to flourish beyond our human stupidity; replaced by simple Love.

The Trouble with Children

APRIL 2013

I'd taken Matthew out of school a day early for Spring Break because of the desperate emotional stress he was suffering. We drove from Wenatchee to Portland to be with Sue for Easter weekend. It was Good Friday and the first sunny day in Portland for months and was Bumped to go down to the waterfront to see if Matt could earn a buck singing and playing the guitar. Who knows, he might be "discovered", was my thought.

Well, Matt had just tuned up and playing a Jack Johnson song when two news reporters flocked to him for an interview; the NBC affiliate reporter saying, "Fox discovered Jack Jr." and she wouldn't try to "steal him" ...

How does this happen?

Angels are working all around us, just listen to the guidance, the mini daydreams that enter your mind telling you where to go and what to do.

So, that night, Matthew was on the Portland, Oregon, Channel 13 News – spirits lifted, hope reignited. But, he'll tell you that the message delivered/received at church on that Easter morning impacted him the most. Returning to Wenatchee to finish his sophomore year in high school... a changed person, somehow; a hopeful life-experience added to his soul.

CHAPTER 15

The Responsibility of Knowledge

"I look forward to a future in which our country
will match its military strength with our moral restraint,
its wealth with our wisdom,
its power with our purpose."

John F. Kennedy

To "love one another" is God's simplest request to each of His children, yet an act that is immensely complicated and interfered with by the socially accepted lies of greed and envy and fear of possessions lost. So, we protect ourselves from each other and forget simple acts of kindness from a source of Love. God wants for our happiness, each equally, universally and has branded our hearts with love, endowed us with unique talents, and deeply forged willpower. He grants us access to opportunities, daily, that are Eternally customized to provide for our families and lead us to productive and fulfilled lives. However, life tempts us to take the "easy way" with diversions that, ironically, lure us away from His simplest designs for our success.

And there are real forces at play in this world that do not favor fair-play and Goodness nor do these forces attempt to take on a disguise that shields us from being gelded by darkness.

Associating and accepting the storyline of these forces makes us accomplices in their nefarious schemes to control the growth of Jesus' simple mission, that we love one another.

It's a choice we make hourly, if not moment by moment; to exist Here-Now in closeness to God or choose to follow the darkness within attracted to the world's glitter. And we become collectively or personally oppressed by those who've become addicted to the social-bling afforded by their stations in life; financial, ministerial, political...

We silently allow dark oppression, fully aware that the oppressors are oblivious to scarcity of which we, the masses, experience in our fundamental daily survival-needs (safe food, pure water, affordable housing, equal access to education and health care, etc.). And we, the unimaginative and placated masses, us each and all, are the willing tools of the oppressors, as the oppressors soar upward unobstructed in their fantasy of ever increasing wealth, as we bob for apples – toothless.

We, the tools of darkness, have become fat in our class-comforts and unworthy of the oppressors' affection; for we are lazy and lessor, in their eyes. So, evil grows unrestricted within those who horde control and that steal unclaimed shares of God's greatest gifts; free and equal access to life, liberty, and the pursuit of happiness.

Do you remember the "economic downturn?" also known as, *"the mortgage and market crisis of 2008 ignited by years of slack government oversight accompanied by deregulations that allowed banks to broaden financial service offerings beyond chartered institutional natures and where money managers on Wall Street perpetrated and perpetuate criminal activities that led to the crisis and will lead to the next; with no common sense accountability for their treasonous activities against their clients, the state, our nation, and the world; rather rewarded with public monies to keep their financial injuries from becoming infected and 'spreading' even deeper in the open wound."*

Yes, that one; where small businesses, marriages, and families writhed under great financial pressures, of which we consumers insist we had no role; we were duped; we're innocent stooges. Yes, that one... in which we each did play an important part in over consumption, overspending, over charging, over indulging... And the resulting and quite surprising "pumped up panic" which justified shareholder's raiding of pension funds and the renegotiation of retirement benefits to accommodate business continuation stripped the trust and hope of our elders' comfort through retirement; now forever shaken, if not lost, to feed the fervor of money-manager's bonus structures; as if these money managers had anywhere else to go, if not bonused; the great canard of '08.

Yes, that one! You remember...

But did you forget our Vets? How often do we think of the physical and psychological pain, incredible unknown loneliness, and hidden emotional troubles faced by our oft forgotten soldiers; men and women who've made it home from the Middle East's terrible wars; wars fought against un-uniformed armies of "enemy combatants", fueled by opposing ideals; ancestrally formed family armies impossible to fight without swelling an increased hatred towards Westerners and our ideologies.

And our Vets return home not exactly in their right minds or anatomy, not the same as when they left. They find themselves betrayed by our Government's insistence on the "necessity of war" and overwhelmed by the broken-promise to provide healing in the form of Veteran's benefits. And thousands of our suffering Vets are left to suffer further; to fend for themselves in a sea of mishandled paperwork; in the Mariana Trench of lost files; deeply crevassed wounds to the soul, mind, and body fester untreated and suicide is a sad commonality.

Those of us who stayed home from war are changed persons, somehow, today from whom it is that we were before the wars began; for better or worse, time changes us. And we may only imagine how dramatically estranged we might become to our previous identity if our daily normality, for those many years, was to survive the ugliness of war.

To know the smell and sounds of a dying brother or sister; how might that change a reflexive physical and emotional response to the sudden crack of a slamming door or how might we cope with the resume-challenges discovered, as we try to re-normalize our identity and resume our war-interrupted career path?

These are times, of which we cannot forget the suffering. Yet, our families and we as a people, in general, follow blindly as our political leaders pass and enforce laws with horrifically selfish, arbitrary, greedy, and egocentric agendas; sometimes masked, but mostly abhorrently and blatantly paraded; the means to reelection and we're too lazy to do anything about it. And our law makers and administrators are well informed of the source of these protectionist directives; directives devised in the boardrooms of powerful Corporations, skillfully and quite deliberately converted to law through favored legislation, administered by the corporate hired guns who now work in the Federal and States' governments, and these corporately instigated laws are upheld as constitutional by our country's Highest Courts?

And we say nothing???

Conspiracies; not theoretical, but blatant and if each of us were asked to give up Cable TV or lattes "for life" to pay down our country's debt or if a military draft were imposed on all able-bodied 18-year-olds, to fill the ranks in the front lines of the desert or terror wars, wouldn't we have railed against the conspirators; risen in protest with more vigor against these home-grown evildoers? If milk and bread disappeared from the shelves, wouldn't we rail against, with more passion, the greed and offensive bonus payments made to executives and money managers, as Corporations hold billions if not trillions of dollars in untaxable cash?

But the shelves in the stores *are* filled with goods and we allow our government to accumulate, for us, 20 trillion in debt. It's great, though, as we're not each asked to endure the pain of repayment, as payments are forwarded to our children and to theirs; accumulating at One Million dollars per minute... hard to fathom.

Sadly, money is the fuel that drives the course of governing and, per the Congressional Research Service report of July 17, 2012; the top 10% of our households control roughly 75% of the wealth in the United States, of which the top 1% controls 35%. The middle class has shrunk, while the rich get richer and access to wealth is made more difficult by laws devised by a well divided and partisan legislature that serves no constituency other than those that keep them in office; the money-men.

"To be re-elected."

... in answer to this question posed to Senate Majority Leader Harry Reid's Assistant in a Daily Show interview, May, 2013:

"What's the most important job of a member of Congress?"

As a whole, we are a placated society with over-filled bellies and 200 channels on TV and virtually nothing to watch, so we do nothing but complain to one another in our coffee shops, at work, and at the bar; as we each watch the favorite news channel supporting our well-healed beliefs and the couch is far too comfortable to leave in protest.

Like swinging a bat at ghosts, we've accepted that no human effort might force needed change; money is too powerful a force and we in the 90%, with only 25% of the available cash/assets, are too scattered to rally real-change. We foster too many important agendas; global warming, changing laws that allow for gerrymandering, buying political offices to forward corporate agendas with laws to limit campaign financing, placing life-time limitations on elected legislators and appointed officials from corporate lobbying, setting term limits of elected offices, enforcing regulations to protect food and drug markets, endless funding for a spiritually-insane industrial war complex, campaign finance reform, global warming, immigration reform, as well as campaign finance reform...

Really! Pick one. It's tough. That's why progressives appear insanely scattered and conservatives simply just say "No" and appear steady and level.

So, except for the professional yellers on both ends of the political spectrum; the loud spitters of lies whom we believe simply because they say the same lie repeatedly with ever more fervor; therefore, it must be true; we, the mostly sane in the middle keep to ourselves and hope, "it will all soon go away." But, it won't without shedding light on the lies with the truth. Remain quiet and we protect Corporations' ability to control the world's natural and human resources that fuel and reward well protected political agendas. And our legislative, judiciary, and administrative Corporately endorsed "tools"; our entrusted "not so trustworthy" Representatives are more able to cement the Corporations' current power structure and we seem to have little, if any voice in the process.

~

Yes, the problems we face are complex and with seemingly infinite levels of darkness that fuels a warming planet, wide-spread malnutrition, and human and drug trafficking. Yet, God's answers are not complex. He wants for our peace; for our success; for our happiness, individually and as a whole; globally. He loves us each and all, but His interest is not in sustaining wealth for a few who insist on maintaining earthly power. So, why do we abdicate the truth to the "official liars" and allow a few to rein havoc over us? As a society, if we will exchange thoughts of fear for that of love, God will take over and lead us out of this incredible financial, ecological, and political mess we've created for our Country and the planet earth.

Remember, we the people *are* the corporations to which we abdicate power, as we cast our ballots in our every choice made to consume products and services. That which we choose to purchase and how often are the two most powerful votes we might apply to trigger change. And while there is much work to do, God does not expect you and me to repair the damage alone. He waits patiently for each of us, singly, to come to Him and together work for Him; nonresistant to Corporate/Legislative power, but fueled by His Eternal Knowledge, Wisdom, Understanding, Counsel, Intuition, and Courage. Fully engaged in this single moment in time and enveloped in His totality of selfless Thought, our actions and words are felt beyond the gravitational pull of pride, greed, and fear.

Alive and engaged, wholly, in this moment in time in being true to the moment, we become the outward reflection of God's Will. As we choose to Will Him a place of honor as the source of our truth and Heavenly-Nudged-duty; today we give Him a platform from which to deliver messages of Hope and Love. And there are many of His assembled soldiers of truth; brothers and sisters; selfless believers within the corporate and government bodies who quietly and humbly chose to fight this battle on earth against the dark forces of pride and selfishness;

against forces that would erode hope and dreams and firmly instill fear in its place.

These spiritually-directed soldiers of God do not make the news. They are not ugly. Their attacks against evil are not vicious. They lead humble lives of nonresistance and love and the battles they wage are not horrifically sensational. They appear comparatively benign influences in their cool non-resistance to fearful battle-cries of the entrenched. And there are hundreds of thousands, if not millions, of these earthly angels on every continent whom we may join in this strategic and somewhat terrifying Game of Money.

~

This Game of Money is played on many dimensions by forces that vacillate between humility and pride; good and evil, of which we may choose to play a conscious or unconscious part. We are born good and may begin our earthly careers rich in hope and with high ideals of changing the world for the better, but with enough time in the frontline's trenches, many are discouraged and become embittered from the callousness and duration of the battle that seems never ending and quite impossible to win.

So, we quite often choose the path of least resistance and join and support the notion that those in power should and must remain in power so that a comfortable life is not disrupted. And business as usual is the lazy way and we become the "other side", as we agree with the status quo in our weekly "shopping circle" to Safeway, Target, and Home Depot. Sure, we may be grateful to the ease of access to the world's resources turned to goods that keep us fed and cozy, at all costs.

However, these costs are too real to "the suffering", masked by physical separation in distance or simple disinterest that we ignore. The human and ecological expense required to create and fill the shelves in the stores and eventually our closets and secured storage units goes unknown without a thought ventured.

Glimpses of our past high ideals and social benevolence may stream through our thoughts from time to time and bring guilt to a simmer for the bad we now endorse, but more often than not, we've given charge of the world to the "money men" and our rage for justice is not brought to a boil.

Or...

We may choose a seemingly more tortuous and progressive path as we mature spiritually and tire of the earthly game and choose to challenge the world's view and enter The Game of Money, as a teammate with our good brothers and sisters and do so from a spiritual framework. We may choose, at any moment regardless of the most recent success or failure, to relinquish control of the outcome of The Game to God. And if we view this battle as a Spiritually Logical game between us and our ego-selves instead of us and them, and it's a Game God wants us each and all to win, assume He wants to be included. So, begin in prayer and join the quietly Bumped Numbers of the invisible and faithful players and take responsibility to act as His conduit of love and hope, in behalf of the hurting, unfairly persecuted, and the unknowing; "the forgotten".

~

It takes six (6) contacts in either direction to sway a Representative's non-pre-purchased vote. So, next time you're pissed-off about the direction this government is headed, pick up the phone and let your voice be heard – every time. And now, in this crucial moment, with God in the Game, let's ask Him to guide resolution to our challenges and strengthen our goal-line stands and allow Him to take over as a player/coach; the role He forever wants to take, but requires only the slightest invitation to accept.

Now, we may be instilled with the appropriate level of courage to make the terrifying "stand" that settles each of our personal and public accounts and we make "the stand" that says, "We're ready to follow God at all costs."

But, how do we guarantee a spot on the Team when we either deem ourselves the "best that ever was" or insist, "I'd rather do it myself" or on the other hand we think ourselves unworthy, inadequate, or incapable of such important work. With these chains around our ankles, how do we run? How do we expect to complete these incredible plays Jesus would have us run in this Game? And these plays become of higher import as our character grows and as we gain valuable life experience that proves our ability to perform beyond ourselves; ever more calm and sure in the midst of intense and insanely difficult life-defining situations; He gives us more and more significantly difficult situations to survive.

When we step aside, we realize that the glimpse of success we experience is but a mere sample of the grandness He holds in store for us. But, how do we begin to trust our abilities to the extent that Jesus does? ... that we might begin to fully realize His limitless desire for our human growth, being the humans we are, and that we might succeed beyond our deep fears of inadequacy, betrayal, rejection, loss, and lack.

Pray!

Yes, pray! And the most powerful prayer may be the simplest; in confusion or desperation say, "God help me!"

And in prayer and meditation, we find a personal communion with God for the truth in this day, we forge our obligations in our hearts, and know our paths are real and true.

~

I've learned a few things in my frenetic chase for the dollar or efforts to do my part in the "great repair". And I pray that God, will keep me on the Team and in The Game and that I'll be mindful of these simple, yet spiritually obvious discoveries found in my search for wealth that money cannot buy; manipulation cannot earn. I pray to remain close to Jesus and that I remember these few absolutes:

First, I'm naked when I'm scared. Not that naked is a bad thing, but I'm definitely not comfortable when I'm naked (scared) in public. And the reason I'm scared is that I think it's up to me alone to master The Game and supply the answers on my own; alone. By alone, I mean to speak of those moments I've forgotten to include Jesus and I've determined that my way is my only choice and I've neglected to include the strengths of my brothers and sisters in our combined quest for personal success and that of a healed planet. And I'm quite visibly shaken.

Secondly, I'm never alone; you're right here with me and Jesus is right here with us. This realization, has been the most difficult for me to accept, yet the most profound; you're here with me and we're in this together and I can only pray that we're appropriately clothed (fearless).

All we have is Now, today, and the only place we may exist is Here. Regardless of the past and unaffected by what has yet to occur, there is no other moment that counts than Now and no other place than Here. In the "Here and Now," we are forgiven and forgiving, loving and loved, and we coexist in the Eternal Hope and Truth that is God.

The dream I've conjured in my mind that defines my life fulfilled falls well short of Jesus' version of success for you and me, my Company, employees, shareholders, and for that of my family. My creation pays for things the importance of which is lost in space and time, while His creation is Eternal, beyond mortal sight. It is Eternally tangible.

Finally, when I walk in Jesus' sandals next to another whom, as well, walks in His Holy sandals and together we determine to negotiate and intertwine our plans to investigate and serve the world, there's nothing to fear. There is no human to fear, as we remain nonresistant to lies and trust in Him, only, and determine to work as part of a Global and Universal Team to fulfill our Father in Heaven's Will. And that goes back to being fearless; clothed in private as well as in public; clothed in Jesus, remembering Him and living that courageous life that chooses selflessness over immediate needs, inclusion over exclusion, and love and trust over fear, doubt, and denial.

~

Globally, if not nationally, we're minnows, yet in the more immediate worlds in which we live and may affect change we are big fish and our small moves towards goodness and fair play create waves that influence others who sit on the fence of selfishness and selflessness and may instigate greatness unknown when good sense is adhered. And with all that I think I've learned, it's difficult for me to get out of the way and stick to the Game Plan when I'm faced with the gnawing and the seemingly endless pains of operating a small business. I become lost as the fear of losing everything creeps into a sales presentation or when I've surpassed projected expectations and pride and vanity stroll through the playing field, arm in arm, with their heads held high and I can't keep pace with my ego's stories of its singular most grand greatness. And I'm the instigator of anger in hurried pursuit that my highest expectations be met; directed by greed or the greatest fears of lack.

This I know; my great ideas and client recommendations are suspect when I submit to mine or another's fears and I honor the view of men who would build fortresses around their success with giant motes; alligators on patrol to protect them from the army of demons created in their minds; demons prepared to loot from them, their pots of gold. And I lie to myself in my laziness to energetically explore the amazing truths to be uncovered in each Now or to faithfully confront, with them, their fears and shed light on the emptiness of shame and fear of shame they've allowed themselves to entertain and that flourishes unrestricted within their souls.

So, who can I trust to be true, if I can't trust myself to remain empty and filled with the Spirit of Truth that I know without a doubt trumps all fears? Why do I walk on spiritual egg shells with a client, when I know the Truth is Here-Now to be had; side stepping inclusion of the natural force of all that is good? Omission of the truth is a lie, so it's true that I live a lie when I exit the moment and cling to the path man insists is the way to safety and security for our families.

It's true that I lie when I betray, unappreciated/untrusted, the odd and sometimes irritating Way God's Grand Scheme leads me to explore. I stop His Will from endangering my plans for greatness, forgetting my most treasured learning that to act Now, in this moment in time, is all we are asked to do and success is a natural outcome to following Him. Living well within His means is much less complicated than going to war with another to fight for my esteemed share. Yet, I have, will, and do.

I awaken each day intending to have a great day and to do and be good, but I'm only mostly good and sometimes ignore or mock the truth, cower in fear in the face of opposition, or otherwise lie out loud. I'd like to think I come from a place of selfless service and that my intentions might even be a lot honorable, but you nor anyone can know that for certain; nor can I. I've admitted that I'm able to screw things up, just as well as the next guy, so how do you discern the truth of my intentions or of those whom you might admire or wish to mentor?

Begin by remembering that we're all in this for the same reason… and doing our best to improve our little corner of the world and to exist peacefully; void of financial chaos. Tolerant of our personal stupidity and in our willingness to help another selflessly, we might exude great patience and experience depth in our peace found in the moment, as we place valued and prayerfully discerned trust in our brothers and sisters and we're less doubtful; with a "Go" from God. We're of an unhampered belief and with a first-faith in our role to serve another, first; our first-faith knows no wrong in Jesus and we succeed together in the spirit of service; first.

When we choose this most difficult path to trust in God's directives, our intuition thrives and we instinctively discern whom we may trust of the many we've been sent to serve. And The Game becomes easier to play, as we've learned to ditch those that only intend to use us and stubbornly hold tight to their knowledge, contacts, and earnings.

We've learned that The Game, played well, satisfies our material and spiritual hungers, regardless of our most previous failure or grand success, as we place our trust, first, in God. By sticking close to Him, we get a sneak peek into the Coaches play-book and it's easier to follow His lead, as we ingeniously follow the Spiritual Logic behind His guidance. And if this great Game is one we must win, and there's room for everyone, why wouldn't we choose, daily, to ask for Him to be our General Manager and Player/Coach, in this Game of Money?

***** Level Five Metaphor Alert *****

If we fall in line with God, together, as if Teammates on His football squad and trust His knowledge above ours or others, He knows exactly when and where to put us in the "Big Game". He knows the pain we've survived that's trained our body, mind, and souls to handle more and more without breaking and He knows the precise moment in which we *must* enter the Game. In this precise moment, which is unlike any other we've been prepped and we're Bumped to speak up and fearlessly say, "Put me in Coach!" "I'm ready God!"

And, of course, He puts you in.

He knows you're ready to run the play and you've put your trust in Him and He's placed His in you. And He's never let you down, even when you've become violently ill for fear of failure. But, He's been in your shoes, so He knows your plight. He's played the game on this playing field here on earth, and He's finally calling on you to run a play He knows you're ready to run. So, in the huddle; He looks you in the eye and says, "We're counting on you. Run this pattern and the ball will be there. You and I know you're ready for this." You may look at the enormity and responsibility placed in your hands and you'll become anxious, but He calmly says, "Listen to me. Trust me. Do as I've asked, run the pattern and the ball will be there."

If you truly love and believe in Him, what choice do you have but to follow Him, agree quickly with a nod… Clap your hands and exit the huddle (as seen on TV) and, with spiritually instilled vigor, run the play He's designed… in agreement, you must do everything in your power to be where He told you to be... just keep your eye on the ball, smile, and make the catch He promised He'd throw; perfectly.

His play design doesn't demand anything from us in the making only in the doing. His Thought, received, instills His vision of success in our minds – deepens the neural pathways in the brain that bypasses those old pathways. Seeing this vision from His perspective helps us trust, but it doesn't come easily, especially when it means trusting that mysterious, unknown, and invisible God. Trust is earned on both sides of "the veil," over time, through small successes in the process of trial and error; playing The Game with and without Him.

He knows us and loves us and knows exactly how difficult it is to survive the human life. So, how can we possibly believe that He'd enjoy sending us into double coverage only to wobble the pass or throw the ball to another player after making a personal promise? He doesn't. The pass is always dead on, right where He said it would be and we succeed when we follow-through and faithfully run the play He calls. And everyone gets a chance to play in the game; everyone that accepts the enlightened path.

With His guidance, I've survived the hard hits in life, quite often on opposing turf; the crowd hissing like snakes and screaming, "Kill 'im!" I've run the gauntlet of defensive linemen, middle linebackers, and safeties crowding and illegally holding and pushing, usually in double coverage – including me against myself, in the rain, mud, wind, and snow, with the sun in my eyes, sometimes sick and alone, incredibly anxious for what seems to be the great and inevitable loss-yet-to-come and time and time again I've learned to "Never give up on the play."

When I stick with the plan He's chalked-out and commit to persevere and I ignore the chants from the crowd and the self-doubt that blasts from the loud speaker in my mind... I'm amazed at my childlike belief and Knightly fortitude and courage and I win... we win... every time... just in time; like He promised. And my Faith grows today, even ever so slightly.

As we learn to trust in Him and the days turn into months and one season gives into the next and we toss another calendar on the quickly growing stack, He begins to count on us more and more to run the more challenging plays He's been eagerly waiting to call for each of us. Over time, the significance of nuance increases exponentially, yet in retrospect ever so slightly and we've gained confidence in ourselves, our ever-evolving Team of Brothers and Sisters, and in Him.

Increasingly, we find ourselves mysteriously readied to manage insanity. We've been honed; prepared in advance for what it is He has in store for us, next.

Today, we're calmer, stronger, and inherently more spiritually-coherent and humanly more confident due to our better understanding and acceptance of His role for us. And we begin to notice a piece of God's shimmer in everything we do; every stranger we accept; every glance of hope we offer. This is the life He wants for us to lead, alive, Here-Now, as we make a Heavenly assured vocal stance and take spiritually-guided action against evil and we love one another by doing so, as would He.

With the Truth realized, we call out the "evil doers" for whom it is that they are, as would He; fearlessly; knowingly; certainly, as we are who we are, by Him for Him – on earth, in His stead.

... and a stranger said, "Is your name Bill?"

May 29, 2016

Memorial Day weekend and Breona, Sue's Daughter, one of my favorite persons, came into town from Portland with two of her friends to explore the Cascades and taste a little of Washington's wine... oh yeah and join the party in Leavenworth (google Woody Goomsba – best tourism video, ever!).

Bre left work a little early, but still rolled in late on Friday night with Beatrix her Golden-doodle, who I love. Her friends came in later, and knowing it'd be tough to find our home on their first time up, I turned on the lights still up from Christmas and they'd more easily spot us, though the pear orchards up Williams Canyon. Sue and I normally get to bed early, around 9:30; 10:30 on a late night, but we always wait up for Bre when we know she's making the drive up.

Spiritual Logic

As per usual Bre was reservedly energetic when she arrived, after a 5-hour drive on top of a full day at work. We hugged, caught up quick, went to our quarters, each too spent to wait up for her friends.

Well, in the morning, I got things going in the kitchen, mixing up everyone's favorite, banana pancakes, when her friends began to stir and join Sue, Bre, and me. I'd never met either, but always enjoy meeting new people and offered them some freshly brewed coffee. I'm flipping pancakes, as we're getting to know each other, the slightly shy Amy and the more outgoing Emma, Bre's CrossFit instructor. I'm telling a story about this or that when Amy gently puts both arms around a sitting Emma and hugs her and kisses her on the cheek. And they both had a comforted smile on their faces.

OK! I can handle an open display of love and affection between gay partners, but it's not so common in my small circle of friends. I try to role with it, be cool, no one gets uncomfortable for being themselves in my house. But I'm in the middle of one of my stories and my mind misses a step, as it tries to process this interesting tidbit of additional and quite unexpected relationship info.

And I think I've been "found out" as I sputter to regain my footing. A quick glance up from the griddle to see the girls still embraced and I realize I've eluded being caught in an embarrassingly judgmental blank glance that might be uncomfortably received; of which I'm innocent on all counts.

Smiles all around....

Cool... I made it. No one's any wiser to my mental acrobatics, I landed on my feet, all but stuck the landing.

I get over it quick, breakfast is ready and we carb up for the tough hike we'd planned for the morning. Sue chose Sauer's mountain trail, it's close, only 10 minutes to the trailhead from the house, and it's a tough one. We've been staying pretty active and, at 56 and 61, Sue and I think we can keep up with the kids – we're not going to get in the way of Bre and her CrossFit instructor. Right?

Sauer's usually takes two hours to get up, power hiking, and hour and half back. We picked this trail, for the views from top. They're spectacular. You get an almost 360° view and a great reference point of where the town of Leavenworth sits in relation to our house and the canyons and mountains we'll explore over the next few days.

It was a grueling march up and back. Dusty from the hike, we make it home to get ready for wine tasting and dinner in town. That's when I discover that the girls aren't actually partners in love, but blood-sisters in love. Yep! They're sisters. I immediately told myself how crazy funny stupid I am, as I smiled and went about my business getting ready.

Our first stop was Icicle Winery, which happens to be near the trailhead of Sauer's Mountain. I was standing on the deck, sipping on a much-deserved glass of wine, gazing at the mountains reflection off the still pond surface as a group of swans mosey by and Amy pulls up and stands next to me. I don't really think the wine had anything to do with it, but I told Amy, that I didn't know they were sisters until we'd come home, after the hike. Then I said, "Amy, I thought you and Emma were gay!"

She about spits wine through her nose, as I told her about what was going through my mind, as I'm flipping pancakes, trying not to blow my cover... And you throw both arms around Emma and kiss her....

It was one of those moments when you had to be there to appreciate how funny it was, especially when she told the rest of the group and from then on, they were referred to as "Sister Lovers".

But, that's not the story.

The next day we chose Colchuck Trail and apparently so did everyone else. Yes, the parking lot was full and most were parking their cars half mile down the road. But, as per usual, persistence and patience pays off and we discovered a spot close to the trailhead. It's a 4-mile hike to Colchuck Lake and a 7 to 8 out of 10 in steep difficulty, so the extra distance to the car with my hurting leg wasn't part of the plan.

Yes, it's a tough hike, so I put my head down and hit the trail lifting my eyes only occasionally not to miss the beauty of the Cascade's forests and jagged peaks. Call it pride or challenge; I wanted to stay ahead of the well trained physically fit Sister Lovers and Bre; to not be dusted; as well as to get pictures of them on their way up the trail. And at points, I could see a perfect backdrop that'd be worth the pose-ask; too many to count.

Onward, I was able to muscle my way up the trail and stay ahead of the pack for the most part. The trail was super busy and as people would

Spiritual Logic

travel down, I'd give them room to pass and we'd smile at each other, with a brief glance into their eyes and a friendly, "Hello", we'd pass. And they'd disappear down the trail, bounding happily away, in small friendly groups.

About two thirds of the way up the trail, a rather large group appeared. They were making their way towards me and as we squeezed by one another, exchanging kindnesses, smiling generously in an expression of what a beautiful day it was to hike; a twenty-something guy pauses and asked me, "Is your name Bill?"

Of course, I stopped and answered, "Yes!" But, I didn't recognize him. I was caught off-guard. "Do I know you?" I asked.

His smiled broadened and he said, "No."

"Well, yes, I'm Bill. But, how do you know me?" I'm thinking maybe from church, as I've spoken a few times before the congregation... it wasn't that.

He went on to tell me that he prays every morning for someone, usually someone he knows comes to mind. But, that morning, when no name came to him, he asked God who to pray for and the answer came, "Bill."

"But, I don't know anyone, closely, named Bill." He says.

I quizzed him, "So, how many people did you stop and ask if their name was Bill, today?"

He says, "I'd forgotten all about it until I saw you. So, one!"

Then he says politely and respectfully, "So, is it OK if I pray for you?"

Comfortable with his presence, I said, "Ya, sure. Let's do this."

And as we stepped back off the trail and stood side to side, heads bowed, arms over one another's shoulders, my mind was a little stunned to be here on a busy trail, with a total stranger, in the middle of nowhere, and within seconds we're thrust into a very real, very deep physical, emotional, and spiritual kinship.

So, he starts to pray for me and right about then, I notice the sisters and Bre and Sue squeeze by and head up the trail and I smile with my head down, as this guy and I are praying. Weird, but I was totally cool with this impromptu prayer moment in the mountains with some guy that wants to pray for me, because he knows my name.

And he asks, "Is there anyone you want me to specifically pray for?" It was only then that I asked him his name. He said, "Matthew." And I said, "OK, let's start with my son Matt." And we prayed and prayed for everyone in my family, each and all.

And as we prayed, we were spiritually-garrisoned in our own little world on that busy Memorial Day weekend train of humans moving up and down a difficult and narrow mountain trail through the high mountain forest of the Cascades. In the incredible beauty of God's creation, two complete strangers bow their heads in an open display of private-prayer, for no reason except by God's prompting to a willing young man, who unashamedly put himself at risk of embarrassment to ask a total-stranger, "Is your name Bill?" And we each were fortified in God's glistening Grace, as we were once again instilled in the knowledge of His Plan for each, in a most "in-my-face" and purely personal way; He called me by name.

CHAPTER 16

Be Your Purpose

"What lies behind us and what lies before us
are small matters
compared to what lies within us."

Ralph Waldo Emerson

Each day lived well is a testament to Wisdom earned through trials and suffering and, as the Gifts of Wisdom are tested against the realities of living on earth, if adhered to, this day may well be the most important day in your life's memory.

Regardless of your physical age, the day will come when you think you've succeeded in life to the point you're satisfied with your position in The Game, yet you'll be Nudged to lift your eyes upward, still. And there it is; a monumental life-opportunity that threatens your peaceful existence and seems completely out of reach based on limited resources or desire to reboot ambition past current comforts.

In an instant, you're no longer on Top of the world or comfortably retired in a position of trust or power. For in this challenging Instant, your peace is threatened as you struggle to believe you've acquired the necessary experience to venture beyond self-set borders. However, climbing Mount Everest, as are each of life's aspirations, is attacked only one step at a time and in certain places it is inch-by-inch and an intelligent retreat to regroup, reenergize, and heal is deemed a success. Just the thought of the innumerous steps and technical climbs required to reach the top may be too daunting and finally paralyze you into inaction, procrastination, or in the relief found in well-earned recreational diversions.

But, when any gigantic undertaking is cordoned off into small parcels, you're more able to find success in each step of the journey and the climb becomes manageable, if not more enjoyable and "the journey" is the dream come-true. And you'll more Instantly take notice of the views along the way and appreciate each earned breath, as you inch nearer the top each day. And another top is reached, an achievement met, and the accomplishment is spectacular.

~

Also, rather than face the challenges in life from the perspective of the fear of failing to achieve "the grand mission", choose to view every new challenge as if inspected through the eyes of Jesus and determine your next moves from His Eternal perspective. In this right mind, ask The Board, as would Jesus, to provide guidance. As He prayed daily, sometimes hourly, remember to model Him to lead you along these very similar and quite treacherous paths.

Jesus has hiked this route to the top and back, since the beginning of time and He encourages us to look past our fears of the unknown as He leads us along the difficult trail that concludes in a job well done, a life well lived. Your trail is being broken right before your eyes and the closer you stay to Jesus the less you'll worry about being overcome by the immensity of the every "next challenge". And you'll succeed in each small step taken towards your journey's home; by constant prayer and thanksgiving.

Jesus made an unspoken promise to us from the cross with His death and resurrection that showed us the Way home and covered our entry-fee, by unearnable Salvation. As you open your heart you'll appreciate the suffering He endured to teach us that there's a God who loves and forgives us and there's nothing to fear by "living in the moment" in thanksgiving and forgiveness; each moment prepares us perfectly for the next. From the Cross, He showed us how to endure even the most horrific death with the strength and power of God that lies within each of us, by His conscious and constant communication with our Father in Heaven; that we may do the same.

He paved the way for us to live and die honestly, in the moment and without defense, resistance, or thought of retaliation. And the higher you attempt to travel along the path on earth, as did He, the greater and more frequent are the challenges, the greater the temptations, and the more hazardous the fall when you take your eye off the trail. Hence, the greater the risks the more often you must pray. The greater the challenge, the greater the reward and the more you must rely on Jesus' assistance to be safe from falling to a prideful death, thinking how great you've become.

But each step you take with Him is a victory and may be a mountain climbed in and of itself; humbly, glorified.

~

We make erroneous judgments each day to determine how far outside our comfort zones we're sure it's safe to travel. You'll sometimes overextend abilities, or so it might seem, as you find yourself absurdly stretched by acting upon His surprising Bumps and Nudges. Yet, He never leaves your side.

Have Faith in the face of extreme challenges as these trials/trails often lead to an impossibly formidable wall to climb. Ask Jesus, in a quick thoughtful prayer, to help evaluate the challenge that lay ahead and you'll be assured that if you choose to climb, He holds taught the rope that keeps you from falling.

In answer to your prayer, He hollers, "On belay."

He tightens His grip, as He's tells you to trust Him, clearly without hesitation and without disguise; He's got you. Notice that He doesn't mumble or mince words; He's quite direct in His offering of Hope and Surety. This is serious business and no time to toy with your psyche as you travel the seemingly dangerous pathways in life that fulfills visions of hope that He's placed in your heart's mind. He promises you safety along the climb if you'll stay close to Him and in the most perilous times you need focus only on one small hand hold at a time, as you ascend the steepest stretches leading you to the next landing along this eternal journey upward.

And when you slip and fall, which you will, He's here with a taught rope that keeps you from smacking your face on the cliff wall or worse, falling to your death.

~

Regardless of yesterday's most calamitous failures and public embarrassments or monumental award winning achievements, you may hear, "You're only as good as your last game" or "your last exhibit" or "your last Quarter in sales". To the degree you achieve greatness or salvage hope from loss, society is in constant measurement of success.

Our loving God, however, does not believe in these human benchmarks. We, you, and I have no idea of how good at anything we are or for how long we must maintain peak performance levels to fulfill our right to be determined an Eternal Success, if that's your true goal. And there's no human that may control these Eternally-marked thresholds or who might be qualified to judge the limits of your capabilities or the significance of knowledge gained by setbacks.

Superficial and demotivating judgments place limits, attempt to control, and, if believed, may personally punish. They chastise your mind and soul with thoughts and feelings of loss even before an attempt is made to achieve and they limit your ambition to grow beyond the most recent or historic defeats.

Failing to meet set goals is deemed failure worthy of shame, if not tribal expulsion. You may have set goals to win and continuously grow business and your personal estates and, if possible, to sexify your physique. But, this comes at a high price and might only add to the human struggle and force you into moral compromise by meeting the demand that these arbitrary and sometimes unrealistic goals be met; immediately, within an unrealistic time frame, and at all costs; you have determined that you must win.

It's up to you and each of us, though, as uniquely designed individuals, to determine how to apply ourselves today and to choose for whom and how to work. When you wake in the morning, prepare yourself to master the-fear-of-the-day and commit to excel in service to your friends, the friended, or friendable; first. And remember that no one may be closer to the knowledge of God's intimate dream for your personal salvation (His ambition) than are you.

So, don't allow another to tell you who or who not to be or what you're able or not able to accomplish. Ignoring the judgment of others, you may take in the long view and envision what God's dream might be in the belief that He's aware of the sticks and rocks on the trail that might trip you up and His knowledge of how to succeed in this single perfect journey is yours; shared by Him.

∼

By your consciously Holy Entrepreneurial service to others and to the world and to God's satisfaction, you'll experience and abundance of "business-miracles" and financial success. Americans carved a nation from the wilderness and fought endless wars against strong enemies and amongst ourselves to guarantee the sanctity of self-determination; the right to liberty and land ownership. Yet, the American dream has evolved and been warped by the unreal imaginings of success, as is well portrayed on TV and in the movies and that protect our "God given Right" to "the good life" to "the American Dream" and we place our faith in alternate-gods from which we seek relief of our problems and that support our selfish quests for glory; in competition, rather than cooperation the ultimate "alternate-truth".

So, we place wreathes at the feet of surrogate gods nearly every day as we worship and honor the gods of securing "the Big Deal" that we must have – those many gods of "Success in Business" that tempt us to manipulate or omit the facts to win every contract – the gods of winning by "Crushing the Opponent" – the extravagant gods of "Big Home and Fancy Cars" – the gods of "Fame and Notoriety" – the gods of "Leisure and Fun" at the expense of finishing the job – the gods of "Finishing the Job" at the expense of time well-spent enjoying family and friends in recreation, leisure, and celebration – the vainglorious "Six-Pack-Ab" god – the clandestine gods of "Pleasing Others" for fear of losing their love or their business and in lieu of honesty – and the overt gods of "Honoring Man" our customers, leaders in business and government, or the wealthy and powerful; for their favor and the expectant security their favor provides.

Honoring earthly gods yanks you out of God's Game and you're on your own. Alone, living a life based on protecting yourself from everything you fear and you'll embarrass yourself, be dishonestly self-degraded, compromised morally, selectively honest, jealous, greedy, angry, worrisome, ashamed, and appear quite the coward in the battle for the truth. And in an unannounced moment in time your motives become transparent and you're immediately found-out.

> "Every day, a piece of San Francisco is on fire.
> And our character is being torched by someone today, as well.
> But, most of San Francisco is stalwart in spirit and magnificently unaffected and likewise, must we be."
>
> Deloris Dogood

~

Problems and issues arise every day and you'll begin to doubt yourself and God's Eternal Plan by their relative immensity. Even as His vision for your ultimate success for this day is certain, you'll question your ability to achieve and might question the purpose of this life that God would have you finish.

Are you truly following God in Heaven or is it a god of your own making? Why does it seem so absolutely clear at times and other times it's foggy as hell? Or is that why? And are you the right person for this job? Why did He pick you? Why does God trust a sinner like yourself? Isn't there someone out there better qualified, with more experience or who is formally or appears to be more formally trained to handle such matters and better prepared for this battle that He's asked you to fight?

Surely God knows of somebody better prepared to tackle this mountainess project and who righteously more deserves of this gift; who is more worthy...

Remember, don't' believe everything you think.

When I'm at my worst, I abandon God's Promise as the immensity of the project seems dizzying. Or I offer my soul to someone for their being-ness, their experience, their investment capital, relationships, or whatever it is they offer that I imagine would propel my ability to perform, compete, and earn. In these internal exchanges, I exit the moment in a state of awe, jealousy, or scheming for another's favor or to close that critical deal. I'm weakened as I look wantonly at the life-rope dangled that saves me from my most galactic fears. And the fear of losing their association or their favor weakens my position and I become a different person as I honor their whims, answer too many questions, talk too much, laugh nervously, or hide my shame in diversion; I defend my words, scramble to produce exponentially, or I dig-in my heels and battle loudly, arrogantly, to protect that which I'm sure I'm entitled to own.

My character and my dreams of creating an historic legacy are immediately abandoned in this honor of a false god that I've created and I cast my vote for a "preemptive war" in Iraq or otherwise make horrendously terrible decisions in business. When I hand another person undue honor and praise or when I fear their departure from a seemingly lucrative association, I accept my innate weaknesses and have justified taking a place below them. And in this uncomfortable situation that I've created, my ego awakens and begins to devise an attack.

And I hate myself for acting such a fool as I cower in fear awaiting the decision from the one I've chosen to honor ahead of God. In these moments of fear driven exploits, I've traveled so far outside any sense of Spiritual Logic that I reckon in ways learned from fear-based survival logic and I say and do things only the spiritually insane might. I speak with false bravado or favor-seeking tone and the smeared face of self-disrespect is a discomforting image of a liar.

And God's angels in human clothing run away and God cannot create through me in these moments of separation that I've chosen to inhabit. All hope of peaceful resolution is lost and *all* parties lose; the oppressor, the oppressed, and the self-oppressed. I have fed their ability to control me by responding favorably to their demands, by my absence and fear of hopelessness that hands this interim-god a controlling interest in Me, Inc.

God, forgive me. I've fallen.

"Don't be afraid of people who can kill the body but cannot kill the soul
Two sparrows cost only a penny, but not even one of them can die without your Father's knowing it. God even knows how many hairs are on your head.
So, don't be afraid. You are worth much more than many sparrows."

Matthew 10:28-31

~

Knowing this, choose to be poor in possessions and true to your awkward-self rather than a slave to the world's view or that of an over expectant venture-capital partner. Our Father in Heaven is your only hope, so pray that you do not compromise His promise to satisfy short-term means-and-ways to wealth. Pray to stay thoughtful in this moment and trust only your Father in Heaven and remember His Promise is your salvation – and Salvation is free of charge and has but only one string attached; the one attached to the truth in this moment:

Love one another.

In this particular moment in time, you're able and ready to accept the Promise, the Surprise, which at times the ease of its access will catch you off guard. But, know it's coming and you'll find it Here-Now, as you stay in tune to recognize God's gifts. Here and Now you'll see the Miracles arrive in packets and bundles and they've become expected; simply part of the Moment; essential pieces to His humanly-puzzling, but Eternally obvious, Plan. And over time, you'll become accustomed to the benefits of His unique unselfish works and find yourself automatically thanking Him throughout the day for the many miracles He proffers that show you His Love is sure. It is within these moments that you'll easily rely on God to keep you in The Game and only in this moment may He count on you to perform without honoring the human-factor of the Grand Purpose.

And the Grand Purpose is merely God's thought fulfilled of which the warning label might read, "Not by my will, but His be done" and "Not in my time, but His."

> "Every moment and every event of every man's life on earth plants something in his soul."
>
> Fr. Thomas Merton

So what?

Well, Now and Here, you know!

And Now and Here, you may more easily surrender to accountability and be Here in this Place – happily. Happily, be a humble martyr to the responsibility of your God-given words and God-directed actions. And Now, because you know about the Now and the grandness of being Here, you cannot blame me or anybody else for your poor choices and, quite frankly, taking blame or credit doesn't change the truth about that which has just happened and you're Instantly Good and good with that!

So, if you want to learn from your mistakes and learn a safer more productive way to conduct your life and better affect the lives of those around you; take immediate responsibility for your mistakes in words and actions. As you mis-step by putting up a defense against fears or in your pride of ownership you find you're owned, fess up, apologize, and let go of your need to possess and control.

And Now, right Here you can do that Great thing you've always wanted to do in your life; that you've ALWAYS known you were meant to do!

And Now, right Here you have every Good reason and God given ability to be that Loving Amazing person you KNOW in your heart you're meant to be! So, be it!

And know this: The lessons you learn today don't end here on earth and the learning may never end, but in "this moment" there is no placemat for self-inflicted struggle and there is no room for another god to glorify. Only in this Moment, Here, is there a constant stream of glorified information from Heaven to be known; extrapolated through human experience; information originated in Heaven and carried to you by angels that allow God's Grand Purpose be fulfilled through you and us. And really KNOW in meditation and prayer – in your quiet Connection with God that you were born to be Great at being you and that means you are Great in serving Him and He knows you're ready and able to be you.

Right Here and right Now with Him, you're ready to be your Purpose. Regardless of your past or fears of the future, right Now, you're right where He needs you to be; perfectly.

~

He's mysteriously created a Purpose for each precise Moment in time, for each of His children, and on this day, He's given each of us Hope for a Way in the Now; and forever, beyond this life. In fact, there is no end to the journey that teaches us to love, first. And in the grandeur of this gifted adventure, our life is just now beginning to unfold, as we live productive and happy lives, as we survive our bunglings on this planet and by our Bumped and Nudged decisions to live life within the Eternal and Spiritually Logical mind that places no god above the Original in business, at home, in Church, politics, education, medicine, or online.

God's Grand Purpose for us is absolute, priceless, and Eternal in the peace and satisfaction we find in this single Moment in time, in service to our brothers and sisters and in our search to know, love, and find God; the Holy Grail; from which we each may drink freely His Love. He gifts us with Grace and when we open our hearts and minds to forgiveness and gratitude and we embrace the adventure. With Him we can be fearless of the horrific mistakes we are certain to make and we're better at being whole with knowledge of His constant Presence; that He's always at our side. He never leaves us alone for He knows the evil we face each day and the Joy awaiting.

So, be Amazing today! Remember that in every step of this high stakes journey to be your Purpose; to the death; He's Here with you. He tells you not to worry, "Be not afraid." And in your sincere prayers for direction, relief, and Hope, He whispers, "I forgive you and I love you… now take that next step and trust Me." "Belay's on!"

Spiritual Logic

the Hope in Entrepreneurialism

THE BOOK OF AFFIRMATIONS

A daily walk through the woods with our Father
and trouble is scrubbed from our struggling souls.

To Begin...

God has gifted each of us, His beloved children, with a clear pane of glass at the beginning of our lives, through which His glory might be shown to the world. We're born innocent and only through a selfless being might He work His miracles to create Heaven on earth; even if only from an infant's smiling eyes, the cutting and honest utterances of Truth "out of the mouth of babes", or a quick jab to the ribs from a colleague to re-center your thinking. God uses our beings, our voices, and our unique personalities, of which He equipped us well, to share and express His love and Compassion towards His every, many, and interestingly odd creations; you, me, our brothers and sisters, our children, and the entirety of humanity and every living thing.

Each uniquely delivered day and in each distinct hour of every day we make a singular and most important decision whether to be that privileged ally in God's honest and simple communication of love; or not. It's that simple, yet a maddening obligation, as our treasured connection with God is mischievously tampered with by our inner demons; our interference in His Plan in fear of doom or distractive ambitions of glory; and our desire to serve is supplanted with fears that cradle loss, betrayal, protectionism, and loneliness.

From the moment of our birth, from this, the most purely honest moment in our existence, we confront mishaps, injustices, and accidents and we're given the freedom to justify the lies of the world by our selfishly reckless words and deeds *or* we may choose to dismiss temptation and hold firmly to our inner most desire to be with God and to serve Him, only. We may choose to inhabit that space and time with Him and act upon the innate desire of which we were created to endear and appreciate, with no thought of reward.

At birth, the panes of glass from which our spirits shine to the world are clean and untarnished, however as we struggle to survive life's many challenges to secure food, shelter, clothing, improver our lot, and to care for our children; we are beaten and nearly destroyed at times and we have failed and we have conquered, but we are influenced nonetheless by the happenings of life that tarnish our once playful innocence; tarnished by fear, vanity, and pride that heretofore was unknown to the innocent creation of which we once were, at birth.

Loss or the mere thought of losing tempts us to escape into the relief offered by the world we've created and we resist God's many Nudges to move forward with Him; Nudges guiding us to peaceful resolutions not of our making. However, in the comfort of habit and while in-hiding from the Truth, the problem compounds itself and our salvation is delayed by primordial reactions to life's challenges that, real or imagined, cast another layer of dinge upon our once clear panes of glass.

Over time, if not rectified (repented and forgiven) it's nearly impossible for God to express Himself through the layers of muck we've allowed to accumulate that surround our innocent core; the pure essence of innocence dimmed by reluctance and laziness. And we become accustomed to this ever-dimming view and choose to do nothing by accepting mediocrity or we bury our talents and seek the seemingly less risky pathway to earth's safety and security. Hiding from our born-mission, hope darkens and our souls lose the energy to cry and we see the world an ugly and scary place to survive and from which to raise children. Sadly, some of us live in darkness and expect that that is our fate; this is the natural struggle called "our lot", so we suffer and struggle and may go so far as to ask others to join us... and with them, we're satisfied that we're not alone; our ignorance justified.

Following are the affirmations I began writing in 2003 while sitting in an emptied home; my family scattered. Writing and reading these affirmations began to subtly reprogram my mind's neural pathways to better thinking and awareness to the Goodness at my core.

As I'd write and read these affirmations, my mind created newly directed channels that ignore fear and disinfect my thinking and ready my mind to seek and accept today's truth; Here-Now. Today, I find that I may smile more frequently, I'm happier with whom I am and whom I am becoming, and I see the world filled with allies rather than ornery antagonists. In my search for today's truth, I'm unencumbered by my need to be right and more readily commit to accept my role in the work required to include God in the processes of living on earth. Thoughtless of me and thoughtful of Him, I'm free of endless repetition of regrettably self-endorsed bad-habits; replaced by His Guidance that leads me to simple acts of service, love, and grace.

> "When you're thinking of something that you must do, you're not doing; you're not being."
>
> Delores Dogood

Good thoughts affirmed in my mind, I've exchanged paralyzing anxieties to fill my day with tasks for His simple Truth; unbearable pain for peace; and fear for love.

I pray that God blesses you on your journey and that your eyes and heart remain open to the Truth found in each moment in cooperation with Him. I pray that these meditations/affirmations work to heal and to lead you to wealth beyond money; to rewards promised from the Grace the Here-Now provides.

Stay true to your odd self and ignore your need to be the answer. Let God's plan find you empty of worldly ambition and you'll be filled with the Universal Power of His presence, Power that's far beyond your making. Alive in Him, it's easier to believe and to know that He thinks you're "worth it". And in this moment of experienced and expressed Truth, you'll recognize coincidences are just another of His many miracles that proves His love for you is endless and reminds you to, "Fear not."

the Hope in Entrepreneurialism

Week One – Truth & Wisdom

Sunday

Focus on this Now

I struggle to be Here, in this particular moment in time, unhurried, yet alert and observant of all that is; alive in this Eternal Now. It is most difficult for me on days that I have a lot on my mind and regret or worry or the exhilaration of imminent success clouds my thoughts with guilt, frustration, or pride. In moments of selfishness, I forget the mission You, God, have for me and my darkest fears of loss and betrayal become overgrown and take control of my being. And worse yet, I've forgotten that You're Here with me and I needn't do this alone; but I think I must and I do.

I pray, today, to be alive in this Moment. In this Moment, I'm focused on You and I know there is nothing to fear; no loss to bear. And there's no thing that is trivial to You, so with every choice and action and word of mine I want You involved. I'm asking for Your affect. And when this mind is filled with regret from my past great failures or from my most recent blunder I pray that I remember to ignore the negative and draw in hope for the positive outcome of Your Promise. I remember to breathe and I experience You in Eternity and I experience Your wisdom and Your peace and together we accomplish every simple and great thing.

Here-Now, I am released from my regrets of the past and fears of the future events that cloud my thinking and that otherwise would paralyze me. Today, I begin with a simple prayer to remain Here, in this moment Now, and I know that nothing more is expected of me. Here-Now, beyond me but fully within me; my life is an extension of You as I experience the height of my abilities and act-out the true desires of my soul; Your Will. Here-Now I can love You, God, with all my heart and might; Now, instinctively able to love my brothers and sisters, as would You; Jesus.

Monday

The Truth stands on its own

I pray that throughout this one day I can recognize and embrace the Truth that You've prepared for me to grasp. I pray that You give me the strength, the mental prowess, and fearlessness to explore and recognize the Truth and that I have the courage to accept that truth without collision; but rather with grace, ease, and candor. I pray that as I focus my attention and energies on this particular moment in time, I am able to investigate what I see, hear, and feel without judgment; without tagging an experience as good or bad or pressing it through "how will it affect me?" and "what might I lose or gain?"

Rather, I observe actions and words with objectivity, free to make unboxed associations discovered along the path You've paved. And I'm comfortable knowing I am in Your hands, guided through the darkest forests, surrounded by Your Angels, indifferent to my fears; sure in Your outcome. I understand that I must be tolerant, patient, and appreciative of myself and my brothers and sister's acute limitations in accepting the Truth You would lead us to face each day. As well, I appreciate our inability to consistently stand up for the Truth or spread it without becoming defensive or trying to own it outright.

Yet, today, I pray that I reach for Your Hand when I'm in doubt of my abilities and You won't let go till I'm safe. I pray to hold firm, as You fill my heart with courage and inner strength to never give up on Your mission. In this, I stand firm; confident in Your Will, confident in Your Truth, and confident in Your Love.

So, when I am called by You or my brother to speak, I pray that I do so without a second thought; but rather that I trust Your Wisdom and that I do not succumb to temptation that drives me to mold the truth or transform it into something more palatable or that sells my selfish precepts; that I speak fearlessly with confidence and I fear not the tough questions asked of me nor of the tough questions I must ask.

As I slip my feet into Your Sandals, today, the temptation to flee or control vanishes. In this free forum and progressive way of living within the light of Your Mind and faith in Your Eternal Destiny for our souls, I have peace in the knowing and have proof of Your Love and Forgiveness. And the Truth is understood and the ugly weight of lies that lead to procrastination, envy, anger, and fear are lifted from my soul.

I can see again and smile in comfort of Your Love and faith in Your Way.

Tuesday

At Peace in the storm

Today, I offer my life fully to the world, as a servant to God and to those whom He would have me serve. When we dance alone, we have nothing to share; no experience is owned solely. So, today I pray that I patiently listen and wade through my mortal thinking and earthbound words to, instead, use the words You choose from Your Eternal Mind. I pray that I discern well, today, as You speak to me through my brothers and sisters; that my mind is open to their unique presentation of Your thought, which is, at times, clearly a message meant for me. And, as these thoughts are spoken from the mouth of babes, my friends, my family, and passing strangers; I seek to listen for Your message and am grateful for the brief shelter I find in the storm of my less than perfect and, at times, chaotic thinking.

So, today, as I am resistant neither to Your thought nor that of man's determined expression of thought born of man, I'm at peace within this moment and am gifted with a free life. In this moment, I am non-resistant to distraction or disturbance caused by neither mine nor my brothers' fears. I pray You to take me to the place of peace within Your heart where my mind and thoughts are one in the same as Yours. And in this place, in this time, and for this reason; defense of the truth is not required. The truth "is what it is" and nothing said or done may change it, no matter the energy I spend in attack or to control any single man's version of it.

Consciously engaged within God's Mind all that is good is possible. And all great things happen, but only as I leave my will that desires to control the Truth and in its place, accept Your thoughts that urge me to pause and stop my mind's wheels from spinning out of control and I accept Your peaceful and certain Way; the simple answer; the Truth. And I relax knowing I cannot change what has happened and You lead me to explore and know what, in fact, is real.

Wednesday

Being Your Will

I am present "Now" with my brothers and sisters and present for my brothers and sisters, yet I am undeterred by neither their nor mine fears of losing; undeterred by unnecessary thinking patterns of the need to accumulate or to protect that which must be owned or from gaining praise, honor, or respect from others. I pray for the strength to remain here in the moment as the day progresses and I am released from my fears and all that I do or say throughout this day is a reflection of Your Will. On this day, I commit my attitude towards life, my energy and time and I pray to distill my desires down to one simple effort and that is to own Your Will and make it mine.

In this moment, I pray that my presence and my word is the outward expression of You and I am humbled by the knowledge and wisdom You entrust in me to convey. As Your words leave my lips, the complete thought enters my mind to what You intend for the moment and I realize that these words are Yours, not mine. And I am honored and amazed by the great and many truths expressed within the depth and breadth of this moment, which is Yours and mine to share.

You have blessed me with consciousness and a personality unlike any others. You have given me freedom to be me; right or wrong. And yet, in those moments when great things happen in my life I invite You to be with me to share my pain and sadness as well as my freedom and joy. I invite You to fill my being and to experience that great thing that I love to do and share that incredible experience that I enjoy.

I pray to be a pure, honest, and energized vehicle to express Your being to the world. So, on a cool crisp February morning as I tighten my boot buckles at the top of the mountain and lean out over my skis to drop off a windblown cornice into the untracked chute below, I pray that You fly with me and ski each turn with vigor in my desire to experience life to its fullest. And when I prepare a speech or presentation and I stand before my brothers and sisters I pray that You give the talk of my life through me. When I paint my house, Your hand guides mine. And as You write this book, I enjoy reading it.

In all that I do, big and small I pray that it is Your experience to express. And I pray to You today that "It is my Will that Your Will be done" and all that I do, I do to the best of my ability with love for my brothers and sisters and an Eternally guided interest in serving them well. As I recognize my calling to serve, I sit taller in my seat, walk with more grace, am deliberate in my direction, and my sense of humor and sage loving smile exudes confidence in Your chosen path for me as I know that Your loving outcome is guaranteed for me, today.

Thursday

Reality is Here & Now not there & when

In this present moment, God is. It is in this moment, only, that I am delivered from my fears and doubts and of those many perceived inglorious outcomes that swirl in my mind that lead to defeat in faraway places. I pray that I forget my selfish and prideful ways and that I act in Your behalf according to Your Will. In this moment, I am the personification of You; truth, beauty, and goodness. I am safe in Your hands and great in Your Thought. Within You, I'm able to discern the truth in every situation and circumstance.

Being with You in this moment in time I am a spark of Your strength and power and can be completely open and honest in the representation of Your truth, I understand my place in Your world, and am at peace within Your wisdom. And I observe the happenings without bias as they are not mine to control. I may not correct the uncorrectable or change the unchangeable; what happened is no longer and what is to come does not exist, except within Your Mind. I fear not, what tomorrow will bring, as You determine what it is that I must do Now; enlightened by the knowledge of a sure outcome; I know tomorrow cares for itself.

My positive attitude towards my life's work, my ability to be happy, safe, and financially secure is found in each moment lived, even in the "waiting place," as long as I remain who I am, Here-Now; with You. My faith grows ever deeply within this great experience of living on earth, today; whether a perceived dark failure or an unexplainable last-minute bailout or grand success; I am grateful to You for my life; for Your Love; for Now. And I will learn and grow closer to You in every shared experience, as I realize the Love You have for me is endless in Your devotion to my soul's growth; in Your Faith that I accept my birthright and appreciate Your Will for me; a loving son; beloved.

Friday

Success

Today, I pray that I raise my children and lead my family, friends, business associates, and detractors to know You and to trust You and to receive You and accept You by my ability to remain calm, patient, and assured of Your plan. And I pray that I lead confidently, humbly, and unhurriedly and I surrender my mortal quests and selfish ambitions to the Truth that is You. Today, I place in a package the complete edition of my ego's version of success that is designed by me to establish my greatness and protect me from my many fears of failure and shame. I take this noxious package and I hand it to You, Father, for disposal and I gladly accept Your free-gift of success that leads me to serve another to the best of my abilities and I happily forget my enormous and full list of needs, wants, and fears.

In this undertaking, this surrender of my fears and acceptance of Your goodness; great success is realized. But the credit due me is only that I have chosen to dismantle my framework and build an Ark for You that my family and friends may be carried through the fiercest storms and roughest waters. In this way of life that I've chosen to live, fully vested in Your Will, I am without fear and I am Your example of success to the world. It is in this unhurried way of living "in the moment" shared with You and with whomever it is You bless me to serve that I live life completely and fully alive. In this moment shared, we are given the chance to truly know each other and wonder not, how to be happy. We have earned the clear channel to Your wisdom as we take Your side in the battle to live in this moment, fully Here. Now, we are showered by Your light, but only in this particular moment in time, not the past nor in the future and all is right and we succeed in all You would lead us to do; today.

Saturday

In Gratitude

I am blessed to be conscious of You and I pray to remember You in each moment in time. It is in this moment that I may find my way and I begin again to be that person whom it is that I have been created to be. Focused on You, I give You honor and thanks and my actions and deeds, my posture, poise, compassion, calm reassuring voice, my inventiveness, my thoughts, my vision of hope, any and all achievement, and my ability to love and share is You in expression. It is in You that I am at my best. I pray that I recognize quickly Your hand in all that is good that I do and I pray that I am earnestly grateful to You and thank You for these amazing miracles, as well as for the lessons learned in my most difficult of times.

I pray that I remember to pray to You all day to include You in every decision and every thought. I am thankful that You are my Will and You are my First Thought and that my dreams of a future are clear and focused on doing that which You would have me do and be today to fulfill Your Dream for my soul. For I am fearless of outcome, happily indentured to You and to my brothers and sisters, my sons and daughters, and all whom I love, all who are close to me. Bless us; all and each of us; and me today, with the worldly-critical mind that disappears and in this Instant, You appear through me with Your spiritually-critical Thought derived from Your Universal Mind.

Today, only, my being and my spirit are honored to become Your Will in expression and I pray that I am stalwart in Your presence, confident when expressing Your words, and poised and caring in doing for You. Today, I gladly give myself to You to serve and to love my brothers and sisters on this planet. On this day, I am forever grateful of any knowledge that You bring to me that reminds me of Your Way and Your ever-loving Will for our combined success, peace, and happiness. Thank you, God, for giving me a mind and spirit from which to envision, eyes to see Your wonders, ears for the sounds of nature; this incredible world you've created filled with beauty, light, and life.

Week Two – Worship

Sunday

Remember our Father in Heaven

God, I pray today that I remember that You are a permanent presence in my mind and my heart and that You are an ever-expanding part of who I am. I realize today that You are not too important to know the details of my everyday life and when I separate myself from You it only takes purpose away from my personal relationship with You and my brothers and sisters. In all that I think, speak, and do today You are here with me and You cannot be here only half the time or when I think the occasion important. You're here whether I think I need You or not, yet, today I unconsciously include You in everything I do and say, as I follow Your guidance and experience Salvation; Your glory, Your Love, Your Forgiveness.

God, I am grateful to You for sharing Yourself with me in my most chaotic and terrifying moments to my most treasured and simple. With You I find truth, beauty, and goodness and in the search for Your Being I find small pieces of You in everything that I am led to touch. God, I can barely envision You and I don't know how to love You, yet I pray that I am doing my best to see You in everything and everyone. I pray that I respect the Eternal Thought You have invoked for each of us to comprehend Your love for us. So, I begin this day by taking a step towards You to know You and think of You and include You in every matter, every conflict, every joy that I experience and that I do so if even slightly more today than could I yesterday; within my ever-growing Faith in You; our Father in Heaven.

Monday

Honoring this Life

At every step, I take today, I pray that I am following You, God, and as I do I pray that I appreciate our time together and that I am learning how to worship, love, and trust in You more and more as I move in and out of strategic, yet seemingly dangerous moments in my life. I am forever grateful to You for the endless Fatherly love and care that You have for me and for each of us. And it amazes me that I have come to a place in our relationship that I expect You to be in every part of my life no matter how small or insignificant the task might seem to be. I know You want to be here with me to experience the greatness in life that this day holds and I pray that I treat this day as though it is my last for You on this planet and that I live it to the fullest. This is the day that You have made and the day that all great things big and small happen. The plan that You have for each of us is real and we truly are Your beloved sons and daughters; so, it is in this spirit that I affirm:

Today I know, love, and appreciate You, my Father in Heaven. In each moment in time, on this one and only day, from now to eternity; my thoughts, my desires, and my intentions are Yours. Now, I pray that

You purify my heart, my mind, and my soul and that my thoughts are truly Yours; excited with the adventure of life, compassion, and love. Now, I make no distinction between mine and Yours; there is no separation between us in my mind. We are one in thought; true, in this moment in time.

Today, I know, love, and appreciate You, Jesus Christ. I accept Your word over mine and it is Yours that I speak or I am silent. I pray that my mannerisms, my expressions, my silence, my compassion, and my evenly-bridled yet enthusiastic words are Yours. I speak today in Your voice, Your tone, and with Your encouraging and positive phrasing without editorial, without overly charged emotion, or thinking overly each situation to my benefit. My agenda is purified of my ego-demands and fears of loss evaporate, as I step into Your sandals and am an honest servant; fair, kind, unhurried, and just. Regardless of mine or my brother's appreciation for the Truth, I remain focused on Your objectives and I courageously state the Will of our Father in Heaven, as a matter of fact.

Today, I know, love, and appreciate You, our loving Holy Spirit. I pray that I am cognoscente of You in every action and deed; every duty I am moved to fulfill, every chore, my work, and in the times You move me to play, rest, and recreate. I'm filled with energy and calm sure confidence that I'm in the right place and in the right time as I pray all day for Your guidance; Your cool calm confidence, Your incessant vigor, and Your true elegance, grace, and dignity. And You and I are complete, arm-in-arm one being in action; at peace in the waiting or passionate battles for truth or simple gestures of kindness that shows blind trust in Father's plan. For I am the sum total of *my* willingness to listen to the First Source and Center that, in my actions and deeds, are a reflection of You.

Tuesday

Gratitude

Thank you, Father for all that You do for us each day and for being here when we need You most, when we are lost and alone, fearful and angry, despondent, confused, or otherwise emptied of life; and You are here, always and forever. I recognize that my salvation has always been Your plan and Your gift to each of us, as I stop and thank you, privately for my daily bread. And You have been here with me through the darkest of times and You have given me hope when I'd none.

I am grateful to You for all You've done and for that which You're doing to save me from myself. God, I especially thank You for this gift of undoing my old self and making me new, today. You have reassured me time-and-time-again through the many great and terrible experiences that I've survived that You will always love me as a father loves his son and that You will never give up on me regardless of how clumsy I might be or how difficult I make things for myself and for others.

And when Your material, emotional, and spiritual gifts are made known to me and I experience great joy in accomplishment, I pray that I immediately and instantaneously realize that all that is good that I do, or disasters avoided, or interesting ideas that I might articulate well; comes from You. All great things that I have experienced in my life have come from my ability and willingness to give up my agenda and allow Your Will to be unleashed to my small corner of the world through my calm sure words and confidant actions. By giving myself and the desires of my heart to You, my rewards are long lasting and real and have no resemblance of my mind's ambitions. Their beginnings coming from You, I pledge to credit You for my success; to anyone who will listen.

Wednesday

Attitude of Impending Victory

Today, I pray that I am living within Your Mind and my thoughts are those of a loving God. In this, I am enlivened and fearless in the face of danger, poised in those times of tense discussion, kind and compassionate in times of despair and sadness, and confident in the positive outcomes You would have for me and us during this day; a life fulfilled.

In fearful and difficult situations, I stop my mind, breathe, relax my eyes, and find You; immediately. I fear no outcome. In these moments of renewed confidence, I treat myself, my family, my brothers and sisters, coworkers and associates, friends and foes with respect, love, understanding, and with Your kindness and loving patience; to I seek You in their eyes and voice.

With each other's help, we win the war against ourselves and we discover You, Your Love, and Your Peace in our small but vital victories over indifference, evil, iniquity, greed, vanity, pride, and laziness. And we begin each trial knowing we have won, simply because we have entered the game within Your presence. And I smile in the face of my worst fears of defeat; knowing full-well Your Way is our ultimate victory and nothing on earth trumps Your Heavenly reward.

Thursday

Fearlessness

When I am timid, meek, and gun-shy; angry, nervous, defensive, and anxious; or over-confident, brash, loud, and cocky; I stop my insolent mind that travels time and choose instead to reside in that place of peace; in the Now. In this moment in time only may You accept my humble invitation to enter my thoughts and, without struggle, I choose to accept Your closeness and agree to Your terms, as You take over the conversation and discard my earthbound manipulative acrobatics and all is well and I am well and we are all well.

I am energized by Your Truth as I plant my feet at the starting line, today. And in this Holy Now, I act and speak with love and admiration for You and Your Creation. And in this strategic moment I am lifted into Eternity and am confident in Your plan, I smile easily, and am composed in the knowledge of Your Love and assurance of Your Outcome. In *this* Holy Moment, I am complete and calmed by Your Spirit, I regret and I fear no thing, I know my purpose, and am poised by Your Grace. In *this* moment, I know full well that You are at my side and that to be happy and to serve Your Creation is the purpose of my life. In *this* moment, I am Your soldier complete in Your Thought, as You blind falsehood with light and explode with inspiration of instantaneous salvation with meanings too deep to ignore value for this particular day.

Now, I am saved from my every fear realized or want unfulfilled. And in *this* singular moment may race continue, as only within this Now may the Truth be an accelerant for my Holy purpose and be my desire realized to win the race against myself; for You; fearless in the course You have set.

Friday

Peaceful Neutral Non-Resistance

Today I hand You, God, total and complete control of my mind, my thoughts, and my emotions. In times of fear or excitement; I honor You, myself, and those around me by letting You control my thoughts, emotions, actions, and words. And I pray to be calmed by Your presence in those emotionally-driven times and I pause and take a deep breath and I find You in the stillness of the moment. In this moment, I find that I am not required to prepare for attack or defend a position or provide a solution to my most pressing issues; for, in conniving and retribution the jailer is in prison as well as the prisoner. In neutral objective non-resistance, I am prepared for the truth within an Eternal perspective, I trust Your outcome, act instantaneously with Your lovingly correct response to an attack, and in so doing I set free my brothers and sisters from an unnecessary battle and am freed, as well.

So, in the silence and quiet and depth of the moment, I am at peace with myself, an enemy or friend, and with my family and I inherently know what it is that I must do for You. In this moment, I fight the good fight in a way that does not resist that does not seek ego satisfaction. Instead, I stand fervently in the face of danger holding firmly to the shield of truth, which is You. Your strength instills patience and unwavering patience that lies within You, alone. Within You, I am confident in the outcome and able to listen, step back, and afford You room to enter the conversation. Inspired inspection of the facts leads to understandings that I could not find on my own and discovery of Truth excites the mind and throws me into corrected action. Unhurried, I embrace these peaceful, resourceful, and timely resolutions; as they cause no damage, do more good, and are far more lasting than mine; as we travel together, on this human journey Home; Now.

Saturday

Deliverance from Me

God, as I enter this day, I am determined to follow the path You clear for me, to listen for Your breathless whisper in my mind that directs me to STOP or to GO. And I place no great importance on my needs over Yours that guides me to serve and that brings me to a safe place of being. When I have succeeded, I take no pride in what I have done, for any great thing I have accomplished is not of my creation. Eternal success comes from following You and collaborating with my brothers and sisters to serve the greater good in this place and time on earth.

If I take the lead to fulfill my agenda, I do so selfishly to claim honor or to fend off financial distress or as I protect what I own or have invented or even as I attempt to counsel or lead a brother to safety. When I take the lead to fill my will, I have chosen a path of my own and have discarded the map God provides for me today that would have taken us to a safe place unknown; that my mind could not know exists. When I'm trapped by my greatest fears of failure I swing the machete more violently at the forest to clear the path ahead and must look quite the fool. But, it is not my job to make up my brother's mind or to intentionally clear the path for him or for me; a path of which I know not where it leads.

In my attempts to skillfully take the lead in full use of my ego designed skills and filled with visions of power, I am lost in my singular version of whom it is that I must be and how great are my ideas, how right is my thinking and who it is I must convince that I am right, who I must compete against, what shame must I hide, how important it is to be honored and appreciated for my works, who must I impress, what reward is my due, what responsibility must I take upon myself to fulfill, what must I fix, what feared task might I put off for a better time or hand to another person, and I get caught-up in the ugly business of protecting what I think I must own.

But, hidden within my being I find You patiently waiting. In You, my need to protect and control disappears and is gone in a heartbeat; in Your heartbeat. In You, I am delivered from myself and I am weightless surrounded by Your love and sweet ambition for our success. There is no serious matter that You are unaware of or have mistakenly overlooked. You have begun untold processes to create a resolution that I am capable to manage for You. In all matters, I am Eternally safe within this intimate moment in time and I find peace and I am alive in the reality of this moment. The anxiety, tension, and struggle are gone and the light guides my thoughts and there is no cause for worry and I am at once at peace within myself; within You. Today, I swear off old habits of control of self and of others and I release us from my worldly position, my worldly aspirations, my worldly conjecture and I become a living breathing conduit for Your Love to enter the souls of men without taking credit nor fearing their judgment of whom it is I appear to be. For in goodness there is no expectation of applaud or anxiety over fair return and I am at peace within Your Greatness and I am free to be me; a dutiful son, uniquely created by an ever-loving Father to live, to laugh, and to love.

Week Three – Counsel

Sunday

Your Words Not Mine

God, when I am hurried or frustrated and have an overwhelming sense dread or in times of celebration when I exude my ego's greatness, I have chosen to walk alone and have not considered Your roadmap for the journey or instructions that would ease the effort for the task at hand. In these times of fear and pride, I have lost my way and my thoughts are corrupted by greed and envy, empty of compassion, filled with worry, and my vision for my day's work is blurred in the rush to compete for first place rather than to serve my client, friend, or family honestly and without thought of reward. I ask, "What's in it for me?" and, "When will I receive my due?"

I am truly fallible, when I choose to exclude You from my day as I step out of the moment and take control. Acting under my humanly and educated direction designed to fulfill every need and want, I make unnecessary work for myself and others that is guided by foolish decisions steered by blind ambition. But, today I must recognize that the same holds true for my brothers and sisters, as I perceive those moments when their egos have full charge of the moment and they strike out or become self-absorbed.

Yet, every day I pray that I learn to understand that we are each placed here to help one another get through these torturous and confusing lessons. If I criticize, condemn, or complain about another or ignore my brothers' often subtle calls for help, not only do I cause trouble for him, I also hurt myself in the process. And that trait, which I so publicly detest of another, is most likely a trait of mine that I abhor in private. Therefore, today, I pray that I quickly forgive myself and others for our lesser ways of being and that I show tolerance and I understand that we are much better than the person whom we appear to be at times; as I lovingly say nothing or confidently offer Your voice of hope.

This week, I will confront evil, lies, and deception without delay. When a brother or sister criticizes, condemns, or complains against a loved one, a friend, or me I pray that You block my urge to defend or attack. I pray that You hold tight my tongue and dumb my thoughts when I attempt to speak from my lower self that I am stopped from hurting another or exposing my more foolish side. Yet, I pray that during those frustrating challenging moments when ambushed by another's thoughtlessness or ambivalence that I come to my senses quickly and can seek Your calming thoughts of peace and I am humbled in this moment as I speak the words You give me that disarm such an attack. I pray that my mind and heart are opened wide to share Your wisdom and love without condescension or offense to my brother, but rather I show compassion in the trust I have for Your words.

Your words flow easily from my lips and amazing things happen not of my mind, but of Yours. At times, I hear Your thought in words that flows from my lips and I immediately recognize the truth that I have spoken to be yours. But I have not before formed these thoughts in my mind, so I thank You for the wisdom You entrust me to express from my being and I am honored by Your trust in me to relay *the* message. Today, I make a vow to You that I will stay in the moment and stand aside and allow the thought that You have for us to be spoken and allowed the time necessary to be processed without editorial.

Your wisdom shines impeccable and there is nothing I might add to Your truth that does not bore with pride. What wisdom could I possibly add that wouldn't attempt to color Your perfect message to prove my value and my worth greater than it is? Will I proudly attempt to take credit? Sure, I'd like to, but "No" I will not. I pray for the strength to stop myself from seeking honor, so that Your messages flow freely from my lips through my unique personality and humble and unassuming, yet confident character. You are made visible for my brothers and sisters through my absence.

Monday

Disappearing Inside of God

Today, I pray to be transparent, as my being disappears completely within Yours and Your love is all that is visible as my ego self is neutralized; I have nothing to hide. Today, I pray that I remember to release my childlike God-created self from my "Made by Me" ego self. Purged of my ego's desires, wants, pretenses, and fears I am freed from my mortal misgivings and misguided efforts so that I might only seek You and Your Will for me. Without my "Made by Me" me, my person may be complete, intuitive, understanding, eternally patient, ultimately forgiving, and filled with the knowingness and being-ness of You.

As I release myself from the shackles of my "Made by Me" limitations, I am freed to accomplish Your Will, to understand and choose Your Way, and am freed to be the limitless person You created me to be. I am no longer trapped in thinking that I must be a certain person, for You have created me without limits. I only discover this as I release myself from the chains of my attachments that limit my mortal thinking. This perspective of who it is that I am and who it is that I must be, the lesser person I'd clung to for so many years is now vanished as I "Now" choose to become Your embodiment of truth. I am composed, confident, compassionate, and invigorated in the truth and this is who I am in expression and action. I am kind, encouraging, thoughtful, and share enterprise and unbridled creativity with Your words.

Tuesday

You Create Through Us

Today I am assured by You that I am on the right path from the subtle signs and from Your loving and sometimes firm guidance. I am more able today to be alive in the moment without placing too much importance or pressure on me to create or protect that which I think is so important to accomplish, as I recognize Your path and sense Your presence in my work. I know that I have but a single part to play in Your great creation and I am amazed by the many and great things that I can do, by You, and for You today. By concentrating my efforts on doing well my small part "Now", "Today" I discover a respect for others for the parts that they each play.

The roles others have been awarded in Your grand scheme are as important to our mutual success as is mine. I recognize that we are each simply doing our best to work and live in peace and succeed in search of truth and the promise of security and happiness in our lives. So, when I speak to a brother or sister I am considerate and respectful of them, for their life's story is rich and their fears of failure run as deep as or deeper than do mine. In thoughtfulness, I honor their struggle and their desire to succeed as I speak Your words, in Your tone, and with Your loving intent; and miracles happen.

Great associations grow instantaneously and friendships are built in this spirit of cooperation and compassion. Energy fills the air in our genuine desire to discover and live within the truth of the moment that we each have been given to share with one another. That great thing You are able to create through us is unhampered by my human judgment and grows beyond my mortal limitations, as my interactions embody You in the Words that flow from my lips. Whether I take the lead or agree to follow Your lead through another; I do so with confidence in Your outcome and I am poised and fluid in my actions that reflect Your absolute authority over my life; of that who I am.

Wednesday

Direct Me

Today, I pray for the clarity of mind to perceive and accept the work that You would have me do. I pray that I am released of my worldly ambitions and fears so that I am prepared and ready to listen for Your thoughts and that I leave nothing undone that is important to You that I accomplish. Today, I give up my personal quest for the gold ring of which I think I deserve. I give up my self-interests, my dreams, my ambitions, and anything I own that I think is important to sustain my earthly way of life. I hand everything over to You and I pray that You give me the words to speak, guide me to the places where You would have me be, and that You take control of my thoughts that they are "Now" in line with Yours and I create on earth for You and experience life for You and step aside and allow You to work through me today forsaking my dream for Your sanity; forgiven when I fail but in sincere gratitude as I succeed.

Thursday

Me Being Me

I pray that I have the strength, courage, and willingness to accept the role You have for me today and my desires are trumped by Yours. In this, I pray that I resist not Your guidance and that my ego is a good loser; that I am freed to easily let go of *my* plans, aspirations, and dreams for the less-selfish, less-prideful, less-fearful, more-freeing, more-serving, and more-powerful way that is Yours, which is Ours; simplified – magnified – glorified. I pray for the courage and strength and determination to openly share who I am with my brothers and sisters as only You will have me so do. I pray that I listen and learn without projecting my agenda and that I am comfortable being who I am; alive in Your time, Now and Here.

Friday

Humility

Thank you, God, for all that You do for us and I am grateful for any success that I experience along with and beside my brothers and sisters and I am grateful for any knowledge of truth that I receive; as all good things come from You; not from my earthly mind and being. Today, I realize that it is more important for me to honor Your desires to serve my brothers and sisters than for me to be honored or recognized for any great things I might accomplish. I am no more special in Your eyes, yet I am loved by You specially, as my wife, daughters, and sons are special to me. And I am unique in how I respect and love You and those I am blessed to know and serve.

Today, I let go of my need to accomplish great and fantastic things or take dramatic actions in the need to produce for my family. Today, I commit my mind's thought, my actions, and my words to everything that is Yours, which are far greater than are mine in search of reward. Nothing I accomplish that is good is achieved alone nor is it gratifying experienced in a vacuum. All that I am – all that we are – is accomplished well from associations made in Your name. So, today I listen closely and am earnestly interested in what I might learn from my brothers and sisters that I might better serve rather than be recognized for my intelligence or humor or my value that I think I might have that earns me a living.

Today I pray for a keen sense of humility and that I muster the civility if not curiosity in life to dismiss notions of my self-importance and I ask questions of others to uncover their abilities and better understand whom it is I am standing beside. When I am moved to boast, seek honor, manipulate the truth, or exaggerate my abilities I pray that my mind is dumbed so that I cannot speak. In lieu of spewing useless words, I pray that You guide me to seek the truth in each moment and that the conversation is centered around this mantra; there is a truth to be discovered within this moment that is for us to receive knowledge, understanding, and to gain wisdom; which transforms and magnifies our miniscule beliefs to the Eternal grandness of our Heavenly Father's.

Saturday

Love for my Brothers and Sisters

Thank you, God, for any knowledge of Yours that frees me from the shackles of my past bad decisions as well as from my concerns over who it is that I think I must be, what I must own or protect, what I must prove, and who I must please. Focusing only on You and doing Your Will gives me less to worry about how I look to the world. In You, I am free to be the person You created and the ego-designed me is instantly neutralized. I pray today that I am that person You would have me be, letting go of my selfishness, vanity, and pride to offer only Your love and that I express only Your thoughts – Your truth. Today, I pray for the strength and sagacity to seek You, so that I am Your word and Your visible light to the world.

I cannot understand the depth and undying love You have for each and every one of us. But I am learning a little more each day how much You want to be a part of our lives and that there's no limit to Your affection for each of us. You desire to be a part of every detail of our lives and I pray today, that I listen closely to the guidance You have for me and that I resist not Your Nudges for me to consider the details that take me to the place where I can best share what You would have me share today. I pray that I take nothing for granted and that I stay in The Game with You to the end and that I appreciate forging Your name on even the mundane details of my existence, until all is accomplished that You would have me accomplish for You, "Now" in this one, single, and only day. So, it is Your name that is etched on everything I say and do in my small corner of the world of which I might affect.

As we travel aside each other, whisked along by Your Will in creation, I pray that I have knowledge of Your many great and glorious gifts along the path to discovering You. I thank You, Lord, for the many gifts You have handed me on my travels and for the many wonderful ways You have found me able to forge Your name. I thank You for Your Eternal love that offers forgiveness for my many failures on this eternal journey home. I am Yours today and for forever and, today, I pray that my many odd, selfish, and prideful ways are forever forsaken, forgiven, and no longer pertain to whom it is that I am. My reality comes from Your perspective and I act from Your Truth and all there is and all that is truly important that I do for You today, I do. I resolve that I tirelessly seek to recognize Your love and in turn I find it easy to love You, accept Your Way, love myself, and that I share this love universally and instantly with my brothers and sisters; for nothing is more important as is this, Your singularly-absolute law: "love one another."

Week Four – Knowledge

Sunday

Surrender

Today, I pray for the strength and the courage to be open and honest with You, God, and with myself, my family, my friends, and my peers as I go in search of and plainly seek the truth that I am moved to discuss or upon which to act. By choosing to live within this ever-expanding truth that is You, in essence, I have chosen a life unencumbered with the concerns of the future outcome of Truth-led actions and words. As I surrender my fears, desires, and hopes to Your Way, I am free to be exactly whom I am, in this moment.

In You, I find safety and I have no fear of an honest examination of whatever it is that You lead me to explore. The Truth is in the Now and I have no power to alter it and I pray that I have the sense not to attempt to color it to my liking. I pray to You, God, that today I simply investigate the facts presented and that I explore the deeper truths You implore me to seek, to fully learn and to know. Today, I pray that I escape my past associations and relationships that had similar facts and circumstance and that I understand and appreciate the full depth and breadth of today's brilliance discovered within *this* moment in time.

I find peace in Your loving arms and safety in the Truth You offer. I take a moment now to pause and understand and I pray that the words I convey are Yours and that these words flow easily from my being. Today, I speak honestly without selling, calmly without exaggerating, and confidently with no anxiety regarding how the Truth might affect me or my dream. I surrender my will to You. I surrender my way for Yours.

Father, today I surrender to You all that I fear and all that I want or think that I need or that I must take, give, prove, or control in this world.

Now, without judgment or bias, I act for You, speak for You, and am for You in service to my brothers and sisters with no thought of reward, accolade, or expectation of kindness that I wish to receive for my greatest accomplishments; for greatness is Yours and, easily and simply, echoes Your Love.

Monday

Discernment

Today, I examine and investigate the facts without bias and I seek God's enlightenment in the deeper truths I might be led to discover. When I am too close to a situation to be objective, I pray that I remember to abandon my ego's desires and that I step back and calmly observe the situation from Your vantage point. From this viewpoint, I have no interest to alter or color the truth to make it more palatable or acceptable or simply to create a copasetic atmosphere. It's not my job to make things alright, happy, or to make the sun shine. My role is to gather information and to remain cool, understanding, and lovingly generous through the acceptance and presentation of the truth; no matter how disturbing or challenging it is to mine or my clients or associates or family's concepts of self-preservation.

Falsehoods and lies are all around us. Perceptions are misguided and strong beliefs have distorted foundations, but the facts are what they are, the truth is what it is, and I pray today that I discern, by the power of the Holy Spirit, what it is that is True from that which is not. I pray for the courage to seek the Truth and that I abide by Your Will of which this Truth is based and that I instantaneously know how best to apply the knowledge I receive and that I speak only these words and that I am stingy with these words as I allow others to inhabit them and that I lovingly listen and encourage Jesus' words to flow easily from all whom I interact. I pray for the gift of discernment that opens my heart and mind to Your Way and that I have the strength to choose the truth over my fear of losing and I fear not Your outcome for I trust You with my life and with my soul.

Tuesday

Love One Another

Today, I am precisely that person God created me to be. His greatest Gift to me is that I love people and love to work to solve problems, ease pains of doing business, and to bring more joy. I enjoy working with people to uncover and refine real problems that may be solved through cooperation, conception, and delivering a solution. I love to listen about how God works in our lives to uncover the true essence of the problems we face and how He works to place us together in the right moment in time to help each other find what it is we are so desperately hoping to find. I love seeing the spark that ignites a thought process when the truth is recognized, of which God has opened our heart and mind to receive.

Today, I seek to be informed and knowledgeable of the issues and pray to remain alive in the moment to listen to God's Nudgings that lead me to pick up the phone and contact the right persons for the job at hand. I am at my best when I allow God's work to be done through me as relationships are formed and answers become reality, but when I make that mistake which leads me to believe I must protect that which we develop I pray that I quickly, readily, and openly accept the truth God has led me to understand. I ask for Your forgiveness God and I pray for the forgiveness of those whom I've inadvertently or overtly or lazily ignored to serve or to rescue or include in our journey. I ask for Your best direction to correct my error – I pray to You, Holy Spirit for the truth and for Your loving hands to reach into my mind to soothe and heal my thought patterns and show me how to love myself and my brothers regardless of our errors; to love others truly as You love us; to guide us beyond our preconceived limitations and to achieve the greatness You envision we have been created to inhabit. I place my trust in You, Father, and live each moment to follow Your lead and do so fearlessly with Your charisma.

Wednesday

Service

Today, I forget my self-driven needs and wants for more and my dramatic fears of having less and I place my thoughts on how best to serve my brothers and sisters to my full ability; instead. Today, I focus my attention on my honing my ability to seek and discover the Truth and respond with honesty to tough and simple questions. I am of utmost honesty in my approach to my work of which I am honored to be talented to employ for others and I pray to be led to the correct sources to gather critical and pertinent information needed to be of highest service, as would You have me.

Today, I seek You to guide me to the Truth for my clients, my business associates, my family, friends, strangers on the street, and those in the world around me in which I live. And I do so without thought of how I benefit personally; other than the sense of well-being I experience in service to others. In loving service, we each succeed and we each find satisfaction, ease, and joy in our labors and this day is filled with miracles that will lead to our combined successes of which we are known and created worthy to receive.

Thursday

Stepping Aside

Father, You trust us more than we may trust ourselves, so today I pray for the Faith to use only Your words and to follow only Your Way. I'll jump from the illusory safety of my existence cluttered with fear to the bliss of Your simplified Way and I'll use the words that You want me to speak and act as You would have me act and easily walk away from the old habits that have fed my fears. Today I am new as I step aside and allow You to conquer my past and draw me into Your lovingly safety from my fears of a virulent future.

I'd rather live with Your outcome than mine and, in so doing, I choose to hand You control of my thinking and my ways and when it is necessary for me to say no, I convey it in an objective and direct manner. When it is necessary to confront a brother or sister I am compassionate, discerning, and repose in my response to mistrust. When it is necessary to be casual, I am. When it is necessary to be quiet, I am. When I must be studious, passionate, angry, humorous, or calming; I am. In every situation, I confront or enjoy inhabiting, I pray that I step aside and allow You to guide my being as I am Your Truth and Your Knowledge and Your Way. And I do so with honest words and non-verbal cues that You have gifted to me to express from my singular presence; right Here, right Now.

Friday

Me

I pray that I no longer fear being wrong, needing to be right, or found inadequate and I pray that I find it easy to accept the Truth of who it is that I am and that I willingly accept the role You have for me today. I pray that I look forward to discovering what it is I might accomplish for You today as I see myself and the world through Your eyes. I know You have no limits placed on any of us. I am the person You created me to be and I am ready, willing, and able to do great things, big and small for You today. I pray for the strength and stamina to stay on the path You have placed below my feet that leads me directly to what it is You would have me do; within the source of all that is good, the Way to peace and happiness for me, my family, my friends, and all whom I am led to serve.

Saturday

Trust in Your Will

Today, I will to accomplish all that is important for You in each moment, in each breath, in each shared interaction, and in my candor and acceptance of the Truth that sometimes lies just below the surface; one question – one answer away from reality. As You open a door for me today, I will follow and I vow to be alive and to enjoy the moment with You. Each day, I am becoming more comfortable in my own skin, comfortable with whom it is that I am born to be and more aware of the value of my ability to accomplish for You that which You've prepared the way for successful ventures and adventures with Sue.

I have found comfort in the knowledge that I am loved by You, forgiven, influenced, and guided by You and that I won't be let down by You. You make no mistakes; I am not a mistake, where I am today is no mistake, who I may serve is no mistake, who I might influence is no accident, and Your Love for me is not by happenstance. In this knowledge of Your undying unfettered Love for me and for us, I have confidence in Your plan and accept the truth You have prepared for me to embrace, today. And I pledge to You my undying devotion and that I appreciate the single moments shared with my brothers as I discover Your Eternal answer to the questions I am moved to ask; within this shared and Holy Instant.

I hand over my life and my work to You today Lord, knowing that You give me the words to say, You'll take me to the places You want me to be, and that You'll guide me to the right action and the right way that is truly Yours; and I am once again whole within Your Being; unhurried, confident, assured, loving, loved, appreciative, successful, and at peace fully within Your Truth. So, today, in gratitude I surrender to You my fears and my plans for success and I declare that it is not my will but Yours be done and I live as I perceive I am; confident in Christ.

the Hope in Entrepreneurialism

Week Five – Courage

Sunday

Non-Resistance

I recognize that our world is a very positive, loving, and supportive place; a work in progress, a battlefield that pits our selfish desires against Your benevolence, between carelessness/indifference and that of definite action towards finding You and serving that stranger who lives next door or who stands next to me in church or who anonymously asks for help or forgiveness. Most people want what is best for the other, as well as for me; some, however, do not. Yet I pray to keep pure, my thoughts, that I am non-resistant towards those whom I will not trust; my so-called enemies. I pray for the strength and courage to appreciate the lessons learned from opposing or combative forces. It is from them that I learn more about myself than do I from my friends and allies who fight to protect me or ease my pains.

In those moments of battle, conflict, and uncertainty I pray that I fear no evil and that I take the opportunity to face my weaknesses and I know that I am strengthened in the process. In the midst of battle, I stand stalwart in my knowledge of Your surety. I place my trust in You, God, our Heavenly Father, the Holy Spirit who guides my actions, and Jesus our Father/Brother whom I pray is my word. Within this moment – truth prevails and I fear no lie of mine nor of my brothers because I, now, trade my version of the truth for God's and for His Eternal wisdom and His most positive outcome.

I pray that I have the quickness of mind, strength of character, patience, and courage to reach for You and recognize the world for what it is; a bridge from this life to the next upon which I will not build a home to call mine. I realize that You are here with each of us, living within and among us to guide us to the safe place where peace is eternal and life is sure. I resist not internal temptation nor an attack from an opposing force, but when I fight I do so fervently for the truth that prevails; truth that trumps pride. My battle is not against another, rather for the truth and against my selfish ambition to be correct. So, I resist not, mine nor another's ambition for worldly gain and I am calmed by the knowledge of the truth of which I know and trust to be Yours eternal and that which instills courage within my being to overcome and to succeed and to win.

Monday

Confidence in Being Neutral

I fear no person, nor do I place anyone above or below me. We are "Equal in the eyes of the Lord" and in my eyes, we are brothers and sisters, equally loved by our Father in Heaven. Though I respect and honor brilliant people for their ability to accomplish great things as they triumph over incredible life defining-challenges, I place no wreath at the foot of their statues. I worship only You, God. I do not honor another above the Way, nor may I surrender my will to another that takes me away from following the course You've laid out for me. I pray for the wisdom and courage to stand with You in the face of lies, manipulation, and deception and I pray that I recognize attempts to hide or color the truth as I am determined to worship only You and remain resolute in Your Truth, only.

By honoring the search for Truth, I am neutral to the outcome of my feared interactions and dilemmas and I remain objectively honest; substantively creative; regardless of my past failures or successes. Today, I judge no man or woman as I seek the truth that resides within them rather than fear, judge, or ignore their existence. Unattached; neutral, I share Your Love more easily as I judge not my brother's appearance or words or my perceived failings and successes and I am endowed with the strength to dismiss the demons of fear, envy, and pride that may otherwise ruin the moment we share. In neutral, I am fearless of the outcomes of my openness to Your Direction as I am confident that, while my death is sure, it is only in Your time that it may occur. I fear nothing with You in charge of my tongue and my actions and I succeed in every chance meeting, business opportunity, and lifelong partnership and friendship You have chosen for me to pursue and exist within, today.

Tuesday

Trusting You

In troubled times, I know You surround me with love and hope and I know that You are at my side ready to take my problems, fears, and imagined darkness away. As I grasp Your hand and cling to life within this moment; I am safe. Nothing in the past can harm me Now and I cannot fear the future, because even in suffering and death – there is peace knowing that You await me in Heaven. Today, I pray for the strength to survive all negative thoughts and insane trials, instead I choose Your Stance, Your Attitude of living for others to bring Your Hope to the world.

Today, I find safety in Your loving arms and in Your thoughts of truth, beauty, and goodness for myself, my family, and Your entirety of creation. And I place my life securely in Your hands and I trust You to clear the path for me and my brothers. Whether You stroll, walk, march, or run ahead of us we know we are safe if we but only follow close behind and trust Your knowledge of the terrain that lies ahead and around the next bend on this sometimes-perilous road; our life journey Home. But only today may I faithfully follow as You lead me down the path at a pace You know I may handle safely; never so hurried or frantic that I lose appreciation for the moment.

Today, as I move in and out of danger, around and through my fears of failure and doom, as I dodge the ambushing thoughts of past bad decisions – embarrassing moments – hurtful times – or as I am tempted to use conniving or manipulation, as I tackle the many problems of the day, I pray that You lead me into battle fully rested, alive, and invigorated in Your dignity, honor, humor, and grace that instantly overcomes my selfish designs. I realize that regardless of my fears, I am loved, healed, and may live today assured by You in Your promise, Your guidance, and the knowingness of Your outcome that instills courage that cannot be manufactured, but only experienced as me being an extension of You in the truth of the moment. I succeed in being with You in this single most important time and place; Here – Now.

Wednesday

In You I am Forgiven

At times, when it seems that I'm alone in this battle and I fear that I might falter and am visibly shaken and shaking, I have let You slip from my hold and I've attempted to solve the most complicated problems on my own. In these confusing and dark times, I pray for the mental capacity, wisdom, and strength to reach for You swiftly immediately and, as each day passes, it's from a well-formed and trusted instinct that I seek You and You and I are together in Spirit and Thought. I pray for the strength to choose You over my habitual thinking that accepts struggle as a way of life; hope paralyzed. Today, I pray that my grip on Your hand is stronger than it was yesterday. God, clear my mind today of my fears of being left to my own devices so that I am secure in the fact that You will never give up on me, Your outcome is guaranteed, and I am forgiven for attempting it on my own if I will but only reach out for You in the slightest of ways all that You would have me accomplish is honorably complete.

Today, I pray that You send me Your Angels to change and uplift my thinking and pull me from the darkness of insecurity, pride, vanity, and the fears of struggle that I believe acceptable. I know that You have a great plan for each of us and You trust me to do my part for You today; forgive me when I fail. So, I pray for deliverance from my uncertain thinking and for wisdom in exchange of my plan. I'm asking You to send me a gentle reminder that keeps me centered on serving others and when I drift from Your tasks, I am guided back to doing Your work. And when I still don't quite get it, I ask You to be more direct if not lovingly brutal to my ego, so that I am sure to get it, because at times I am deaf if not blind and dumb. I trust that You'll guide me to the right place and that You'll let me know when I'm getting fat, lazy, or overconfident in my ways.

Whether my life is in turmoil or going amazingly well, I pray that I seek You and Your outcome over mine. I am lost when I insist that I'm right, but everything is only right when I give up myself and enter that safe place within Your loving arms that guides me. And Your grace and forgiveness gives me hope that there is nothing from my past that cannot be healed in this moment in time and Your Will is fulfilled. I pray that You forgive me for the wrongs that I have done and I pray that those whom I have hurt, hurt no longer and that we now may walk together or arm in arm with You in eternity, in the living Now. All that I strive to do today is not that which is conjured in my mind from habit or envy, but is truly Your Will for us and I succeed in Your mission and I am fully alive within this moment that is Your Grace to experience.

Thursday

Forgiving and Forgiveness

With the help and guidance from Jesus and the Holy Spirit, I am easily able to forgive my enemy, my friends, and myself for the trouble we've caused each other. Today, I pray for the courage and the will to love others and care for them as though they are my own blood; as though they are my son or daughter, brother or sister, or mother or father. They are part of me and I them. We are one church in Christ, spiritual brothers and sisters and we are at our best when we work together to create for You; each in a special way; with our unique personality, flavor, and voice. And we allow and support each other to perform our parts independently and to fruition.

Today, I fear not being taken advantage of or being disrespected or dismissed and I forgive myself and anyone else who has hurt me; instantly, now, and forever. I give the Holy Spirit any and every hurt that I have for another and I pray that Your Spirit heals that betrayed, hurtful, and unruly piece of my mind, body, and soul. I pray that those wounds that run deep and that have left such scars on our combined souls are healed and no longer exist. Today I surround myself and my brothers and sisters in the Holy Spirit's arms, in our Holy Spirit's Love and we are enlivened with the courage to work together, to do Your Will.

Today, I ask those whom I have hurt for the courage to forgive me and I ask You, Father to fill me with the courage and strength that I freely and immediately admit my wrongs and humbly disclose my shortcomings. I pray that I am stopped from doing harm to another, that I cannot attack another for the position they deem important, from defending the indefensible lie that I cannot let go, and that I am stopped from forcing another into a place where they must pray for the courage to face me. For all whom I have hurt, I am sorry for what I have done to you and I only wish that I'd done better for you as your ally, business associate, boss, brother, husband, son, father, and friend.

Friday

Doing Your Will

Today, each of my ambitions, quests, self-interests, and all that I have pursued for so long that I think so important that protects my convictions or the things that I think I must own or goes to create more wealth, an estate for my family or that assures my success, attain higher social status or to be more respected or more beloved by the world and by You; all of these things that I aspire that I believe make me who it is that I am – I pray for strength, wisdom, and for the courage to give it all up and hand it to You – God.

Rather than admire the rich and powerful, or seek methods to gain their approval and favor, or compromise my being by placing great importance on the acquirement of that which I think I must own in comparison or to achieve for others that which I think I must to gain acceptance or to be do and speak from intellect for the world's validation of my work my character or being; I pray for the courage to seek that, which You desire for me in each moment in place of my ambition.

Today, I strive to discover what it is exactly that You desire, that which You know is best for my family; my brothers my sisters; and for me. Energy spent otherwise is for not; the outcome of all other effort is left to chance and in comparison, to working for You; the result is in a bag filled with empty acquirements. But in Your plan, I am rewarded with the satisfaction of me being fully me in this specific moment in time. The prize is Here-Now for all whom You would have me share its grandeur and I am once again the comfortable servant; smiling; loving. Trusting You and Your outcome; I may be Yours to express to the world all that You desire in Your manner and with Your words and phrasing.

Saturday

Hope

By giving up my selfish quests and fear driven tactics, I change my focus from me to You and I easily find Your Way to the Truth. In Your Truth, I find hope and in Your Way, my thoughts are Eternally fluid and I'm more open to receive the many gifts You've stored for me. In the madness of life, I stop and take notice of the small miracles that enliven my spirit and I find peace that I easily may share and I realize that You love me beyond my ability to know. In these many miracles, I find hope and I recognize the simplicity of Your Plan; my plan; for this day.

As You hold me in Your hands and heart today, I trust in You with confidence in these daily tasks that, regardless of scope, each leads me closer to that incredible outcome, which I can barely imagine its relationship to the most mundane task You would have me endure for my brothers and sisters; sons and daughters. The Holy outcome is Yours, nonetheless; a result of a Holy Communion that is fulfilled in seeking You and doing Your Will today, one small step at a time. In the process, I am rewarded with a life filled with truth, honesty, adventure, and excitement. My being; my body, mind, and spirit is enlivened and energized by Your hope for me and for us.

Thank you, Father, for I am honored to be Your pawn in this immense, multi-layered, and complex plan that fulfills Your Will for the whole of us today and that sets the stage for a safe tomorrow. By me allowing me to be Your son; by me being who I am, only; I am a person filled with hope and that You may instill in my being the programming that thwarts evil and distrusts and, instead, seeks Truth and Justice. And I survive beyond the shortsighted dwellings of my mind's fearful conceptions and I live beyond my shortsighted dreams; in a place that trusts You to provide all that I need to exist and to succeed; and to fulfill Your vision of a life lived well. In this, I am at peace in Your being, today.

Week Six – Understanding

Sunday

Focus on Success

I pray today for a fixed mindset to an instantaneous agreement to live my life for others, to seek to know and to discover the subterranean meanings that help me to understand the needs, pains, and joys of my brothers and sisters; my family's. Their good health and success is my good health and success and Your Ultimate outcome revealed.

You have gifted me with a multitude of talents that I have yet to completely explore, align, and focus because this single most important day has not yet come with its unusually distinctive fears to conquer; that

I have been prepared to overcome. In this single most important day I am about to live, my talents, honed by experience, wrought by failure and success, culminate in whom it is that I am and how I might best offer myself to You, Father, to selflessly serve Your children; my brothers and sisters and sons and daughters; my wife.

We are each gifted in so many unusual and varied ways that go mostly unexplored. Our search for truth, security, and happiness has us each explore our worlds and stretch our abilities in ways we mostly fear but in ways You insist we are safe in succeeding. Every day, in every way, we may become better and better and yet, I know that my truth goes mostly non-actualized when I focus my attention on my inherent weaknesses, perceived limitations, and my most feared negative outcomes.

We are each tormented by thoughts of many and great past moments of failure, sadness, and, more often than not, incredible moments of stupidity. In our moments of weakness, these thoughts clutter our mind's ability to perceive the success You envision we freely inhabit. Understanding our innate childlike fears helps me to realize, as I meet a brother or sister, that I may ignore their imperfections and instead I may choose to seek the truth, beauty, and goodness that is much more true to whom it is that they are. I forgive myself and my brother for our shortcomings in fulfilling God's role and with this understanding, I may be more true to whom it is that You created me to be; today.

I forgive and am forgiven; I love and become loveable. I serve and appreciate being served; I teach and learn and learn and learn… and we succeed together within the endless Grace that is Your Gift to each of us.

Today I focus my breath, my mind, and my will to appreciate my brothers and sisters and myself for whom it is that we are, in reality. I will to thank You, Father, for this simple blessed moment in time that I share with each member of my earthly family and I pray that we each seek the Truth You would have us claim in this shared experience. And I pray for the ability to exist, only in this moment, completely, with each person whom I am led to associate and that I experience my life completely as I openly extend myself to the world; no thought of return; no fear of what I might lose. In prayer, I'm reminded to appreciate this moment in which we together share with You, God, and I know this moment is true. In this true moment, I am without fear of loss or of being manipulated or betrayed, but rather I have won this inner war and my interactions and transactions with my brothers and sisters serve the world perfectly; unobstructed by fear, invigorated by love.

Monday

Respect my Brothers and Sisters

I resist not the distractions in my life that confuse me and take me away from Your mission for this day. I pray to remain focused on completing my journey and that I may do so calmly and confidently; assured of the ultimate prize. When I face a challenge that seems to have no immediate resolution or that stupefies my ease of thought, I immediately reach for Your hand and remember that there's ample time to discover the truth and to work with my brothers to foster an answer for the problem that includes the thoughts and desires of many who share my space; my good desires.

And, I resist not my foes who might become my best teachers as I learn to investigate my shortcomings and I am a better person for the effort.

I live not to change another or criticize, complain, or to condemn another for their weaker actions or words. I am respectful of others' opinion and for their journey; on one hand, I desire to learn from them that which I could never learn from my own journey's experience and, on the other, in non-resistance to their follies, as well as mine, we're more easily able to reach solutions from broader backgrounds. Living Now with my brother at my side, rather than opposing him – asking and answering the tough questions – I may more readily understand him; respect his plight and concerns, better appreciate his talents and dreams. As I look to discover and enjoy great truths through the many interactions with my new-found friends, together, we may share in failure and success – neither the more powerful – each equally important in the process of achieving God's greatness on earth. Living truthfully in the brotherhood of man; but one success is ultimately sure; living peacefully and wholly within the Grace and Mind of God.

Tuesday

A Blessing

This morning, we are seated here at God's banquet table that He has invited us to share in His abundance. Today, I serve my brothers first and only then will I sit and eat with them. I pray that You bless my brothers and sisters with Your Abundance, Your Wisdom, Your calm reassuring Voice, and Your Love – for everyone I see, everyone I meet; I offer Your Blessing; Your Understanding; You.

My Family:

My Friends:

My Coworkers & Business Associates:

Bless the new persons in my life and the strangers I may never meet again; I pray that You bless me with good intentions and the courage to act and speak as my voice expresses a sincere and earnest offering of peace, hope, and love that we all may be better for the experience and come closer to being that person whom it is You have created us to be; for You, for me, each other, and all of Your Creation.

Wednesday

Attitude of Appreciation

Today I ask questions of others rather than tell them what it is I think I know or what it is that I think they need to know. I reserve judgment of others forever and, except for evildoing, I ignore disrespectful actions and words and, without need to correct another, I stay focused on the direction God would have me travel in the moments in which I exist alongside my brother and sisters. By asking questions, rather than offering my self-perceived wisdom, I am less caught up in the stupidity of glory-chasing or correcting another. I remain calm in my thoughts of God's purpose and I allow others to be fully who they are without accepting, rejecting, or dismissing the importance of their most immediate concerns or insanity or choice of self-satisfying need to celebrate.

The Holy Spirit leads me to ask the perfect questions and tell naturally tethered stories, but I offer His wisdom only as I am moved or when asked by another or invited to provide a solution. Today, I pray that I am humble in my quest to do Good and I realize that, while it *is* my job to correct my past mistakes of my foolish ambition, it *is not* my role to insist another is doing or being good by my standards. I also will not heap praise upon another for simply doing what it is God has gifted them to accomplish nor will I attempt to change or deconstruct anyone for that which I do not agree or that which I find absurd or quirky, but rather I appreciate my brothers and sisters evenly for whom it is that they are and offer only a truthful honest comment of hopefulness, as I might be moved to so do.

As I seek to learn from those I'm blessed to associate, I become a part of them and they add to me; their better side; that childlike side, the child God asks us each to be. In these realizations of Truth by associations and with appreciation and gratitude for gained Wisdom, we each are made better for the experience. So, I pray that God, You may easily live through me and Love the world through my emptiness and through these peaceful eyes and a relaxed smile I may exude an agreeable attitude towards being corrected when wrong; humble when correct; eager to learn from another's experience; thankful in living well; driven to do Your Will to serve the world; that my work provides well for my family; that I am nourished by my love for my wife; and I am wholly that rare person You created me to be, today; only.

Thursday

Ego-less

I am admittedly wrong in my human thought, so I must be non-complaining, non-condemning, and non-critical of others as we each struggle to swim against the currents of fear, doubt, and worry. As I see a sister or brother struggle and point out their misgivings, I find myself naked and appear all the more foolish for the effort. But, as I leave my grandness behind and seek to honor God and His creation, I am wiser and more assured of the Truth exposed in these moments shared, as we attempt to understand what it is like to be in the mind of our creator, of all that is good, wise and fair; in the mind of God.

Without regret for what I've done in the past that I fear will affect my life today, without fear of what this day might bring from a lifetime of ego-led adventures, without fear of abandoning habit's comfort and disabling my ego to wander this world within God's adventure, without these lies that hurt and hinder my ability to be honest, without this crutch I've created that props me up when I know I am less, and without fear of being less – I abandon God's adversary that I've created that causes such pain; pain none should endure. I abandon my ego-self, made-by-me life, and today I live my life freely within God's wholeness humbled in His Way. Today, I am complete, whole, and prepared to serve without thought of self, of self-preservation, of fear, or shame. Egoless, I am freed to serve those God would lead me to serve and today my words are true, my being is at peace, and my actions are right within this Holy Instant; prepared for me to appreciate – eternally in advance by God, Himself.

Friday

Knowing my Brothers and Sisters

When I am with another person, I wish to do more than interact cordially in a superficial manner. Today, I choose to look into my brother's eyes and speak and listen to their souls. I refuse to react to their point of view or defend my position or strategize over my next move in anticipation of theirs. Today, I step back from my inner struggles and selfish aspirations for success and fame and, instead, strive to discover with whom it is that I share my time. I pray to remain in the moment without conniving for position or exerting concern about filling the voids in my life with their approval or friendship, or receiving remuneration from their pots of gold or good favor from their positions in life; their knowledge; their wisdom-estate.

Today, I have decided to let go of my dreams and have become empty of manipulation, as I pause my mind's thinking and ask God to take over the conversation with His brand of silence and honesty without conjecture, but with a question to clarify and understand and appreciate another's perspective; not from judgment, but from a loving place.

As I look into the eyes of their souls, I silently ask "Who are you... really?" and "What are you trying to find?" As I attempt to search their souls in search of what it is that's so important to them, I seek to find greatness within my brothers and sisters. As I yearn to see the world from their perspective, to walk in their shoes, see the world through their eyes, and hear from their ears; learn from others what it is that moves them and what gives them life. In this Holy interaction, I become alive and have been given life. In these Sacred moments, we share, I have become that loving person You created me to be and I easily extend the love You have for them. In this shared moment, I understand their pain and joy and my compassion for the situation or the person is discerned and authenticated by You within my spirit and the moment is mutually experienced; more than words, life is shared. And together, we experience God's Grace.

Saturday

Beauty in Diversity

Today, I give up the song and dance I think I must perform to fulfill ambitions, that I might gain approval from those who directly affect my income, or that I might be thought highly of or, at least, accepted socially by friends and strangers. On this day, I choose to redirect my energy to simply doing good and being good rather than constantly outpouring energy to gain honor, attention, or appreciation. In self-acceptance of our Father's Gift of life, I find serenity in knowing each of us is different and this is how it is supposed to be; I am a boundlessly unique and perfectly odd Creation of a limitless and perfectly Perfect Creator. And there is harmony to be found by understanding that we each are created with sometimes severely odd differences and that with my ability to love without thinking, live without controlling, and appreciate, honor, and respect myself I may more easily love my brother as I do myself.

Today, it is my will that I appreciate people for who they are and for whom they wish to become and that we each are simply striving to discover the place God has set for us in this world. Our diversity and the friction it creates drive us to reach beyond ourselves to understand another's point of view and takes us to places we would not have gone alone, with and from our simply singular point of view.

Like sand poured onto the smooth iron rail that give a train's steel wheels' traction when climbing the steepest grades, resistance and friction gives us the ability to grow beyond our minds comfort. We can only move forward as we appreciate and allow a melding of our differing points-of-view and ways of being and we are each made better by the shared experience. Our lives are made fuller and more complete in this broad and glorious tapestry of human individuality. By being myself completely today unashamed, unplugged; I offer the world yet another truth, yet another view and in this simplicity of being, something great happens that is beyond my making; beyond my control. Today, I expect God to guide me to Heaven through my acceptance and belief in the beauty of our vastly eternal differences.

Week Seven – Intuition

Sunday

Trusting His Path

When I face difficulties that seem impossible to overcome and tasks that stymie my thinking and I've struggled to see clearly my way and anguish timeless to trust in Your Way, God; I pray: Today, God, open my heart and mind to accept Your goodness and be Your goodness filled with strength and courage that I can fight one more of eternities endless

Spiritual Logic

battles between my selfishness and Your total selflessness. Strengthen and enlighten me to honor and accept the goodness of Your selfless path. You know me better than anyone could possibly; I mean well, but so many times I choose the way of the world and allow my personality viruses of pride, vanity, or fear to prevail. I attack a brother or I defend a non-defendable position or otherwise find a way to foul up a great relationship; as I hide from the truth or cowardly speak; untruthfully, lie, camouflage shame with an argument, abandon an ally, or blissfully ignore an injustice. When I choose failure, and ignore time with You and dismiss comfort in You and the Grace You provide; I begin to shake, my eye twitches, my uneasiness constricts my spine, and I'm at my worst and nothing goes well nor may my life be correct.

God, it's for these things that I have done on my own in my name that I am truly sorry and I pray for Your forgiveness. In my purely human reactionary mind, the material world tempts me to believe it has the answers to my prayers. So, today, when I'm going in the wrong direction and about to make a fool's move in my belief in the world, I'm asking You to gently guide me, whisper to me the word, make the street lights red, stub my toe or, if You must, throw a bomb into my plans. Do what You must to stop me, do it quickly and I pray that I recognize Your guidance that Bumps me to move in Your direction to save my family, my brothers and sisters, and me from myself and my selfish ways.

As I learn to trust these signs, I fear less the outcome of my trials. Trusting You, I fear less what it is that I am sent to do and am more eager to discover what it is You have in store for me and my family and friends; and I find that I may love and be loved; but only as I remain in this single moment in eternity with You. So, regardless of how poorly I've acted in the past or as I slip today, I trust that You forgive me without thought of reprisal, but with Grace. You are here for me in this new moment to make myself whole and I have no worry of what the future holds nor do I regret my past mistakes. When I or my brother masquerades as the creator and the truth is threatened and I am moved to defend my dream or retaliate or protect my version of the truth, I pray for the strength and sagacity to release myself and my brother from attack and in its place offer peace in eternity, which is, in fact, the truth that is discovered in this exact moment in time.

Your version of truth and destiny happens in spite of my exasperated efforts to control the outcome and war is avoided and in its place a home filled with peace and love. And I'm confident today, in Your presence through the process and I'm alive within Your loving ways.

Monday

Jesus was Never in a Hurry

When things get hectic and out of control in my life, I pray to remember that You assign me only tasks I may complete well and that You know full of the new learning I have been prepared to absorb without resistance. As I am reminded of this, I take a deep breath, time stops, and there's no need to hurry to the next moment. No matter how crazy or upset I am, in a troubling thought, in timelessness, I've taken a vacation from my fears and have chosen to be fully activated and intimate within You as I interact with others in this moment; the Eternal Now. Today, I pray that my will to be me and to serve others is strong and that I am alive "Here" "Now". I may be quick to respond, work fast and efficiently, fight valiantly, play with vigor; but I do so, only as I live completely within this moment; unhurried, coolly fearless, fully alive, and unsurprised by my ability to perform well, beyond my long-formed illusions of self-restricted abilities.

I pray that in this moment, I move with care, deftness, and dexterity and that I am efficient in communicating Your thoughts and that I portray well the gifts You expect me to share with the world. But, no matter how important I envision my role or how pressured I am to meet a deadline; I commit to focus my full attention on this singular "Now". I am fulfilled within this moment with You and I move in time no slower… no faster than "Now". In this moment, I am here for You and You fill my life with bigness that I can't imagine as I hand You my regrets of the past and fears of the future. I give my dreams to You and I am honored to act Now for You as You entrust in me to do.

As I walk with Jesus today, I notice that everything that is happening in my visible world is as it is; outside of my need to influence, control, or make things right. Yet, I fear no fight God would have me fight. I must only be right with You in the face of lies and misunderstandings of truth. Evil, sin, and fleeting thoughts of treachery and betrayal fills the minds of men and I am blessed to examine my failings and judge not the basis of the lies others may tell. Today, my role is that of a son of God and my mission is to clearly discern the truth in "this moment" and there is no reason to fight or argue with the insane on a battlefield of their choosing in a war against their worn-out misconceptions and anxieties. God's truth requires neither defense nor a loud or angry display; it need only be spoken to be understood. And without thought I dismiss mine and all others' fears of loss and I place my being in God's hands for His Will to prevail through my selfless actions and words. There is nothing to fear, there is nothing that I must have, there is nothing that I must own or control, and there is everything to gain within this moment; unafraid, unhurried.

Tuesday

God is the Eternal Now

Today, I am conscious of myself and of others and I am conscious of You, God, and I pray to see no distinction between our Will, as I strive to live completely; within this moment in time. It is in this precise moment that I find our Father in Heaven's Will and know that it is created for me and that it is mine. But, as I drift away from this consciousness, I pray that You guide my thoughts and that I return to the moment, deliberate in finding You; Here-Now. In this one single and Holy day, in this single solitary breath, I am reminded of the ease of this place and time and I discover unimagined peace and as I frequent these moments filled with amazing discoveries, I am comfortable to explore the depth and breadth of Your Will.

As I flow more easily with the currents of life, conflictive personalities become less abrasive to my soul and my fears disappear in the thought of God for in this moment I trust You, God, with my being and I'm alive within this Now. In this Now, I have no fear of the future nor do I regret my past failings, *as I have only this moment to consider*; not the next nor the last; only this.

Now, right now, I am filled with Your wisdom and understanding and I have new insights to the sure outcome of the path You would have me travel, today. My intuition is keen in this moment in time and my road is blessed with the knowing. Embodied within Your loving Way and guided by Your insights, my spirit is freed to explore this world and I care for the details and act decisively, as I realize that I have every right to be happy and to enjoy the work within the journey You have had for me to begin anew for You; today only and every "only" day.

Wednesday

Harmony in the Zone

In the Now, I am in harmony with You and Your Way. In this moment, I am connected to Your Eternal Mind and unhurried, energized, and all that I do and say comes from You; I'm in the "Zone" in these single moments and I'm Your son and act and speak and exist as Your son is. It is only when I slip out of this moment and relive the past or prepare for the future by editing my actions and words to protect what I think I must own, I find I am alone and I struggle in daily living and everything that I do is wrong. My life is a chore and mishaps lead to spiritual uneasiness and soulful frustration becomes the order of the day.

However, in this present moment, I have no thought of worry or trouble, nor do I fear failing to accomplish anything that a loving father desires of his son. As I step away from my thoughts of fear and selfishness and enter the moment that resides within You, Jesus, I am completely within Your loving thought and that thought guides me to the best place for my family, my friends, and for the world in which I may and do affect. Within You, within this moment in time, I intuitively know what to do and I am great at it. My words have been chosen for me by You and my vision is clear and my soul is at peace. Here-Now, I'm in harmony with Your Will; alive in Your arms, I know how to live well, enjoy others, and I wholly love and tirelessly serve my brothers and sisters, as would You. In service, Your Will is alive through my actions and words and I am alive; I am Your loving son filled with gratitude for His loving Father.

Thursday

A Thought without Thinking

In this moment in time, I am a part of Your Truth, as You have created. Today, I pray that I may live within this truth without the pressure to provide an answer or make something work that seems to be broken. Playing "In the Zone," I'm out of the way and fully within You,

God, and You are unhampered by me and able to express Yourself to the world through me; a loving student. Here, within You, my ego is completely and absolutely absent and there is no hint of fear, pride, or vanity. There is no grey, only truth and the truth is easy to experience once accepted.

The truth requires nothing from me to create it, only determination, humility, and courage to seek it fearlessly, to uncover, and to face it without thought of how it affects my ego's agenda. In this moment, I am at the height of my ability to be as You created me to be; absolutely. In the Now, my highest thoughts bypass my human fears that would otherwise attempt to color or otherwise dictate my spin of the truth and Your truth is intact and pure; pure as the driven snow.

In the zone, my thought is without thinking, I listen actively, I am without being, my actions are fluid and sure, and my words flow undistorted and unedited.

In this moment, the truth is clear, innocent, and pure and I discover You in that first, that initiating thought, that leads to all other thought. That initial spark of truth; the first thought in a line of thoughts drives me and is visceral and most true to whom it is that I am; it's Your creation not mine. I neither designed, imagined, nor do I claim ownership of this first thought. I only pray to You that I recognize it and recognize it swiftly. It is in "this moment" that Your thought excites my mind and, today, it's my will that Your thought becomes mine. It is in this moment that Your thought, Your outcome becomes ours and simply, thereby, just becomes. The result, that happening, simply IS. What the mind of God creates within my mind, in my selfless and complete absence and acceptance, becomes my vision for the day and Your greatness becomes my reality and becomes our success. What the mind creates; IS. So, what is Your Thought for me today, Now? I pray to know and accept.

Friday

Prayer

As I commit my life to being Your Will and leaving mine behind, I pray to stay out of the way and let You create the world You envision; through me. I make this request in prayer to You today that I realize You are with me, right now, so that I may do that right thing, use that right word, and I act immediately to Your prompting, honor Your correcting thoughts, and that I find strength to face my most sublime as well as exaggerated fears of loss, pain, and failure. With You at my side and in my heart and mind, I am absent of fear and filled with might that examines the facts and faces the truth without falter. My fearful thoughts disintegrate, as I breathe consciously and live consciously within this moment. Being near to You, I find the way when I am lost by that simple act of giving up my vision of what it is I must do or protect and I place my complete and total trust in You.

Today, I pray for the courage and strength to hand to You my will and to be resolutely subservient to Your agenda, in each moment. Today, I free myself from me. I pray to discover Your thought and the truth and I know, by You, what it is that is most important that I create and I avoid the trappings of *my* controlling thoughts and I live Now; tuned to Your clear channel enlivened by Your Word.

In this prayerful moment, the monsters in my life that I would avoid become unmasked and the light of truth shines on them and reality exposes that there is nothing to fear; a child's fearful dream vanishes in the light. I Now see the simplicity of Your truth and the hope You have for me and those thoughts of the worst possible thing that could possibly happen no longer has a hold on my creativity; as my simple prayer is answered…

"God, I belong to You. Today, I am no longer. In this moment, I give me to You. When I speak, I speak Your Words and they are spoken with Your Love and Respect for my brothers and sisters and when I listen, You receive and filter out the noise and Your Discernment leaves me with only Truth and I respond to insanity assured, as I reflect Your Confidence in the Glorified outcome that is Yours. Today, I am alive and I thank you, Lord for this breath."

Saturday

God's Vantage Point

Today, I am determined to trust You with my life, my business, my family, and my today. As I concede to succeed in those things great and small that You've prepared for me to accomplish, I am grateful to You for leading me to the satisfaction of accomplishing for You, Your Will; which I pray I recognize is, in reality, my will; Heavenly ordained.

Spiritual Logic

Listening, believing, and acting to Your cues have led me to many incredible places and to my beautiful wife, Sue. While on this adventure I have found peace, truth, beauty, and comfort for myself and those around me in the world in which I work, live, and create for You. When I'm successful at anything, great or small, it is only because I have stuck with You, trusted Your lead, explored Your Will, taken ownership of it, left mine behind, envisioned Your outcome, and have had an attitude to thrive within it.

I am happiest when I give up myself and accept Your Will as mine.

In prayer, I find the strength and clarity of mind to appreciate Your design and the challenges become not a chore, but rather a great redirection to serve. I once again am fearless in the pursuit of the truth that lies within each moment, which is now unencumbered by fear or pride; rather my actions and my word is that of hope and love.
In prayer, I remember that it is in *this* Moment that I am triumphant as I express Your Will to the world. I am a beloved son who coexists in Your SUCCESSES, albeit, sometimes guised as FAILURE. But, in the end there is no good nor is there bad, only the truth found in an experience that gives us each a shot at being our best and doing our best in this particular and peculiar Moment in time; for the highest good. As I end each day I am grateful, a little bewildered and exhausted at times but none-the-less astonished and appreciative of the many blessings You have given me to experience. In gratitude, I commit my being, my thoughts, my soul, my work, my love, my adventurous spirit, my ambition, my needs, wants, and dreams, and my entire will to You – that today, I am alive within You and in Your journey, together, we explore Your Universe; sharing Your inspiration, compassion, and Love.

the Hope in Entrepreneurialism

Spiritual Logic

A Testament to my Faith
A Prophesy

This is the boldest testament to my Faith that I'm able to proclaim.

    While writing this book on how to be successful in business, I've been mostly broke; funding my business ventures, bootstrapped, only by the Faith in God's ultimate care for my family's health, wealth, and safety. I'd write about my "Adventures in Businessland" with the firm belief that by telling my story, in real-time, you'd witness the Faith I put into action; living proof that God's Promise is inevitable. And you'd be inspired to step out on the scary and precarious ledge of your dreams and know that, "in God all things are possible."

    That being said, here's my Prophesy of Faith, written on the 3rd day of February, 2017 the 14th anniversary of writing the first words of this book:

> I've written this book unknowing of the vastness of my future wealth or from where it might come. While I'm not financially wealthy, I full well know that it is coming. I predict that within a few short years, I'll be as financially wealthy as I've come to be Spiritually. I know that someday, with all humility and thanksgiving to the Source of all that is Good; even in my reluctant acceptance, now become profound in Jesus Christ that He is my Lord and Savior; God will prove to you and the world the Truth's presented in this body of work.

    And this book will be a reference for me to point when someone asks, "What do you attribute, Bill, to the 'over-night' success of the Spiritual Logic Foundation for Entrepreneurialism?"

    And I'll smile and reply, "Here's the roadmap!"

    My prayer is that God provides for you more than for me by your study of this work. And that He endows upon the success and rewards due you and your family; to be fostered and shared by you for this planet and all His Children. Thank you, in advance, Jesus for making this dream become my reality.

Spiritual Logic

ABOUT THE AUTHOR

Really?

You can't be serious.

What more can I say?

Spiritual Logic

www.ingramcontent.com/pod-product-compliance
Lightning Source LLC
Chambersburg PA
CBHW071410180526
45170CB00001B/47